Shortfall

Shortfall

FAMILY SECRETS,
FINANCIAL COLLAPSE,
AND A HIDDEN HISTORY OF
AMERICAN BANKING

Alice Echols

THE NEW PRESS

25 YEARS

NEW YORK
LONDON

Requests for permission to reproduce selections from this book
should be mailed to: Permissions Department, The New Press,
120 Wall Street, 31st floor, New York, NY 10005.

Published in the United States by The New Press, New York, 2017
Distributed by Perseus Distribution

ISBN 978-1-62097-303-5 (hc)
ISBN 978-1-62097-304-2 (e-book)

CIP data is available

The New Press publishes books that promote and enrich public discussion and
understanding of the issues vital to our democracy and to a more equitable world.
These books are made possible by the enthusiasm of our readers; the support
of a committed group of donors, large and small; the collaboration of our many
partners in the independent media and the not-for-profit sector; booksellers, who
often hand-sell New Press books; librarians; and above all by our authors.

www.thenewpress.com

Composition by dix!
This book was set in Fairfield LH

Printed in the United States of America

2   4   6   8   10   9   7   5   3   1

In memory of my mother

Shortfall, *n.*
A falling short; the amount by which a supply
falls short, shortage, deficiency. Also, a decline;
a shortcoming, a fault; a deficit, a gap; a loss.
—*Oxford English Dictionary*

Contents

Prologue

Captain Nothing

George Bailey. It's a name that most Americans, or at least those of a certain age, recognize in a flash. With just a bit of prodding ("You know, Jimmy Stewart . . . *It's a Wonderful Life*"), even those who have never watched the 1946 film in its entirety usually know whom it is you're talking about. George Bailey is the small-town banker at the center of Frank Capra's classic Hollywood movie. A man filled with dreams of a big and exciting life, he finds himself, when his father dies suddenly, stuck in his hometown, Bedford Falls. This untimely death shackles George to his father's struggling building and loan association (B&L). Consigned to what he disparagingly calls this "business of nickels and dimes," he tries to make the best of it, albeit grumpily at first. Kindhearted, altruistic, and willing to take on Henry Potter, the town's evil banker, George is the sort of person most Americans have rarely, if ever, encountered in the world of financial services.

At the same time that George Bailey was doing his best to bring the American dream of homeownership to the working people of Bedford Falls, Walter Clyde Davis was operating a different kind of building and loan association in Colorado Springs, Colorado. George Bailey was a beloved figure, whereas Walter Davis aroused in others feelings of wariness, sometimes even dread. Yet Davis turned his building and loan into the biggest in central Colorado, with 3,600 depositors. His success enabled him to buy into a tony neighborhood, drive luxury cars, and finance summer-long European vacations for his family. And then there was Davis's mistress, another telling difference between the real-life B&L man and his fictional counterpart.

Each man faced financial calamity during the Depression. But George Bailey selflessly handed out his own honeymoon money to forestall a bank run engineered by his nemesis, Henry F. Potter. By contrast, Walter Davis went on the lam before news of his association's failure hit the papers. Back home in Colorado Springs, investigators discovered that the town's "financial wizard" had left his business with a jaw-dropping $1.25 million shortfall. In today's terms, that translates into nearly $22 million.[1] When detectives arrested him that December, newspapers across America carried the news. Journalists knew the scandal would resonate with Americans who had come to view bankers as a species of gangster, or "bankster," as they were sometimes called. Here was a man, argued one journalist, who had passed himself off as a captain of finance when he was a mere pretender. "A cabin boy, strutting the bridge in a captain's uniform," Walter Davis could now be seen for what he was: "Captain Nothing."[2]

The building and loan industry, once a central part of our country's financial fabric, is barely remembered today. What has lived on in our cultural memory is George Bailey, who has become a fixture in books about banking and finance, homeownership, and the Depression. As for Walter Davis, well, he's pretty much gone missing from our history books.[3] You certainly won't find him in the standard histories of the "thrift industry," the term used for the building and loan industry and the modern savings and loan business that succeeded it. According to these accounts, the vast majority of building and loans survived the Great Depression, and

In studio photographs, Walter Davis looks like someone with whom one would prefer not to tangle—very much the anti–George Bailey. (Author's archive)

Midway through *It's a Wonderful Life,* just as newlyweds George and Mary Bailey are heading off on their honeymoon, something goes terribly wrong—a bank run at Bailey Brothers Building and Loan. It's 1932. The depositors are desperate but restrained, until they learn of Old Man Potter's offer to pay fifty cents on the dollar for their B&L shares. George tries to win back his depositors by explaining the power dynamics behind Potter's offer. However, the run only comes to an end after Mary hands over their honeymoon money to George, who selflessly distributes it to the crowd. (Image courtesy of Getty Images)

those that didn't failed because of the collapse of the country's real estate market, not because of any financial impropriety.[4] Indeed, a number of scholars who have written about building and loans depict them as noble institutions—"banks with a soul"—and write as if the fictional Bailey Brothers Building and Loan Association was actually representative of the industry.[5]

Yet among building and loan men of that period Walter Davis was hardly anomalous. Neither was his failure or the circumstances surrounding it. This is no small thing. During the Great Depression the industry's cratering brought untold grief to millions of depositors. Despite this, the history of the American thrift industry during the interwar years remains hidden, buried in the bowels of state archives and local libraries.

My discovery of this forgotten financial history did not begin in the archive, however, but with an almost chance conversation some twenty years ago. I was home, visiting my parents, when the dinnertime banter one evening went too far. After my mother left the table, slamming shut her bedroom door for good measure, my father explained the roots of her cellophane-thin sensitivity. He spoke about her family, particularly her cad of a father. His was not a story with a Capra-like happy ending. Our conversation that night was my introduction to the man at the center of this book, a man whose name I did not yet know. Within our family everything about him—stories, photographs, and memorabilia—had been banished. Walter Clyde Davis, my grandfather, had been scrubbed as clean from my family as he was from the history books.

It's embarrassing to admit, but until that evening it had never occurred to me that it was weird how little I knew about my mother's past. Even though I grew up surrounded by her parents' possessions, I don't recall ever inquiring about them or how they had come by all their swanky stuff. The room-sized Oriental rugs, the salmon-colored Art Deco chaise longue, the mahogany furniture—all of it was strikingly at odds with the midcentury blondness of my friends' homes. And so it was with our pantry, crowded with variously sized Wedgewood plates, cups, saucers, and bowls, not to mention an array of delicate stemware for every conceivable kind of alcoholic drink. Some who have written about family secrets report a disjuncture between the accepted family narrative and their own perceptions, and others of being haunted by an unknown knowledge, what psychoanalysts have dubbed nescience.[6] For example, in another book about real estate and lending that pivots on a family story, historian Beryl Satter writes that as a child she often felt as though she was "living in the aftermath of an explosion whose source was obscure."[7] Admittedly, the shattering events in

her family's story were not at a generational remove; still, how was
it that I never registered as strange our home's faded, antique opu-
lence or our family's conversational voids?

It would take several more years before a friend, another historian, persuaded me to start digging. Even then, it was she who
did the first bit of spadework by searching for my grandfather in a
bound volume of the *New York Times* index at the Santa Monica
Public Library, then copying and mailing me the relevant articles.
That was how I learned that Walter Davis was generally understood to have been an embezzler rather than the victim of the Depression that my father's account had led me to believe.

Making sense of my grandfather then, in 1999, was much harder
than it would have been even a few years earlier. By this juncture,
my father was dead and my eighty-nine-year-old mother had an
uncertain memory and was struggling with an unnamed neurolog-
ical condition. Moreover, I had not yet broached the subject of the
scandal to my mother, who was unaware I even knew about it. I
could think of only one person—my father's sister, a former nun—
who might provide some useful information. What she had to offer
was a vague memory of having been told that her sister-in-law's
father had owned large swaths of Wyoming. As for my mother's
relatives—or those who had lived through the scandal—they had
all passed away, and nothing of their personal archive seemed to
have remained. Then, a few years ago, a tiny collection of letters,
diaries, and memorabilia belonging to my great-uncle, Roy Davis,
a prominent local politician, found its way to the local Colorado
Springs history museum. This tiny bundle represented a sliver of
what was once his archive, which had been tossed into a dumpster
after his death.

As it happened, I was just getting interested in investigating the
scandal when my mother's decline forced her to move into an assisted living facility. That meant putting our house on the market.
We had moved to Chevy Chase Village from an adjacent Maryland

suburb in the mid-1950s. Over the years, many of the houses in
our neighborhood had been McMansioned. Ours, however, looked
exactly as it did when we moved in. Little of what we accumulated in the subsequent forty-three years had been given away or
junked. After a serious attempt at culling, my sister arranged for
the remaining stuff in our basement to be hauled away. In the process, several mildewed trunks, whose contents our mother had described as worthless, became part of the junk heap. In the end, my
sister unearthed several boxes of family memorabilia and I gathered up a handful of my mother's designer clothes from the 1920s
and a batch of family photographs, all of it from the sole surviving
trunk—a beautiful, slightly worn Louis Vuitton that for decades
sat closed, but likely unlocked, in one of the few dry spots in our
basement.

The woman who bought our house, realizing that our mother
was unable to clear it and that her daughters were unlikely to do
so, and believing the house could do with a makeover, bought it "as
is." A year later, my sister and I were on the phone talking about
the old neighborhood. She had recently spoken to neighbors who
told her that the new owner was gutting the house. In passing, my
sister mentioned the seventy or so boxes she had told the movers
to leave behind in our attic. My sister had no idea I was weighing
whether to research the scandal, so there was no reason she should
have shared with me what was now a galvanizing detail.

Of course, the boxes *would* be in our attic, a space that always
made me uneasy. It was where we stored our Christmas deco-
rations, and when air-conditioning was finally installed, where
some crucial bit of that system was located. Twice a year my father hauled a ladder in from the garage and made his way up it
to retrieve and store again the unwieldy boxes that held our tree
ornaments and Styrofoam Santa Claus. The combination of the
wobbly ladder and my less than totally nimble father always made
this a nerve-racking exercise. But I now wonder if some of my

nervousness resulted from having picked up on my parents' anxiety about what else was stored up there.

Whatever the source of that old anxiety, I was now fixated on those cardboard boxes. It turned out the renovation on our former house was proceeding so slowly that the contractor had yet to empty the attic. After I explained the outlines of the scandal to the new owner, she promised that once the boxes were downstairs she would open up each box and look inside to see which contained family papers and memorabilia. I would have preferred going through them myself, but I did not have the chutzpah to ask. A few weeks later we spoke on the phone and she reported that most of the boxes contained nothing worth keeping. A few of them, however, looked very promising indeed.

In those boxes were a seventy-page transcript of subpoenaed family telegrams, newspaper clippings, diaries, scrapbooks, correspondence, and photographs, including many of my self-regarding grandfather. Some of this material, including a bookstore clerk's scribbled message to put aside a copy of Theodore Dreiser's *American Tragedy* for Mrs. Walter Davis, seemed almost too spot-on. Often the most telling scraps had been tucked away inside diaries and books, one of them a copy of *Poems That Have Helped Me*, a gift that my grandfather sent to my grandmother while he was on the lam. All along an intimate archive of the scandal had been cached inside our house.[8] My mother held on to it all, even though doing so risked the possibility that one of her daughters might eventually discover her family's secret. Why hadn't she thrown it all away when she moved east?

The material inside those boxes was indispensable, as was my grandfather's two-hundred-page FBI file, acquired through a Freedom of Information Act request. Just as important were my mother's contributions. The floodgates may not have opened when she first spoke about the scandal, but she became remarkably forthcoming. Several weeks into our talks she announced that she was granting me "permission" to write a book about the scandal. Sometimes, particularly after lengthy discussions that touched on parts of the story that had long since faded from her memory, I felt she regretted having given me her okay. Yet she continued talking to me about it, and over a period of two and a half years the scandal became a conversational staple. These were not structured interviews recorded on tape, but rather informal conversations. Her memory often failed her when it came to the details of the scandal, but parts of that experience remained indelibly with her. She often told me about coming downstairs for breakfast one morning and finding her father in a panic about the bad news in that day's newspaper. "He saw it all coming," she said. And then invariably she would add, "He blamed it all on Bubbles!"

My mother never could tell me who this Bubbles character was, but quite a lot of what she did tell me was borne out by my research. Was she really almost the victim of a kidnapping at the hands of depositors desperate to force her father's return? Yes, that story made the front page of the local papers. Had her father's grave been left unmarked out of fear that it might be desecrated or dug up in the hope that some part of his fortune had been buried with him? When my wife and I visited the cemetery where the Davis family is buried, we found that both of my grandparents' graves were without headstones. Sometimes my mother's memories were self-contradictory or at odds with what I discovered elsewhere. And I would not rule out the possibility that on occasion she tailored her story to fit what she believed were my expectations. But her recollections of her feelings were fairly consistent. For a book such as this, which tries to impart a sense of the emotional textures of that time and place, and of the feelings of those most intimately connected to the scandal, her memories prove crucial.

Shortfall uses the building and loan scandal, particularly as it played out in Colorado Springs, in order to explore the relationship between capitalism, class, and conservatism in America. It asks why it is that when it comes to stories of financial failure, particularly stories of "bad capitalism," forgetting seems so often to set in.

That I became less interested in what happened to the missing million and more intrigued by what the scandal might tell us about our country owes a lot both to our current economic and political landscape and to the nature of research itself. For me the shift began as it so often does for historians: squinting at a microfilmed copy of an old newspaper and finding myself drawn to a nearby article, one with no apparent relation to my topic. From these semi-distracted glances I would sometimes recognize a name, which occasionally led to unanticipated connections, be it to the Ku Klux Klan (KKK), which successfully "kluxed" Colorado in the 1920s, or to the violent labor wars that preceded Klan activism there. As my research expanded into seemingly disparate corners of our country's past, this book became not only my excavation of a buried financial history or a long-forgotten chapter in the history of a small Western city (or for that matter my own family's history) but also a timely, on-the-ground history of twentieth-century American capitalism.

The first discovery I made as I researched the scandal was that the crash of my grandfather's building and loan was not singular. By the summer of 1932 every single building and loan association in Colorado Springs had collapsed. With all four of its associations shuttered, the city was hit with an avalanche of failure.[9] "What am I to do I can't fathom," wrote one penniless depositor. "I am nearly insane."[10] An unusually large number of Colorado Springs residents—between five thousand and six thousand in a city with ten thousand heads of household—were depositors in one of the four failed associations.[11] The industry's collapse hit with the force of a natural disaster, and residents frequently likened the financial meltdown to just such a catastrophe. However, what they experienced did not feel impersonal or random in the way that the loss from a tornado or an earthquake would. The Great Depression, which was key to the failure of the building and loan business, was a global phenomenon, but to those victimized by this industry's collapse, there was nothing invisible or anonymous about it.[12] That's because the men running these associations were often trusted neighbors, fellow congregants at church, and sometimes even their children's Sunday school teachers. They were not big-time, anonymous tycoons in faraway New York. Anxious about foreclosure, terrified of life with little or no financial cushion, association members absorbed what was happening to them as nothing less than a personal betrayal.

What happened in Colorado Springs occurred in countless communities across America. During the Depression the building and loan industry suffered terrible losses, in large measure because of the calamitous downturn in the real estate market. There were contributing factors as well, which included poor accounting, lax regulation, inflated interest rates on deposits, bad loans and low-down-payment loans, balloon mortgages (a much-touted recent innovation), and financial misconduct.[13] State records show that in Colorado alone 60 percent of all building and loan associations closed their doors during the Depression years. Half the population of nearby Pueblo, a working-class city and home to the Rockefellers' huge steel mill, was directly affected by the crash of the town's mega-B&L—the biggest in the state.[14] In Texas, home of 153 associations in 1929, there were only 54 building and loans still operating in 1944.[15] California also had more than its fair share of trouble, including the spectacular $8 million embezzlement of the behemoth Hollywood Guaranty Building and Loan Association with its 24,000 depositors.

Estimates of B&L failures nationally vary widely, but one recent study posits that nearly one-half of the associations that were in operation at the onset of the Depression were out of business by 1941. Those associations that managed to survive often just limped along.[16] To be clear, not all closures were the result of financial improprieties, much less embezzlement. Moreover, depositors were not always left empty-handed when their associations became frozen, were liquidated, or were forced into receivership. That said, in very many cases depositors found they were unable to recover more than a slender fraction of their money. But, again, you won't find this in books about the building and loan business, largely because the thrift industry boasted a powerful trade group that planted upbeat stories in the press, lobbied Congress, reinvented itself as the "savings and loan" business, and played a role in the publication of seemingly objective and authoritative histories of the industry, which scholars have too often taken at face value. And then there's *It's a Wonderful Life*, a box office flop that became a cultural phenomenon decades after its release. It wasn't Capra's intention, but his movie has managed to cast a long and protective shadow over the thrift industry.[17]

The collapse of these associations, like the all too common failure of state-chartered banks, affected millions of Americans. At the time of the stock market crash, one in ten Americans belonged to a building and loan association. B&Ls were a crucial component of America's lending and investment landscape, helping to fuel homeownership and the consumer revolution of the 1920s. It was through these associations that ordinary Americans often came to see themselves as homeowners, consumers, and investors. In the process they developed different expectations about money, believing that it should work for them rather than form a lump under the mattress.

Despite the overwhelming importance of the B&L industry to American families and its spectacular cratering during the Great Depression, there is, remarkably, no history of how it all played out for depositors in even one city. *Shortfall* unearths this unknown chapter in the history of American capitalism. Swindles and ripoffs are hardly unusual in finance and banking, but the episode I recount here ranks with the worst in the history of modern finance, all the more so because its victims were regular Americans. The mission of these building and loan associations was to facilitate working-class homeownership on affordable terms. Originally part of a wide-ranging cooperative movement, B&Ls were even called "poor men's banks." And yet as the industry grew it shifted as sharp businessmen ditched the original semi-philanthropic B&L design for a different business model, that of the lucrative for-profit corporation. They took to luring customers with offers of inflated rates of interest on their deposits—rates that were unsustainable even had the thirties roared like the twenties. As B&Ls transmogrified, the people running them were increasingly apt to operate them not as a "cure for poverty" but rather as "honey pots" in order to line their own pockets.[18] By de-romanticizing the world of building and loans, *Shortfall* pushes back against our self-congratulatory national narrative and raises the possibility that the playing field in America was tilted more in favor of the wealthy and well positioned than is usually acknowledged.[19]

This book also calls into question the presumption that the problems with American banking and finance begin and end with Wall Street. It asks: What if Main Street, home to the very businesses meant to embody the best of American capitalism, has not always worked well for ordinary working people?[20] Certainly in Colorado Springs and elsewhere, much of the suffering during the Depression was caused by Main Street businessmen, who lacked the sophistication of big-city stockbrokers and banksters but who were their rivals in greed. In the years before New Deal–era financial reform, banking, big and small, was often characterized by what one legendary financial reformer called "legal chicanery" aided by "beneficent darkness." Many accounts have detailed the rot at the core of Wall Street in these years, but far fewer have looked beyond it.[21] Decentering Wall Street allows readers to see that the problems with banking and finance in this period were systemic, not the result of a few bad apples in lower Manhattan. Indeed, uncovering the hidden history of the building and loan business in this understudied corner of the American West goes some way toward challenging the Frank Capra–like equation of smallness with virtue. This is to say that the little guys were not always the good guys, and that shortages did not always stem from absentminded employees like George Bailey's Uncle Billy.

A lot of writing about the thirties treats it as the "red decade," when collectivism and faith in big government triumphed over the ideologies of free enterprise and rugged individualism.[22] It is true that the Great Depression witnessed fundamental reform that was in some ways far more profound than anything achieved in the wake of our own Great Recession. And yet the episode I recount here may surprise readers accustomed to stirring Depression stories of working people subverting farm auctions, blocking rent evictions, and participating in sit-down strikes on factory floors. Depositors elsewhere in the nation did fight for government regulation of the B&L industry and often supported New Deal reform, but in Colorado Springs the story unfolded differently. There, the idea that people move through the world as "self-contained, contract-making individuals," best left to their own devices, unaided by government efforts to diminish inequality—an idea associated with our own neoliberal times—had already taken root.[23]

What I discovered in Colorado Springs led me to see the thirties' social-democratic turn as more contested and less settled than the lasting political recalibration that I had taken it for. The portrait of the thirties that emerges in these pages suggests that the New Deal ideals of collectivism and economic justice were born of catastrophic economic failure and, still, were resisted by many Americans, not just wealthy businessmen.[24] The story of aggrieved depositors I tell here goes some way toward filling in the backstory of modern American conservatism, and indicates that in some places the rightward shift of the white working classes has a longer history than we have known.[25]

Some readers might argue that Colorado Springs is hardly representative, even of the West. It is true that from the beginning the city sold itself as the antithesis of the typical wide-open Western town. Drinking, gambling, and factories were all relegated to adjacent Colorado City. Until a nearby gold strike transformed it, making it top-heavy with millionaires, Colorado Springs was primarily a health resort town, and a predominantly Anglo one at that. The city's evolution into a bastion of free-enterprise conservatism owes a lot to the 1891 gold strike in Cripple Creek, some twenty miles away as the crow flies but forty-five by road. The gold there produced fortunes (and the expectation of more to come) as well as fierce wars between capital and labor.[26] During the years that Cripple Creek produced more gold than anywhere else in the country Colorado Springs was the American dream on steroids. America might boast of streets paved with gold, but the downtown streets of Colorado Springs were actually paved with gold. In 1920 fifteen hundred carloads of crushed low-grade gold ore from the Vindicator Mine in Cripple Creek were added to the city's paving mixture, making the town's streets gleam.[27]

So at the turn of the twentieth century Colorado Springs was not precisely your typical Western city. And yet, every bit as much as Cripple Creek or other mining towns in the area, Colorado Springs was transformed by the capitalist logic that reduced nature to a "collection of commodities," by what historian Patricia Limerick has characterized as "the attitude of extractive industry—get in, get rich, get out."[28] The story I tell here is very much a Western story in other respects as well. That is because over time many cities of the West would increasingly come to resemble Colorado Springs, with its service-sector economy, non-unionized workforce, and reliably conservative electorate. And moving forward into the 1940s, the far edge of my time frame, the town's militarized economy presaged what would happen in much of the West, loaded today with military installations.[29] If anything, Colorado Springs prefigured what the West became.[30]

To be clear, if my mother's hometown was prototypical, its rightward trajectory was never a foregone conclusion. Yes, the mining and milling interests came to enjoy an outsized influence there, but even that was not preordained. After all, the Pikes Peak region, where organized labor is now virtually banished, was once a hotbed of radical unionism. W.S. Stratton, who became a mining millionaire, started out as a carpenter and remained a proud union man. Moreover, in contrast to most of the state, Colorado Springs fought off the KKK. The Pikes Peak area was also once home to militant suffragists and Populists, and even some socialists. Although the period covered in this book is one in which conservatism held sway, the city's longer history demonstrates it was not hardwired for conservatism.

The strains of conservatism I track in *Shortfall* first took hold in those parts of the American West characterized by non-unionized labor, plentiful and cheap land, minimal business taxes, and a political system controlled by the business elite.[31] The region's politicians have long attacked the federal government despite its aid in subjugating native peoples, fighting labor unions, subsidizing the construction of the railroad and dams, and stabilizing local economies through the development of a military economy. Of course, plenty of Americans, as historian Michael Kazin has observed, "hate big government and love federal spending—as long as it benefits them and anyone else they regard as morally worthy."[32] However, the involvement of the federal government in the development of the West, and particularly in the *regulation* of its development, elicited a response from Westerners that one historian

has characterized as "politically schizophrenic." Despite (or perhaps because of) the New Deal's largesse toward the West, which
received three times the national average of federal expenditures,
Westerners' response to the federal government went something
like this: "Get out and give us more money."[33]

Still, Colorado Springs seems to have had a head start on other
Western cities, even Barry Goldwater's Phoenix, when it comes to
conservatism.[34] Consider this: the city's founder, General William J.
Palmer, modeled tax resistance in 1884, a mere thirteen years after
establishing the town, by announcing that he was leaving El Paso
County and would no longer be paying personal income tax there.[35]
As is the case today, there were competing strands of conservatism
in play. There was the slash-taxes-and-eviscerate-government crew
of conservatives who foreshadow today's Tea Party activists. And
then there were the city's elite businessmen, most of whom were
among neoliberalism's early adopters as they deployed the rhetoric
of free enterprise while developing pro-business tax and regulatory
climates. The bottom line is that if you want to understand the
history of conservatism in the United States, you might want to
familiarize yourself with Colorado Springs as well as Kansas, the
subject of Thomas Frank's important 2004 book.[36]

Thinking about the relationship between capitalism, class, and
conservatism means grappling with homeownership. America can
rightfully boast that, historically, homeownership has been achiev-
able here, even for millions of working-class Americans. Those very
same Americans, many of them immigrants, viewed owning their
own home as the surest path to family security and the best buffer
against the uncertainties of industrial capitalism.[37] When building
and loan associations were gaining a foothold in America in the
post–Civil War years, they did so as nonprofits. In those B&Ls
guided by the principles of mutuality and cooperation, members
found that this promise was often kept. But as *Shortfall* documents,

the culture of building and loans shifted by the late nineteenth century, and the cooperative movement of which they were a part waned. Buying a home, for those with few resources, became more of a gamble—and more of an individual enterprise than a community endeavor. Increasingly, buying a home meant buying on contract or dealing with a dodgy loan man like my grandfather, and in both cases a forfeiture clause was standard.

In his 1906 novel *The Jungle,* Upton Sinclair exposed the rip-off—the "trap of the extra payments, the interest, and all the other charges that they had not the means to pay"—that for many working-class families was the reality of real estate.[38] Studies of housing in Chicago indicate that Sinclair's fictional account described all too well the pitfalls for the working classes of owning property.[39] By the turn of the twentieth century the foreclosure rate for Chicago's working people stood at a full 50 percent.[40] Despite this checkered history, it is an article of faith in America that homeownership is an unambiguous good, a surefire path toward upward mobility, even in the wake of our own disastrous subprime mortgage crisis. That homes can be (and have been) our ruin is simply not a part of Americans' cultural memory. And in later chapters I ask if homeownership may affect more than our pocketbooks—if it may, indeed, change our political understanding of the world we inhabit.

Understanding class requires getting at its emotional undertow. For the most part, American historians have ceded this territory to novelists, playwrights, and screenwriters.[41] Jay Gatsby, Clyde Griffiths in Dreiser's *American Tragedy,* Mildred Pierce, Willy Loman, and George Bailey are among their most memorable creations. Mildred Pierce builds an empire of restaurants, but the "smells of grease" from her kitchens betray her lack of class and make her repellent to her haughty daughter. Jay Gatsby can throw swanky parties and use leisure-class lingo such as "old sport," but it's Daisy Buchanan, the woman with the voice "full of money," with whom

he is infatuated. And who can forget that scene on the train plat-
form in *It's a Wonderful Life* when George realizes his brother,
Harry, is reneging on his promise to take over the B&L? In those
moments before he pulls himself together, his face registers the
dismay and the pain of being consigned for the rest of his life to his
dad's shabby office.

As these examples signal, class is relational. It plays out in intimate spaces as well as workplaces, and class feelings are not read-
ily shed. None of the aforementioned characters is stereotypically
blue-collar, yet class is hardly negligible in their lives, and so it is
with the people in this book. Some of the folks who turn up in these
pages, such as the unionized millworkers in turn-of-the-century
Colorado City, saw themselves, at least briefly, as part of a politi-
cized working class. But this book takes on board a range of people whose occupations, neighborhoods, educational backgrounds,
and income levels lie outside the conventional parameters of the
"working class." Salesclerks, stenographers, seamstresses, secretaries, contractors, carpenters, stonecutters, waitresses, barbers,
even struggling shopkeepers—they were blue-collar, pink-collar,
and even white-collar, which is why I describe them as "working
people" or the "working classes." If they shared a disposition—and
I can't say for sure that they all did—"getting ahead" may best describe it.[42]

A hybrid, *Shortfall* ranges across subfields of twentieth-century
U.S. history—labor, conservatism, the West, and gender. It features a braided narrative: a financial history, a community study,
and a family history. British writer Alison Light has described family history as a "trespasser" that disregards multiple boundaries,
including those between the private and the public.[43] Readers of
this book will surely experience this dissolve between public and
private. What this means in practical terms is that, throughout,
the narrative toggles between the micro and the macro. A passage
about an intimate family detail might give way to a discussion of

fringe financing. But in a narrative in which both an individual family and the American economy are moving inexorably toward ruin, this back-and-forth approach underscores the fact that despite our best efforts to deny it, the boundaries between intimate life and business are sometimes surprisingly porous.

Part One

1

Advertisements for Himself

Walter Clyde Davis's name first turned up in the Colorado press just two months after he relocated there. It was the fall of 1905 when news of the twenty-four-year-old's marriage appeared in the local press. The mention in the *Colorado Springs Gazette* played up the romantic angle. Separated for two months—with Davis in Colorado and his fiancée, Lula Gilham, in Indiana—the young couple married the very evening she stepped off the westbound train in the Springs. Gilham was said to be from "one of the most wealthy and influential families in Indiana," and Davis was described as having practiced law in his home state. According to the write-up, they were from the Hoosier state's more cosmopolitan cities—she from Indianapolis and he from Columbus. The *Denver Post* approached the story differently. "Pleading at Bar Wins Heiress for Colorado Lawyer" was the title of its account of their marriage. Here, the "very handsome" twenty-one-year-old bride was said to have struck a hard bargain with her suitor, agreeing to marry him only if he won an important lawsuit in Indiana. "If you win this suit, you win me," she declared. Davis prevailed, the paper said, with one of the arguments of his life.

So how far from the truth did these Colorado marriage

announcements stray? Was my grandfather a hotshot lawyer and my grandmother an heiress?

When Walter Davis arrived in the Springs at age twenty-three he carried with him business cards that described him as a lawyer in Greensburg, Indiana. He carried something else as well—two letters of reference. The letter writers, both of them prominent judges, were generous in their praise of him. Yet it was as an "office man"—a stenographer and typist—and not as a lawyer that the judges recommended him. It turns out that Walter Davis had worked as a court reporter, and before that as a barber in his father's well-appointed tonsorial parlor. It was his father's tuberculosis that precipitated Davis's move to Colorado Springs, where the clean, dry mountain air was thought to cure the disease.

Lula Gilham was raised in Greensburg as well, but in a hardscrabble part of town. The daughter of a stonecutter and a dressmaker, she was orphaned at age ten. Over a two-year period, tuberculosis wiped out her family. A drugstore clerk, likely the one who sold her bottles of cough syrup, became her guardian. After living with his family and nearly finishing high school, she got a job as a clerk in a department store before moving to Indianapolis, where she secured work repairing fur coats in a ladies' tailoring shop. At age eighteen she should have come into a modest inheritance when her guardian gave her some part of the $1,000 insurance payout due her and any money from the sale of her parents' run-down cabin.

I cannot prove that my grandfather composed these self-serving Colorado marriage announcements, which are among the few scraps in the family archive that chronicle my grandparents' lives when they were young. I do have the handwritten version of a more restrained marriage announcement that appeared in the Greensburg press, and it was composed on stationery Walter had used in the last job he held in Indiana. How he managed to persuade the Colorado papers to run these stories when wedding announcements were typically two to three sentences long, I don't know.

Davis family, circa 1888, in a Greensburg, Indiana, photo studio. From left: Lizzie, Ray, Roy, Walter, and Allen. Even at this age, Walter seems tightly wound, perhaps because the staging made baby Roy the main attraction. (Author's archive)

In this school picture, Lula Gilham is in the back row, second from the right. (Author's archive)

However, we see in this bit of misrepresentation his determination to use the move west in order to reinvent himself. In this respect he was no different from many other transplants. That said, how many newcomers would go so far as to pass themselves off as members of the moneyed professional class?

There is no fathoming Walter Clyde Davis without understanding Colorado Springs. Likewise, it is impossible to make sense of Colorado Springs without situating its story within a larger narrative about the development of the American West, a region that in the aftermath of the Civil War figured prominently in the national imaginary. The West was a place where people like my grandparents came to reinvent themselves. And it was also the place where some believed the nation itself could be reimagined. These were years of promise and peril that pivoted around fundamental questions of freedom, equality, and national identity. Would the Union hold together? How expansively would citizenship be defined, and would it be extended to African Americans, immigrants, and women? What place would Native Americans have in this reconstructing nation? And by 1877, the year of the Great Railroad Strike, there was no avoiding another great divide—labor versus capital. Was it possible to reconcile the country's republican ideals with the growing industrial working class, much of which labored and lived in deplorable conditions that rivaled those of Europe? Was American exceptionalism sustainable? For many, the West, with its grand, unspoiled vistas, held the promise of renewal and redemption.

Few people invested more hope in the West than the founder of Colorado Springs, William Jackson Palmer, an engineer, a railroad executive, and, by the end of the Civil War, the highest-ranking Quaker officer in either army—a brevetted brigadier general in the Union Army. Like other railroad men, General Palmer saw the development of a transcontinental railroad system as critical to a number of projects—postwar reconstruction, the conquest of

Left: Even when he was young, Walter Davis radiated attitude in studio portraits. (Author's archive). *Right:* A young Lula Gilham. (Author's archive)

native people, the opening of Asian trade, and the expansion of trade relations with northern Mexico. However, what most excited him about the railroad's development was the role it would surely play in the discovery and exploitation of coal. As secretary-treasurer of the Kansas Pacific Railway, Palmer promised to bring what he called the "star of empire" westward into an area whose coalfields he would make among the most productive in the world.

Palmer was an evangelist for "mineral-intensive industrialization." Powered by coal, the Mountain West would undergo, he argued, an industrial revolution that would rival that of England. Of course, Colorado was no stranger to mining. The Pikes Peak gold rush ("Pikes Peak or Bust!") had already played itself out by the end of the Civil War. Ultimately, the gold mines had not produced as much wealth as they had consumed. The prevalence of hucksters had undermined the region's standing in financial markets. If that wasn't bad enough, locusts were destroying the crops. In 1869,

one on-the-ground observer went so far as to warn that a "prema-
ture decrepitude" threatened the region. But at the same time that
others were writing the area off, Palmer was envisioning it as an
industrial powerhouse whose growth was virtually guaranteed by
the apparent inexhaustibility of coal there. He also believed that
the region's rugged and remote terrain would inoculate it against
economic competition, which he blamed for many of the country's
problems, particularly its labor woes. If industry were organized
paternalistically, he argued, workers would feel as though they
were a part of a family rather than at the mercy of some "soulless
corporation."

Palmer did more than daydream about the future of the region.
He left the Kansas Pacific and formed a new railroad, the Denver & Rio Grande Railroad (D&RG), which would run south of
Denver. And he set about surveying and buying coal land. Palmer
bought thousands of acres of such land in southern Colorado,
enough to power the D&RG, and enough to eventually make his
Colorado Coal and Iron Company the largest coal mine operator
of the Mountain West. Indeed the acrid smell of burning coal was
a familiar one to Coloradans in the period between the 1860s and
1910s.

At the same time that Palmer pursued the intensive exploitation
of these coal lands, he also yearned to make the area "a home in
nature," one that would bring together the "best features of the
Western wildness and European refinement."[1] In all his Colorado
dreaming Palmer does not seem to have sensed any contradiction
between his advocacy of intensive coal mining and the preservation
of the nature he so loved. And yet Palmer knew, especially from
having visited British coal mines and some of the industries they
powered, that industrialization could damage both workers and the
surrounding environment. In personal terms, Palmer would manage to have it both ways. The town he founded, Colorado Springs,
would remain a bit of paradise on earth because wherever mining

was happening, it was happening on the town's outskirts, not inside it.[2]

Palmer decided he had found his home in nature in 1869 when he first came to Monument Park, at the base of Pikes Peak. Besotted with the place, located about seventy miles south of Denver, he rhapsodized to his fiancée that life in this place could not help but be "poetry." He toyed with the idea of calling it "Bijou" to signify its preciousness. Palmer found its majestic mountain views transformative, and he thought others of his station might feel "elevated by them into a lofty place of thought and purpose." And yet he wasn't going to leave this to chance. A place so divine could not be allowed to become like other Western towns with their bawdy amusements—saloons, brothels, and gambling. When he established the Colorado Springs Company in 1871 to promote and sell land there, he stipulated that this was a place for those of "good character and strict temperance habits." He hoped the rich would flock there, as they had to Eastern resorts, but ideals mattered to him.

And yet as Palmer and his associates moved ahead with planning their new community, they were not motivated by idealism alone. It may have been "Bijou," but that doesn't mean that Palmer and the rest of the men in his outfit would permit the truth to get in their way when it came to turning a profit. Unable to resist the temptations of hype, they called the new community Colorado Springs despite the fact that the closest spring was a good six miles away, in Manitou. The town's founders outlawed gambling, but in naming the new development they were betting that the white settlers whom they were trying to lure there would not be too bothered by that sleight of hand.

The Colorado Springs Company moved quickly, buying ten thousand acres of land for a dollar an acre. By the summer of 1871 it had driven the town's first stake at what would become the intersection of Pikes Peak and Cascade Avenues. Only three months later the D&RG was offering rail service between Colorado Springs and Denver. By the end of 1871, more than 150 structures (many of them portable houses shipped from Chicago) had been erected, and quite a few cottonwood trees had been planted. However, the first visitors were not always enchanted with what they found. It may have been called Colorado Springs, but Marshall Sprague, who wrote a loving history of the town, admits that the town site was "treeless, bleak, brown."[3] Two years later British journalist Isabella Lucy Bird traveled there and pronounced Colorado Springs "a queer, embryo-looking place" whose treelessness appalled her.[4]

Sales were sluggish at first, but a shrewd advertising campaign in the British press, selling the Springs as an ideal place for everything from cattle and sheep ranching to regaining one's health, was so successful that the town came to be known as "Little London."[5] Wealthy men from the East who were suffering from "neurasthenia," a nervous condition associated with exhaustion and linked to the demands of modern American commerce, also arrived. One of the era's most widely read doctors prescribed that such men head west and engage in physical activity. He was the same doctor who devised the "rest cure" for women stricken with neurasthenia, the "cure" that Charlotte Perkins Gilman exposed in "The Yellow Wall-paper."[6] The opening of sanitariums and hospitals, and the growing reputation of Manitou's mineral springs—said to cure any number of ailments—brought more and more health seekers to the area. The opening in 1883 of the Antlers Hotel, a luxury hotel with Turkish baths and central heating, further enhanced the Springs as a tourist destination.

Still, Colorado Springs remained a sleepy resort town until 1891, when prospector Robert Womack discovered rich gold-bearing quartz in a cow pasture known as Cripple Creek. Thirty years had passed since the conclusion of Colorado's gold rush, which had started in 1858. Only twenty miles from Colorado Springs, as the crow flies, the mining district was six miles square. It was

The Antlers hotel and downtown Colorado Springs, circa 1915. In the mid-sixties the Antlers was demolished and rebuilt. It is now a thirteen-story behemoth that from Pikes Peak Avenue obscures the stunning view of Pikes Peak. (Courtesy of the Andrew J. Harlan Photograph Collection, the Pikes Peak Library District, 402-45)

located in the crater of an extinct volcano that was filled with great quantities of lava and granite that contained dry quartz filled with pure gold. This was not the sort of "picture rock" that had caught the eye of earlier prospectors, but once the nature of the deposits was understood, gold production in Cripple Creek exploded, from $2 million worth in 1893 to sixty times that amount by 1902.[7] Nowhere else in America produced more gold that year than Cripple Creek. During the era of Cripple Creek gold fever, bank deposits in Colorado Springs increased ninefold, and the town's population tripled. More often than not, the mine owners moved away from the mining district and took up residence in Colorado Springs, often on Wood Avenue, which was soon dubbed "Millionaires' Row." At the turn of the century Colorado Springs boasted that it had the greatest number of millionaires per capita anywhere in the United States.

Already a town that leaned in the direction of the leisure class, Colorado Springs was remade by all the gold. As conceived by General Palmer, the Springs was meant to be an ennobling place that would function as a refined retreat from the crassly commercial. But with Cripple Creek, the town embraced the speculative.[8] The Colorado Springs Mining Exchange became the financial hub of the town. By 1899 it was handling more than 230 million mining shares valued at over $34 million.[9] Some of that mining money found its way into the town's parks, roads, medical facilities, cultural institutions, and transportation system. Highlights included the elegant opera house, the Antlers Hotel, Colorado College, nearby Monument Valley Park, numerous shops and restaurants (including a vegetarian eatery), three sanitariums, and a state-of-the-art trolley car system that took passengers nearly everywhere, including the recently opened Zoo Park, an amusement park in Cheyenne Creek. As for the Cripple Creek District, its growth was off the charts, although there were plenty of businesses there that General Palmer would have regarded as disreputable. By 1900, its population stood at almost twenty thousand, with nearly sixteen thousand residents employed in the mines.

By the 1910s Colorado Springs was unrecognizable from the days when it was a "dreary stretch of sagebrush and yucca."[10] With its red-light district and industrial sector relegated to adjacent Colorado City, the Springs could be said to be in the West, but not completely of it. In many ways it was, as it advertised, a "Spotless Town," just as General Palmer had envisioned.[11] And of course its surroundings—Pikes Peak, the Garden of the Gods, Manitou Springs—would always make it special. A Western town that in some ways played against type, it prided itself on its sophistication. A "rare combination of climate and culture" was how one piece of boosterism put it in 1917.[12] This was something grasped by many

In 1897 Cripple Creek was a thriving mining town, a far cry from what it became in the mid-twentieth century. In 1952's *The Price of Salt* Patricia Highsmith described it as a "tiny disorder of a town." (Courtesy of the Cripple Creek Photograph Collection, the Pikes Peak Library District, 174-3476)

"cultured" foreigners, including the Englishman who named the Springs one of the only two civilized places between the Atlantic and Pacific Oceans (the other was Chicago) because it offered polo, good society, and, on occasion, even decent tea.[13] Many residents and visitors would have agreed with a leading city planner who in 1905 claimed that the Springs belonged to a "very small, very highly favored class of city."[14]

All the gold money that streamed into Colorado Springs did more than just prettify the place. Some historians have argued that gold helped shift ideas of success in America, following the California gold rush of 1848. "The old American dream, the dream inherited from ten generations of ancestors," writes H.W. Brands, "was the dream of the Puritans, of Benjamin Franklin's Poor Richard, of Thomas Jefferson's yeoman farmers: of men and women content to accumulate their modest fortunes a little at a time, year by year." In the wake of the gold rush, Brands argues, tempered expectations were supplanted by a "new dream . . . the dream of instant wealth."[15] Recent work on the great California gold rush complicates Brands's view. However, I would argue that for the men who became mine owners during the Cripple Creek gold rush, the dream of striking it rich (or richer in the case of those who arrived on the scene already moneyed) was often a powerful lure.

All the millions made off the gold strikes skewed expectations as the town's leaders and boosters came to expect that the Springs enjoyed a lock on success. Colorado Springs was too rich, and with too beautiful a surrounding area, to fail. Yes, there might be periodic downturns in Cripple Creek mining, but as long as there were gold strikes that resulted in mines like Winfield Scott Stratton's seemingly inexhaustible Independence Mine, the money spigot would stay firmly in the on position.[16]

Gold rushes shifted consciousness in another way, too. "Mining set a mood" in the West, as Patricia Limerick has argued. Even after gold mining was played out, "the attitude of extractive industry" persisted.[17] Frank Norris captured this predatory disposition in his novel *The Octopus*, which focused on the agricultural entrepreneurs of California. The San Joaquin Valley farmers at the center of his book "worked their ranches as, a quarter of a century before, they had worked their mines . . . To get all there was out of the land, to squeeze it dry, to exhaust it seemed their policy. When, at last, the land, worn out, would refuse to yield, they would invest their money in something else; by then, they would all have made fortunes. They did not care. 'After us the deluge.'"[18]

In Colorado Springs nature's beauty and nature's bounty were inextricably connected. The inseparability of the land's beauty and its commercial potential was unintentionally captured by then vice president Theodore Roosevelt who, upon traveling on the old Short Line railroad from Colorado Springs to Cripple Creek, a route of stunning views, reached for a financial term to describe the experience. The trip was so beautiful, he remarked, it "bankrupts the English language!"[19] Over the years the specialness of the land underwrote schemes large and small—resorts, hotels, spas, sanitariums, and eventually the military installation cum nuclear bunker known as NORAD, built deep into Cheyenne Mountain.[20] One such scheme was the brainchild of a Chicago politician who in 1905 spent $75,000 building a "Coney Island resort" in Ivywild, a neighborhood just south of downtown. With dazzling lights, a roller coaster offering lightning-fast rides, and a small zoo featuring an elephant, a bear, and a "sacred cow" that was said to be from India, the amusement park attracted upward of five thousand people on weekends. Its closure a decade later exemplifies what sometimes happened to those big dreams. Both the zoo's sacred cow and the bear were purchased, butchered, and sold to the public as meat. In the bear's case, it was chained outside a popular downtown restaurant for several days as an attraction—a "wild bear," the management claimed—before being slaughtered and fed to its customers.[21]

Of course, more than anything Colorado Springs owed its success and its preciousness to the exploitation of the land in the Cripple Creek mining district. Cripple Creek's gold proved difficult to reach; it required industrial methods and legions of miners who toiled underground and for a wage. It was labor and time intensive, and, unsurprisingly, it took money to bring it off.[22] Although there were some exceptions—most notably Winfield Stratton, an enterprising carpenter who became Cripple Creek's first millionaire—a number of the men who made their fortunes in Cripple Creek hailed from wealthy or at least influential families.

Still, there were differences in mine owners' class backgrounds and political allegiances, and they were not negligible. Despite their physical proximity, with many of them living clustered together in the North End of the Springs, the area's mining moguls did not always stand united. At opposite ends of the pole were the aforementioned W.S. Stratton, who retained a strong identification with the working class, and a group of younger, mostly Eastern-born men—Charles Tutt, Albert E. Carlton, Charles MacNeill, and Spencer Penrose, whose brother Boies was the very powerful U.S. senator from Pennsylvania. Their privileged backgrounds earned them the sobriquet "the Socialites."

Despite his outsized wealth, which by the turn of the century stood at $16 million, W.S. Stratton had no truck with the Colorado Springs millionaires' club. Rather than build a mansion on Millionaires' Row, he moved into an older frame house he had once worked on as a carpenter, a house unfashionably close to the business district.[23] He also made a point of paying his workers between $3 and $5 a day because in his view it wasn't right for a former workingman like himself "to take advantage of the necessities of his fellow men."[24] An iconoclast, Stratton supported free silver presidential candidate William Jennings Bryan, even though it was not in his own financial interest to do so. He was generous—outfitting the city with an up-to-date streetcar system that ran forty-one miles, donating Cheyenne Park to the town, and giving lots of valuable land to the county and the federal government. Long after he had made his fortune, Stratton underscored his alienation from the town's elite by joining the Colorado Springs carpenters' union, local no. 515. As a final nose-thumbing to the town's establishment, he directed that upon his death most of his vast fortune should go to the creation of a poorhouse—a comfortable one where El Paso County's orphans and elderly would receive ample, wholesome food and quality care from the home's nurses and doctors.[25]

Stratton's egalitarian vision of the American dream was not shared by the Socialites, who reportedly kicked back with the working-class men and women of Cripple Creek in the early days of the rush, the years when it was all gambling and booze and brothels, but who did not identify with those men and women or their struggles. Philadelphians Spencer Penrose and Charles Tutt enjoyed a long-term business partnership, and they would have an enduring effect upon the region. After striking it rich and selling

Spencer Penrose is fifth from the left in this undated photograph. (Courtesy of the Margaretta M. Boas Photograph Collection, the Pikes Peak Library District, 001-277)

the C.O.D., their Cripple Creek mine, Penrose and Tutt (along with partner Charles MacNeill), did what so many mining magnates did: having extracted what they could from the land, they moved on to fresh terrain. In their case, they moved into the business of refining gold ore, which seemed more lucrative than mining it. They secured financial backing from Philadelphia capitalists as well as from local men, including Stratton. Their new business, the Colorado-Philadelphia Reduction Company (later surpassed by the United States Reduction and Refining Company, or USR&R, a refining conglomerate), built its first plant on the outskirts of Colorado City, at the eastern edge of Red Rock Canyon. A chlorination mill to refine the gold coming out of the Cripple Creek mining district, it was the largest of its kind in the United States, and it marked the beginning of what became an empire of refining mills.[26]

Colorado City was the region's industrial hub. Briefly the capital of the state before the outbreak of the Civil War, Colorado City was hardly robust by the time General Palmer founded Colorado

Springs. "A decayed looking cluster of homes" was how journalist Bird described it in 1873. However, twenty years later the gold strikes in Cripple Creek had transformed Colorado City into a bustling town, albeit a very different kind of bustling town compared to Colorado Springs. Located between Manitou and Colorado Springs, Colorado City was the place to which everything deemed undesirable by its tony neighbors to the east—the drinking and carousing and the dirty mills—was consigned. Virtually every corner sported a saloon, and the south side of Colorado Avenue between 25th and 26th Streets was pretty much nothing but dance halls and barrooms with passageways that reportedly connected to a tunnel system that led to the area's popular brothels. With four big ore-reduction mills at one point located there, likely employing upward of six hundred men, it was where much of the area's working class worked and lived, sometimes in fairly shabby circumstances.[27] To unionist "Big Bill" Haywood of the Western Federation of Miners

In this 1901 photograph, the Standard Mill is on the left and the Philadelphia Mill, formerly the U.S. Reduction and Refining Company, is on the right. Laborers there wore shoes to which blocks of two-by-four were attached in order to avoid having their feet burned by the hot ore. (Courtesy of the Margaretta M. Boas Photograph Collection, the Pikes Peak Library District, 001-2193)

(WFM), the place was a "forlorn little industrial town of tents, tin houses, huts, and hovels."[28] Today this area is home to some fine historic buildings; it is also home to a fair number of dilapidated cottages from that era.

The men who profited from the mills lived in Colorado Springs, and increasingly they invested their money in other parts of the West. "None of the refined gold was left here—nothing but waste and slum" was unionist Haywood's grim verdict.[29] And whenever the wind blew, the chemically treated gold tailings left in huge piles by the mills created "immense clouds of dust" for residents of Colorado City and west Colorado Springs.[30]

As the writers of the WPA Guide to 1930s Colorado succinctly put it, "Colorado City did the work, but the great fortunes went elsewhere," specifically to Utah, where Penrose and company would make yet another fortune mining copper.[31] In the process, they joined forces with Cripple Creek titan and Socialite A.E. "Bert" Carlton, who controlled the transportation of all that gold. And before long they moved, with him, into sugar beet production. Penrose and the Tutt family would become known for their philanthropy, but not immediately. And along the way the two men took a position toward labor that was strikingly different from Stratton's.

In the early years of the boom, particularly while Stratton was still alive, there was a substantial middle ground between the Socialites, on the one hand, and Stratton, on the other. But in the wake of Stratton's death in 1902 that shifted, and the jockeying for dominance grew more intense. Something else shifted as well—the remaining mine owners no longer felt constrained in their dealings with an increasingly militant labor movement. Cripple Creek workers had long resented the mines' absentee owners, and when they referred to the Springs as "Little London" they did so with a sneer.[32] But starting in the 1890s, labor, particularly the radical Western Federation of Miners, began flexing its muscle—both at the workplace and at the polling station. When workers went out on strike in

Business partners Spencer Penrose and Charles L. Tutt Sr., circa 1895. (Courtesy of the Andrew J. Harlan Photograph Collection, the Pikes Peak Library District, 001-366)

1894 to protest management's demands for wage cuts and a longer workday, Colorado's pro-labor Populist governor, Davis Waite, supported them, and the strikers won. Relations between management and labor remained tense, however, as Colorado become what one observer called a "storm center in labor troubles."[33]

The actions of Governor Waite had the effect of energizing conservatives, including the men behind the *Colorado Springs Gazette*. The paper routinely denounced Waite as a dangerous radical and the WFM as a violent outfit. The mine owners and operatives in Colorado Springs worked especially hard in these years to cultivate political influence in state government. With the collapse of Populism in Colorado by 1896, organized labor would find itself in just a few years facing a very different political landscape. The period also witnessed another change, the "industrial integration of mining and smelting." Competition between these titans of industry was often ruthless, and meant that the region's big industrialists did not always move in lockstep. Still, the next big strike in the region, which began in February 1903, nine years after the first strike, brought very different results.[34]

None of the owners of Colorado City's three mills could have been pleased when in August 1902 the city's millworkers formed the Mill and Smeltermen's Union, which was part of WFM District Union No. 1, the union of Cripple Creek miners. In response, Charles MacNeill of USR&R hired a Pinkerton detective who provided him with the names of forty-two union men at the Standard, the company's lone Colorado City mill. It was only after the USR&R then fired those men that the Mill and Smeltermen's Union called a strike. The Mine Owners Association (MOA) hired strikebreakers and Pinkerton detectives. The MOA also persuaded Colorado's Republican governor, James Peabody, to call up the National Guard, despite the opposition of Colorado City's elected officials, including its chief of police, George Birdsall. After little more than a month the owners of the Portland and Telluride mills settled with the strikers, and on terms favorable to the union. However, MacNeill refused to bargain, and the strike at the USR&R mills dragged on. The WFM was not eager for a strike, but by early August 3, 552 miners in the Cripple Creek District elected to go on strike at mines that continued supplying ore to nonunion mills. "Everything seems to be on strike in the State of Colorado" was General Palmer's gloomy response.[35]

This time around the MOA had the governor of Colorado in its corner and the support of a surging movement of businessmen, the Citizens' Alliance—a virtual arm of the Republican Party. There

Armed miners, possibly members of the Western Federation of Miners (WFM), on strike in 1904 in Victor, Colorado. (Courtesy of the Cripple Creek Photograph Collection, the Pikes Peak Library District, 192-4293)

were Citizens' Alliances across the country and in Cripple Creek its members were dedicated to defeating the WFM. As the strike dragged on there was an escalation in violence on both sides. One historian has described this period as nothing less than a "miniature civil war."[36] But the governor's actions—establishing martial law, suspending civil liberties, shuttering a free press in affected areas, calling in the National Guard, appointing to his military staff USR&R's Charles MacNeill and Spencer Penrose as aides-de-camp, allowing the company to pay the salaries of additional deputies, and choosing anti-union mining manager Sherman Bell to lead the troops—were blatantly one-sided and doomed the strike to failure.[37] Bell made clear his intentions: to "do up this damned anarchistic federation."

The strike stretched on, and in early June 1904, after one terrible, violent incident that the MOA blamed on strikers, lawyer and MOA secretary Clarence C. Hamlin orchestrated the deportation of WFM members who were found guilty by kangaroo courts presided over by members of the Citizens' Alliance. Approximately 263 men were loaded onto trains, which took them to either the Kansas or New Mexico state line, where they were deposited. The union men, some of them homeowners, were told to never again return to Cripple Creek.[38] The withdrawal of pro-employer troops that August did nothing to improve the situation in Cripple Creek and adjacent mining areas. Instead, it unleashed what the *New York Times* called a "reign of terror" as union sympathizers in the Cripple Creek area were subjected to mob violence, to which the governor turned a blind eye. In the Cripple Creek mining district, those opposed to unionism seized control of the local press and all municipal and county offices. In the future, all employees at the Cripple Creek District mines and the Colorado City ore mills were required to sign MOA cards. It was rumored that promotion in the mines would now be contingent upon being both a Republican and a Mason. Within two years the population of the once-vibrant

Cripple Creek was significantly smaller, as some mines never re-
opened, gold production slowed, demand for miners fell off, and
committed unionists left the area.[39]

The WFM's defeat would precipitate the formation of an even
more radical organization, the Industrial Workers of the World
(IWW). But the IWW would have no impact in Cripple Creek or
Colorado City. In these towns the defeat of the WFM did more
than alter the conditions of work in the mining industry. It remade
the political landscape as well. Voting Republican in the Cripple
Creek District was now virtually mandatory, with the result that
Teller County went Republican. It was the first time since 1899,
when the district had broken away from Republican-dominated
El Paso County to become its own county, that the Democrats
had lost it. The result: Clarence Hamlin was elected its new district attorney and Sherman Bell its sheriff. It was as if the city had
been taken over by a permanent occupying force.[40] As the publisher
of the *Colorado Springs Evening Telegraph*, which he acquired in
1903, Hamlin was already a powerful man. The town's two newspapers, the *Gazette* and the *Telegraph*, changed hands a good deal
during the early twentieth century, but they were often in the
hands of mine owners or those friendly to them. And in 1923 both
newspapers came under the control of Penrose, Tutt Jr., Hamlin,
and T.E. Nowels Sr. Doggedly anti-union, the papers' management
apparently went so far as to fire a newsboy it believed to be a "labor
agitator."[41]

Throughout the strike, the MOA, the Citizens' Alliance, and the
militia presented themselves as victimized by the WFM and its
supporters.[42] The MOA's narrative of the strike parallels the way in
which, a decade earlier, Wyoming cattle kings, many of them Ivy
League–educated Easterners and British aristocrats, characterized small homesteaders as rustlers, illegally encroaching on their
rights. Take the example of the hugely popular western *The Vir-
ginian*, which was written by Penrose family friend Owen Wister.

In his novel, Wister transformed an actual incident—the killing of two cowboys outside of Casper, Wyoming, by cattle kings and their paid mercenaries—into something entirely defensible, indeed necessary. In Wister's hands, what was actually "a brutal murder by a power elite" became instead a proverbial case of what historian Christine Bold calls "heroic individualism"—"'your ordinary citizen' taking back the power of the U.S. constitution on the wild frontier."[43] As historian Patricia Limerick has pointed out, Americans' tendency to cast themselves as innocent victims goes all the way back to the East Coast's colonial elite, but it was nowhere more developed than in the West, where white settlers saw themselves as innocent pioneers. "An empire of innocence" is Limerick's verdict.[44]

Governor Peabody's handling of the 1903–4 strike is symptomatic of much of the American West of the early twentieth century, and particularly in Colorado: a fusion of corporate and state power. In progressive circles, Colorado was known as a "corporation-ridden state." The effects were hardly abstract. For example, one reason that coal-mining deaths in Colorado were twice the national average was the weakness of the state's regulatory efforts. According to a 1914 report by the Congressional Committee on Mines and Mining, the political influence of the state's coal operators led to ineffective regulation and to dangerous working conditions of the sort "in existence in scarcely any state except Colorado."[45] Striking coal miners in 1914 called it "government of the companies, by the companies, and for the companies."[46] One leading Democrat, and a moderate at that, went so far as to attack the state's corporate chiefs as "anarchists" who used money and influence "to corrupt the ballot."[47]

During one interlude when the *Colorado Springs Gazette* was not controlled by the mining and mill trust, the paper savaged Republican Simon Guggenheim. All the "pin-headed little millionaire" had to do to win his Senate seat in Washington, claimed the paper,

Save Colorado from Socialism

VOTE THE REPUBLICAN TICKET

The choice between Benjamin Griffith and William E. Sweet is the choice between Americanism and Socialism. Griffith, the Republican nominee, is a builder and bulwark of constitutional government; Sweet, the Democratic nominee, a theorist and believer in the communistic schemes that wrecked Russia and bankrupted North Dakota.

Sweet is known throughout the state as a parlor Socialist. He openly praises his Socialistic warehouse plan and says he will invite such Bolshevik agitators as William Z. Foster to make Colorado their playground.

He is the son of Channing Sweet, for years a prominent Socialist; he is a personal friend of Eugene V. Debs, and is a member and admirer of the radical Denver "Open Forum."

It is so plain that Sweet is a Socialist that the Socialist party has withdrawn its candidate for governor and urges its members to vote for Sweet, and the radical wing of the Farmer-Labor party has filed a ticket of near-Bolshevists with Sweet at its head.

"The aim of Socialism," says the encyclopedia, "is to gain political power in order to convert private property in land and capital into collective property."

That is why the Socialist party, unable to seize the government in its own name, captured the Democratic party, put a man of its own stamp at the head of that party, and then rallied all the forces of disorder and revolution to his support.

Misery and famine followed the introduction of Socialism in Russia, and disorganization and bankruptcy followed its introduction in North Dakota. Similar consequences will follow if it wins in Colorado.

Benjamin Griffith is the ONLY candidate for governor, regardless of party, who stands for real American government in this election. To protect the sacred liberties of constitutional government from soviet sympathizers he must have the support of both executive and legislative branches.

Put GRIFFITH in the governor's chair and back him up with friends or Americanism, enemies of Socialism.

VOTE THE STRAIGHT REPUBLICAN TICKET

This 1922 Republican Party attack ad assails William E. Sweet, a progressive who advocated a living wage. It ran in the west-side newspaper, the *Independent*, which became the mouthpiece of the Ku Klux Klan. Despite being red-baited by both parties, Sweet won the governorship. (*Colorado Springs Independent*) was to "hang around Republican headquarters in Denver and make a noise like the rustling of a pile of bank notes."[48] This may seem hyperbolic, but as one student of Colorado's labor wars notes, Colorado really had "evolved into a massive company town," presided over by the state's very influential mining magnates and the businessmen in charge of the powerful Colorado Fuel & Iron Company.[49] In 1917, one advocate of cooperatives argued that Colorado harbored a "deep and powerful opposition to anything savoring of Co-operation," and the opposition ranged from the "big Rockefeller interests down to the small retail merchant."[50]

The strike shaped Colorado City and neighboring Colorado Springs. By the end of 1905, moderate mine owners were completely outflanked by the anti-union Socialites and those who did their bidding. The millworkers union that had taken hold at two Colorado City mills was now dead. Going forward, this would be the new order. In 1922 local business leaders chose none other than Charles Tutt Jr. to head up a new group that was taking root across America. The Open Shop Society was committed to promoting the "American Plan," which mandated that all workplaces be "open shops" in which union membership would be optional.[51] The National Association of Manufactures, a conservative business group, was the first to push for the open shop, which was, effectively, a crucial first step in getting rid of labor unions. It was so popular among businessmen and Chambers of Commerce across America that Sinclair Lewis included it in his bestselling send-up of get-ahead 1920s business culture, *Babbitt*.[52]

As for those striking workers, the union had meant considerably more to them than an annual Labor Day march. We know from Elizabeth Jameson's study of Cripple Creek that the strike's failure there had a devastating effect upon many of the district's working people. It meant the death of an idea and an ideal—that workers might constitute an effective counterforce to the power of the mining and mill barons, both at the workplace and in the voting booth.

More work needs to be done on working-class Colorado City, but there is no reason to think that defeated strikers and their support-ers there experienced it as anything other than a crushing blow. After all, the strike originated in its mills.[53]

With many of the region's most militant unionists deported and new anti-union rules in place, most of the remaining radicals very likely left town. One exception was a Danish socialist who after being deported from Cripple Creek settled in Colorado City. He continued to agitate, but then, he was a writer, not a millworker. For those who had gone out on strike but then had signed the hated MOA cards in order to work, they surely struggled to absorb the defeat. "Fear and accommodation" is how historian Jameson char-acterizes labor's relations with management, which held the upper hand, especially as gold mining and milling in the region began to wane. In 1905, with gold production slowing, the USR&R's MacNeill, declaring the mill could not be run "on atmosphere," announced the indefinite closure of the Standard, throwing two hundred men out of work. Soon the plant was sold to a competitor, who shut it down permanently in 1911 just three years after the opening of the Golden Cycle Mill, which introduced an improved and cheaper method of milling.[54] Socialite Bert Carlton bought the Golden Cycle Mill in 1915, but as gold production continued to decline so did the need for smeltermen and millers. Once again the population in Colorado City fell off.

Under this new regime in which unionism was banished, the white working class had limited ways to assert themselves. One way in which the residents of Colorado City continued to contest at least some aspects of the status quo was in the pages of their weekly paper. The *Colorado City Independent* (renamed the *Colo-rado Springs Independent* after the Springs annexed Colorado City in 1917) positioned itself in open opposition to the two Springs newspapers, which its editor derisively called "The Daily Twins."[55] It fought the city's high taxes, which west side residents found especially galling when their neighbors to the east were the ones with the good parks and schools, and the dust-free air. During Prohibition the paper attacked the Colorado Springs police chief, calling him "General Harper," and the man he was said to be protecting, the openly "wet" mining magnate and Broadmoor Hotel owner Spencer Penrose.

By 1924 the *Independent* had become an organ of the Ku Klux Klan, and this was yet another way in which the westside weekly expressed its hostility to the "big men" of the Springs, who were resolutely anti-Klan. The frequency with which the mine and mill trust had used immigrants (and sometimes African Americans) as strikebreakers goes some way toward explaining why, even twenty years after the de-unionizing of the Pikes Peak region, so many white working-class residents flocked to the Klan, which in this iteration targeted immigrants, Catholics, Jews, bootleggers, and African Americans, among others.[56] By 1926, Colorado had been so effectively "kluxed" that a *New York Times* journalist observed that the "invisible empire" wielded more power in Colorado than any other state, with the possible exceptions of Indiana and Kansas.[57]

The KKK enjoyed considerable and enduring support in old mining towns and on the west side of Colorado Springs.[58] At its peak, the El Paso County klavern attracted two thousand members and even boasted a Junior Klan and a women's Klan that featured an all-female orchestra. It ran a slate of candidates—the so-called American Ticket—during the 1925 municipal elections, but the Springs political establishment went all out to ensure its defeat.[59] The Klan was defeated, but Klan involvement was a way westsiders could provoke the Springs establishment.

To be clear, the political shift of the white working classes of Colorado City took time. As late as the mid-twenties the *Independent* opposed the establishment of ROTC in area high schools on the grounds that it would encourage militarism, which it blamed on the "greed and ambition" of the wealthy and government officials. The paper's stance may have reflected residents' memories of how the militia had been used against union men two decades earlier.[60] Class tensions persisted beyond the 1920s, but as later chapters demonstrate, by the 1930s politics in the Springs tended to be characterized by cross-class organizations. A widely shared "pioneer" identity, which included the prosperous and the working class, and the participation of so many men in lodges went some way toward mitigating the area's class tensions.[61]

Nearly twenty years separated the failed strike of 1903–4 and the rise of the KKK, and certainly other factors help explain the popularity of the Klan in those areas where unionism had been strong. That said, the trauma of the strike, coupled with the shriveling of Colorado City, likely reverberated across generations. There are parallels between what happened in Colorado City and what happened in many communities, particularly in the South in the wake of the failed Great Textile Strike of 1934. Workers there, unprepared for management's hard-line response, which brought unemployment and eviction, turned their backs once and for all on unionism. The legacy of the failed strike lingered there, undermining any effort at unionization.[62]

By the time the Davis family turned up in Colorado Springs in 1905, Colorado City still had its red-light district and many of its mill jobs. But by that point the anti-union regime was in place. The new order would not have transformed Walter Davis into a company man. After all, he arrived in town a stenographer located uncomfortably in the lower middle class but fully committed to joining the capitalist class.[63] Nonetheless, the changes that followed from the crushing of unionism transformed the town where Walter Davis would make his name. In a town where the elite felt entitled to run the show, the realm of the permissible widened for all businessmen. This was perhaps especially true of my grandfather, many of whose earliest customers were working-class residents of Colorado City.

Of course, there is no way that even as ambitious a newcomer as my grandfather could have immediately grasped the nature of power in Colorado Springs. During those first few weeks in town, at least when he was not trying to secure employment, he was probably taking it all in—particularly the comings and goings at the Mining Exchange. With a population of 21,000, Colorado Springs was more than three times the size of his hometown, and if not quite the jewel of Palmer's original dream, it still made Greensburg, Indiana, seem poky. His new home must have felt like a place of plenitude, where talent, cleverness, and ambition might win out.

Yet even as Colorado Springs offered opportunities to smart, go-ahead men, my grandfather would have soon discovered that its class boundaries at the upper end were rigidly drawn and meticulously maintained, much more so than in lethargic Greensburg. From its earliest days the Springs had cultivated a sense of its own preciousness, which was accentuated by the Cripple Creek mining boom. As a consequence, a kind of gold ceiling settled over the town, determining which men belonged to the El Paso Club and which families were members of the exclusive Cheyenne Mountain Country Club (where Teddy Roosevelt played polo) and participated in the world of gala parties, debutante balls, and charity events—all lavishly chronicled in the local newspapers.

Breaking into this world whose participants vacationed for "the season" in Europe, wore custom-made clothing, and hobnobbed with celebrities would have been daunting for a man of solid accomplishments. This was a world way beyond the ability and means of my twenty-four-year-old grandfather to crash. Nothing demonstrates just how far out of his league he was than those ludicrous marriage announcements in the Colorado papers. He also arrived with what felt to him like a liability. That would have been the rest of the Davis family—his father, fifty-one-year-old Allen; his mother, forty-five-year-old Lizzie; and his three siblings, twenty-one-year-old Ray, nearly eighteen-year-old Roy, and seven-year-old

The swells of Colorado Springs, otherwise known as the members of the Cheyenne
Mountain Country Club, in January 1913. Spencer Penrose is in the back row, fourth
to the left; photographer Laura Gilpin's father is in the middle row, to the left of the
man holding the trophy. (Courtesy John Lipsey Photograph Collection, the Pikes Peak
Library District, 304-4170)

Willard. Family finances were sufficiently tight, even in Greensburg, that only Walter had finished high school. Younger brother
Roy's schooling ended at the eighth grade, and it's a good bet that
Ray's did as well. On their first day in the Springs, Roy was sent out
to search for work, which he did, finding a job as a package wrap-
per at Hibbard Department Store. Although Walter had helped his
father set up a new barbershop, it was his brother Ray, who had
also worked with his dad in the Greensburg tonsorial parlor, who
joined him in this new venture.

The sale of his home and business back in Indiana enabled Allen
Davis to purchase a house and a small three-seat barbershop in
downtown. Walter and his father had scouted out possibilities for
another tonsorial parlor in the Springs, but the competition was
fiercer than they had faced back home. By the time they arrived in

Colorado Springs the town already had twenty-three barbershops, some of which were elaborate affairs offering all kinds of amenities, even baths. They did manage to rent space for the shop in the business district, but it seems unlikely that it enjoyed an A-list clientele. Still a barbershop today, with the old-style barber's pole in front, the space is both cramped and gloomy. Given Allen Davis's illness, he may also have had a difficult time keeping clients unless, of course, they were other consumptives.

The people of Greensburg may have been unconcerned about a tubercular barber working in close proximity to his customers, but the same could not be said for some other parts of the nation. Once medical research revealed that tuberculosis was, in fact, communicable, attitudes toward the disease began to shift. By the turn of the century, TB, once deemed an almost fashionable illness, was increasingly understood to be a poor people's disease, one that particularly afflicted immigrants crammed together in airless and germy tenements. Public health officials, alarmed at the disease's spread, advocated the registration of people sick with tuberculosis. And by 1904 sixty cities, including New York, required physicians and other health providers to supply their health departments with the names and addresses of patients they were treating for TB. Officials even considered restricting the interstate travel of people with TB, although no action was taken. Even if people with TB did not entirely internalize the censorious judgments of health officials, they knew the sting of ostracism. "Your friends will treat you so low down," sang blues musician Victoria Spivey in "TB Blues," one of several such songs to carry this disheartening message.[64]

Attitudes also began to shift somewhat in Colorado Springs, even though the town originally had been promoted as a resort for well-to-do consumptives. By 1900 over half of the town's residents reported that either they or a family member had moved to the Springs in search of a TB cure. TB may have been the town's first real economic engine, with its sanitariums, hospitals, and tent cottages, but not all of its residents were comfortable with such a large population of consumptives. After all, the town had a well-burnished reputation for cleanliness, too. Apparently one reason that the commercial hub of downtown—Tejon Street and Pikes Peak Avenue—was hosed down every day was to minimize the risk of tuberculosis spreading to healthy residents.

By the time the Davises arrived in Colorado Springs the police were just as likely to give the boot or a train ticket to an indigent person suffering from tuberculosis as to let him camp out for free. Hotel clerks and landlords often denied lodging to those who were obviously sick because too many such people arriving in town were utterly without resources.[65] There were local laws mandating the fumigation of houses where TB sufferers had lived, and, as in many other locales, laws banning promiscuous spitting. Still, Colorado Springs did establish the Sunnyrest Sanatorium in 1910, which offered free care to people with TB, despite the fears of some that the town would be flooded with indigent consumptives. It is perhaps not surprising that the town courted affluent sufferers, many of whom stayed at the Cragmor Sanitarium, described in one account as having the ambience of a cruise ship, with rollicking parties late into the night.[66] As one Denver physician (and a person with tuberculosis himself) observed in 1904, "TB is a good respectable disease if you have money, but without it, it is a mean lowdown business."[67]

As a property-owning businessman, Allen Davis did not, one imagines, fall into the ranks of the shunned. But for my socially ambitious grandfather, having as his father a consumptive barber felt like a liability. Then, in January 1908, after two and a half years in Colorado, the mountain cure stopped working and Allen Davis ceased being a worry to him. Ray and Roy accompanied their father's body back to Greensburg, where Allen wanted to be buried. Why wasn't Walter, the eldest son, the one traveling back to his hometown and taking charge of his dad's funeral? Initially I

assumed he stayed behind because he was creating distance between himself and his family, but then I examined Allen Davis's
probate record. It turns out that Allen's will stipulated that Roy,
Ray, and nine-year-old Willard (through his guardian, Lizzie) each
receive $1,060. The will made no provision for Walter. One possi-
bility, I thought, was that Allen had already given Walter a substantial sum, effectively his inheritance, upon marrying Lula. But had
that been the case Walter would not have challenged the will. In
fact, he went so far as to question his father's soundness of mind
back in 1906, when he had made out his will. Walter's legal challenge proved unsuccessful, but it may explain why, at age twenty-
seven, he decided to go it alone. Or maybe Walter had already
pulled away from his family, perhaps even in marrying Lula, and
that accounted for his disinheritance. However events unfolded, it
seems likely that Walter's disinheritance, which was, after all, tantamount to being labeled a black sheep, hardened him.[68]

Walter's father was no longer around to be an embarrassment to
him, but the rest of his family was. As long as they were all in the
same town, there was no way my grandfather could shed his roots.
In fact, twenty-five years later, shortly after Walter fled town in
1932, a newspaper serving the working-class west side (formerly
Colorado City) called attention to his "humble background."[69] Allen's death did not throw Lizzie into poverty, but she was a struggling widow who worked well into her sixties. At least a part of the
sons' inheritance was likely tapped five years after Allen's death so
that she could buy a big if undistinguished house on Nevada Avenue, on the northern edge of the business district. It was there that
the Davis family—minus Walter and Lula—lived for some years.
As her sons got married and moved out she turned her home into a
boardinghouse. She also worked across the street at the high school
as a matron, providing help and counsel, likely of a scriptural sort,
to female pupils, who called her "Mother Davis." Upon retirement,
she had her house divided into a duplex so that her eldest son, Ray,

and his wife could live next door to her and her youngest son, Willard. Meanwhile, Ray took over ownership of Allen's barbershop, which he ran for twenty years before becoming a traveling auditor for the Fraternal Order of Eagles. As for Willard, after serving seven months in the military during World War I, he held jobs as a gardener, embalmer, and ranch hand before settling into a job pumping gas at the local Conoco station.

It could not have been easy for my grandfather to refashion himself as a middle-class professional man when most of his immediate relatives were common "working people." It wasn't just that they had fewer resources than he did, although surely that mattered. They didn't drive the right cars, live in the right neighborhood, wear the right clothes, or work the right jobs.

There was one exception, however—Walter's enterprising younger brother Roy. Savvy, hardworking, and folksy, Roy was a gifted salesman. At age twenty-three, after only six years in the Springs, he opened up a typewriter shop. Perhaps the inheritance helped with that. One year later, in 1912, he was advertising aggressively in the city directory, with expensive bold-print ads featuring his stylized signature. Soon his eponymous shop dominated the local market in office machines. Selling typewriters paid the bills, but Roy harbored political ambitions. In 1919 he was elected to a seat in the lower house of the Colorado General Assembly. Two years later, in his second term, he was chosen Speaker of the House. At age thirty-three, Roy Davis was, the press boasted, the youngest person in the United States to have held such a position. In 1922 he scored an important legislative victory by helping to push through stalled legislation for the construction of the Moffat Tunnel.[70] The controversial tunnel was meant to give Denver the improved rail access west that its business leaders were demanding, and which nearby Pueblo already enjoyed. Roy's maneuvering earned him some enemies in his own Republican Party, but by 1928 he was back in politics after being elected to the Colorado

Roy Davis before the scandal. In the thirties, the combination of the scandal and the Depression nearly killed his typewriter business. He made ends meet by grading civil service exams for the state. (Author's archive)

Senate. He was subsequently elected to a second term, and was chosen president pro tem in 1931.

Roy owed much of his success to his feverish participation in the town's many clubs and fraternal organizations. By 1914 he had already served as both the president and the vice president of the Fraternal Order of Eagles, and as the clerk of the Industrial Order of Odd Fellows. Soon that list would expand to include the all-important Scottish Rite Masons, the Knights of Pythias, the Loyal Order of Moose, Modern Woodmen of America, the Rotary Club, the advisory board of the Salvation Army, and the Shrine Club. He later served as director and vice president of the Colorado Springs Chamber of Commerce. This is only a partial list. He made himself a ubiquitous presence in the town's civic life, which served him well, especially come election time. He may have belonged to more clubs than most, but ambitious men of that era usually were clubmen. Membership in fraternal organizations was about to take off across America. Participating in these clubs brought real benefits. For example, Rotary Club membership ensured that other members would feel compelled to patronize your business rather than that of a non-Rotarian competitor. The growth in these organizations is inextricable from the get-ahead culture of those times and the expectation that influential contacts of all sorts would follow from membership in prestigious organizations such as the Masons.[71] Sinclair Lewis was careful to give a different name to Babbitt's club, but it was obviously modeled on the Rotary Club, whose members "never lost sight of doing a little more business."[72]

You might think that Walter would have appreciated that one of his siblings was making something of himself and thereby raising the family's profile, but this was not the case. After all, Roy was six years his junior. If Walter had met with more immediate success in Colorado Springs, he might not have felt so resentful of his younger brother, but nothing had worked out as he had hoped. He listed himself as a lawyer in the city directory, but he was never admitted

Davis listed himself as a lawyer in the city directory even though he appears to have never worked as an attorney. (Author's archive)

to the bar, and I have found no evidence that he ever practiced law there. Instead, he worked as a stenographer for a real estate firm, then for the city, and finally on a freelance basis. I don't want to overstate the modesty of my grandparents' circumstances. Even if their house on East Willamette Street was in an unpretentious area, and even if Lula's inheritance helped to finance it, they were not renters. Still, how was it that a man this obsessed with making it ended up playing second fiddle to his younger brother?

After all, other men had used their position as secretary as a launching pad to wealth or at least influence. Take the example of the financier and energy magnate Samuel Insull, the son of a London dairyman who began his career as the private secretary to Thomas Edison. General Palmer worked with at least two private secretaries. After Palmer's death, his longtime secretary on the East Coast, George A. Krause, became the president of the

Colorado Springs Company and the Antlers Hotel. Palmer's other secretary, William Postlethwaite, may have had only a high school education, but he worked for decades as the treasurer of Colorado College (and was known as an amateur anthropologist), which brought him respect if not wealth. The most famous of all these office men was Oliver Shoup, the private secretary to Verner Z. Reed, the thirty-seven-year-old real estate man who earned a $1 million commission when he sold Stratton's mine, the Independence, to an English syndicate in 1901. Shoup began working with him before that sale, and eventually moved from managing Reed's multiple business interests to partnering with him. When Shoup left Reed it was to establish an oil company, which was just the beginning of his far-flung business empire. He leveraged that success into two terms as the governor of Colorado, serving from 1919 until 1923. Finally, there was Edward Sharer, a graduate of the law school at Kent College in Chicago, who would later join the ranks of building and loan heads. Sharer worked for many years as a private secretary to J.R. McKinnie, a legendary pioneer of the mining business in Cripple Creek.

All of these local men were better educated than my grandfather, who when he was on the lam presented himself as a retired lawyer with a college degree.[73] They also had been lucky enough to find employment with very wealthy men, and at a time when the gold supply from Cripple Creek still seemed inexhaustible. Moreover, they came to office work when it was accorded a higher status, before it became feminized. By the time Walter arrived in Colorado Springs in 1905 office work was undergoing a transition. Even though 1910 marked the year in which there was the greatest number of male stenographers in the United States, the job was becoming de-skilled through the mechanization and routinization of office work.[74] With the introduction of office machines, men like my grandfather were finding themselves replaced by women, whose paychecks were considerably more slender. We can see the effects of these changes in Colorado Springs, where the 1906 city directory listed seven stenographers, only one of whom was male. Tellingly, Walter Davis never listed himself under the heading of stenographer, although he worked as one. By 1911 the total number of stenographers listing themselves in the city directory had dwindled to five—all of them female. To make matters worse, his brother Roy was selling the very machine that was helping to render obsolete the one real skill his eldest brother possessed. The Corona typewriter "shut up like a knife, a lesson to stenographers," as one newspaper columnist noted.[75]

Walter's stalled ambitions only made him more standoffish with his family. He looked down his nose at his brothers, even Roy, whose marriage to a waitress at the Acacia Hotel he criticized. And yet Roy's wife left the paid labor force upon marrying him, whereas Walter's wife, Lula, worked for a number of years by her husband's side. Even after the birth in 1909 of Dorothy, their first and only child, Lula worked in his cramped office in a bank building. Her work there isn't noted in the census or the city directory, but a century ago women who "helped" their husbands in the office or the store did not count as working people in their own right and were not part of the official record. My mother remembered spending long stretches of time in a dresser drawer in her father's office, and a surviving photograph bears out her memory.

For my mother the fact that even as a baby she was not at home in a crib or a cradle, with her mother nearby, was the best evidence of how steep her family's climb had been. Indeed, it says a lot about how Walter was faring financially that he needed Lula working with him at the office. The idea that the home was women's and children's sphere—inviolate, and separate from the ruthlessly competitive and morally compromising world of commerce in which men moved—still had traction, particularly in Colorado Springs,

During the workweek, a bureau drawer in her father's office served as my mother's crib. For her, this stood as definitive proof of her parents' very modest circumstances. (Author's archive)

a place so alive to improprieties. So even if Lula and Walter were doing well enough, the very fact that the Davis's worlds were not scrupulously demarcated meant that bourgeois respectability was beyond their reach. The ideology of separate spheres, with men notionally in the larger world and women in the home, never described the lives of most Americans—particularly those who were working class or, like my grandparents, not middle class. But even if it was a trope rather than an exact description of reality, those whose lives did not conform to prevailing notions of respectability were nonetheless affected by the condemnatory attitudes of those better positioned.

My grandfather had come up short, but he was determined

Lula Davis with baby Dorothy, on the steps of their East Willamette home. (Author's archive)

Dorothy Davis as a child in her front yard in Colorado Springs. (Author's archive)

to turn things around. He may have even considered moving to Pueblo to advance himself. The second-largest city in the state, Pueblo boasted the first and the only integrated steel mill west of the Missouri, which is how it came to call itself the "Pittsburgh of the West."[76] Walter and Lula hosted a dinner at one of the city's better hotels, the Hotel Maine, for a group consisting mostly of Pueblo professionals and their wives. As an orchestra played, Walter, Lula, and their guests dined in an area discreetly screened by palms, at tables decorated with arrangements of cut flowers, ferns, and smilax. Eighteen people turned out for the event, including a department store owner, a prominent surgeon, a banker, a contractor, and an accountant. The surviving news clip is undated, so I don't know if Walter was still trying to drum up business as a lawyer. Nonetheless, the event usefully illustrates the differences between the two brothers—Roy methodically earning a reputation for reliability, hard work, and charitable endeavors, and Walter blowing his wad on a splashy gambit. But my grandfather was not about to follow Roy's path to power.

Over time their starkly different styles and lifestyles likely hardened into positions, with Walter playing the cosmopolitan, self-consciously modern man and Roy the throwback—the Bible-quoting, civic-oriented, family man. Walter loved to travel to cities, while Roy preferred his cottage at nearby Carroll Lakes. Walter was a philanderer, while Roy was the most faithful of husbands. (His fellow legislators in the Twenty-Third General Assembly demonstrated just how well they understood Roy when they presented him with a gift: a fourteen-karat-gold watch with a picture of his wife and daughter on its dial.) Walter chose the most extravagant anything—car, restaurant, or hotel—whereas Roy always opted for the merely functional. It's not surprising that the staple machine at Roy's store was the Royal—the typewriter equivalent of Henry Ford's Model T. And once he was successful Walter loved to throw money around, while Roy was notoriously tight-fisted. In one newspaper article, Roy warned American Legionnaires traveling to Paris about the aggressive "tip-seeking practices" of that city's waiters, which led the paper's regular columnist to observe that, "even in the United States here and there, tips are expected."[77]

The more successful Roy became—and he was hailed in at least one newspaper as a "gifted genius" conversationally, especially when scriptures could be cited—the more of a know-it-all he was. The *Gazette* noted that he steered legislation through the state senate in nothing less than a "Napoleonic" fashion.[78] Within the family Walter, who had been garrulous back in Greensburg, receded, preferring silence to competing for space with Roy, who increasingly behaved as though he was the eldest son. Well into the twentieth century people routinely kept scrapbooks, which in the articles cut and pasted can reveal a good deal about their assemblers.[79] In the case of Walter and Roy, the two men disliked each other so much that each kept a scrapbook whose pages largely chronicled the other's defeats.

Roy and Walter Davis each had an idea of what it was that he was pursuing. For both of them it involved pulling themselves up by their bootstraps and earning the respect of others. Yet theirs were fundamentally different versions of the American dream. Roy wanted to make his mark in politics, and while there was nothing modest about the man, he positioned himself as someone motivated by the "common good" even if that extended only to a portion of the population. As for the material world, his desires were, as he often said, simple. It was comfort and security he sought. For my grandfather the common good seems to have remained a distant concept meant for someone else, no matter what his building and loan advertisements claimed. He wanted nothing so much as the experience of being wealthy, and the respect that came along with it. He wanted what the wealthiest men of Colorado Springs enjoyed—the sense of rightness that comes with being able to navigate the cultural parameters of class. For sure, having money was essential, but it was about having the cultural wherewithal to pass as wealthy.

Walter and Lula shared the dream of making it . . . and the worry that their roots might stand in the way of those dreams. They passed their dreams and worries on to my mother, a woman who to me always seemed most at home at upscale restaurants and department stores. But one day as we were talking about her parents she interrupted me. "I don't mean to upset you," she said, "but we really were nobodies come from nowhere." My mother did not explicitly reference *The Great Gatsby*, where a version of that phrase is used, but I knew she had read Fitzgerald's novel. Any doubts I had about how fully she had internalized her parents' shame were dispelled when she said, "You know, we weren't from the best stock." Several weeks later, just days before she died, she revealed that she was of Irish descent, a real drawback if you were socially ambitious.

America was meant to be a country unlike all others, where stock held no sway, where people were judged on the basis of their character, talents, and achievements, not where they came from. But even in America one's character was never entirely separable from one's roots, and at no time more so than in the early twentieth century, when pseudo-scientific hereditarianism was highly influential in public health, medicine, and beyond.[80] The idea that criminality was hereditary, for example, was common. It surfaced in 1930 when depositors of the Hollywood Guaranty Building and Loan Association learned that its head was guilty of a shocking $8 million embezzlement. News of that Los Angeles scandal provoked bomb threats both against the embezzler's family and against the state's building and loan commissioner. One furious depositor, expressing what I suspect many depositors thought, wrote to the jailed B&L head, "You dirty rotten crook . . . your dirty blood runs through your son's veins." He vowed to make it his life's work to rid the community of "this rotten strain."[81]

My mother could never quite bring herself to blame her father.

Perhaps she felt herself too compromised, too implicated. She remembered him as a tragic figure, victimized by his adopted town—the town of millionaires—and perhaps most of all by his desperate desire to vault over the distance between his roots and where he saw himself headed.

2

The Loan Man

Six years after moving to Colorado Springs, Walter Davis ditched stenography and embarked on a new career as a small moneylender. By 1912 he was using the moniker "The Loan Man" in the local city directory. He continued to advertise himself in the directory as an attorney, but it was as a moneylender that he first made his mark in the region.

The early twentieth century world of moneylending is often characterized as "fringe financing," and in the larger scheme of things it was. Personal indebtedness was still at the fringes of the American economy. Nonetheless, to those millions of Americans whose survival depended upon them, moneylenders were essential. Nearly 25 percent of all families in New York City made use of small-loan facilities in 1907; for families with annual incomes of less than $700 that figure rose to almost 50 percent. Likewise, in early twentieth-century Pittsburgh between 20 and 25 percent of that city's families borrowed from a loan business in any given year.[1] And it wasn't just poor people who resorted to small moneylenders. Many government employees—police, firemen, and white-collar workers—as well as skilled tradesmen and foremen sought their services.[2]

This undated photograph of Walter Davis was taken in his cramped walk-up office.
(Author's archive)

Small moneylenders were central to the twentieth-century revolution in consumption, too. Beginning in the 1880s, working-class
immigrants began to buy "on time," a practice that put the American dream within closer reach. Sometimes the terms of these
on-time contracts were surprisingly lenient. Take the case of the
installment-plan purchase of a sewing machine by one immigrant
family living on New York's Lower East Side. The husband purchased the machine from a neighborhood peddler, who agreed to
let the couple pay it back at the rate of 25 cents a week over a prolonged period, which stretched into eighteen long years. The family
sometimes failed to make its weekly payment, and yet the peddler became a trusted family friend. This sort of intimacy between
neighborhood peddlers and "their" families was not uncommon.

Indeed, buying on time made sense to those who spoke little or no English, found American culture perplexing, and had little money.[3]

Installment credit made its way into the middle class, too. Many such people bought on time in order to purchase the accoutrements of a middle-class lifestyle: a sewing machine, furniture, carpets, a piano, a stove, and an encyclopedia set. Installment contracts took the form of a lease or chattel mortgage that enabled retailers to repossess the goods in case of delinquency. Customers who fell behind on their payments and were anxious to avoid repossession often sought the services of small moneylenders, which is why their ranks grew in the late nineteenth century.[4] Moneylending was not yet a critical component of American capitalism, but in terms of the numbers it served and the role it played in democratizing credit, there was nothing fringe about it.[5]

Small moneylenders were usually described as loan sharks, businessmen who charged extremely high rates of interest, with the aid of deceptive or coercive methods, and in ways that skirted established (if routinely ignored) law. Loan sharks were reviled. They operated under a "cloud of illegality," but they varied in style and in business practices. One of these was Denverite Charles E. Stratton, whose loan shark operation stretched all the way from Helena, Montana, to Los Angeles, California. Even the *Collier's* writer J.M. Oskison, a well-known muckraking journalist, admitted that Charles Stratton was a "man of wealth, some refinement, and culture." If Stratton was, in his view, the best of the sharks, Harry Leven of Colorado Springs was the worst. The owner of Colorado Springs Weekly Loans, Leven was the kind of man "who keeps a revolver in a pigeonhole of his desk and has the crevices of his office walls stuffed with newspaper to prevent people in the adjoining offices from overhearing him."[6] He was an unabashed loan shark who listed his occupation in the city directory as "Money." Leven, whom Oskison described as a "one-eyed Russian Jew," confirmed

the anti-Semitic stereotype of the moneylender, one that was sufficiently widespread that the editor of *Jewish Social Service* noted
with considerable relief that when residents of Cleveland formed
an anti-loan-shark movement they found not even one Jewish firm
among those that had been prosecuted.[7]

Our lending landscape is, in some respects, not that different
from what prevailed in the early twentieth century. However, the
business of moneylending, as practiced a hundred years ago by my
grandfather, differs in key respects from today's vast and astonish-
ingly lucrative world of payday loans, pawnshops, subprime automobile loans and auto title loans, and check-cashing operations.[8]
What unites past and present is need. Much of the popular literature about loan sharks stresses the newness of indebtedness in
Gilded Age America. However, the idea that earlier generations
of Americans lived largely debt-free is a myth. The Pilgrims were
no strangers to debt and neither were colonial planters, including
some of the nation's more notable founding fathers. Farmers, who
are often assumed to have been the most self-reliant and therefore
the most virtuous of all Americans, were actually among those most
dependent on credit. If anything, "a river of red ink runs through
American history," as one historian recently put it.[9]

Certainly the demand for credit grew with the spread of wage
labor, which rarely permitted workers to practice "anticipatory
thrift." Borrowers went to loan sharks for a variety of reasons, including staving off repossession of installment purchases. Many
borrowers also did so when they suffered a loss of income due to
illness, an industrial accident, or unexpected medical bills or funeral costs. And of course there were layoffs—some temporary,
others permanent—and these were particularly characteristic of
the boom-and-bust world of mining.[10] Working people's dependence on loan sharks also owed something to the nature of banking in the early twentieth century. Commercial banks did not offer
personal loans to low-income, high-risk borrowers. They catered to

those who already had money and could afford to pay more on the money the bank might lend them than they earned on the money they had on deposit.[11]

The scarcity of credit meant that many ordinary Americans resorted to loan sharks, who secured their loans either through a chattel mortgage (that is, on movable personal property such as appliances, vehicles, and jewelry) or through wage assignment. Pawn dealers were also part of the moneylending landscape; they were actually in a more advantageous position than loan sharks because they had in their possession whatever had been pawned, be it jewelry, clothing, or a quilt.

Like today, usurious rates and deceptive and exploitative business practices were common. Loan sharks' rates were often predatory—usually a simple annual interest rate between 20 and 300 percent, although rates could be considerably higher, especially if the loan was small.[12] Loan men were also anything but transparent in their dealings with borrowers. According to one widely circulated article, small moneylenders were "suave and persuasive." They were known to talk "blandly" while giving up almost nothing by way of details. And yet by the time the transaction was over, the borrower would have attached his name to as many as six documents. This article offers some sense of the paperwork a borrower might encounter:

> There is a "mortgage of personal property," which specifies the amount of the loan, but avoids any reference to the rate of interest. Ten or twelve paragraphs, safeguarding the lender's rights, are found, but hardly a sentence relating to the equity of the borrower. There is a note or bond accompanying the mortgage, with the rate of interest disguised by provisions for weekly payments. You will find a bill of sale and a power of attorney ample enough to permit the "shark" to sign the client's name to any document that he may think desirable.

Finally, the article warned people off of salary loans that could lead to their wages being garnished for an indefinite period.[13]

When borrowers ran into trouble repaying their loans, loan sharks employed techniques of intimidation. We know something of how this worked from a 1922 exposé of the loan shark business, which was still thriving in the twenties despite concerted and prolonged efforts to shut it down. The reporter, who worked for the business magazine *Forbes*, managed to obtain one loan company's "confidential instructions" about how best to collect on a loan. With the delinquent borrower seated across the desk from you, lay into him, the memo advised, and stage a fake phone call to an attorney so he believes the firm is plotting legal action to force repayment.[14] That fake phone call was one practice my grandfather could have dispensed with because his customers would have believed he was an attorney. This is perhaps why he continued to list himself as a lawyer in the city directory.

The smooth talk, the deceptive pitches, and all the perplexing paperwork that often proves ruinous to borrowers typified fringe finance, then as now. And so did the self-justifications that fringe financiers relied upon. Loan sharks frequently defended their work on the grounds that it actually benefited poor people and those who had fallen on hard times.[15] They often portrayed themselves as misunderstood businessmen who were enabling working people to realize the American dream. In one article from a trade journal, a moneylender pushed back against the accusations hurled at his profession. Being a loan man didn't make you hard-hearted and callous, he argued. If anything, it had put him in touch with human frailty, thereby "sensitizing" him, making him "feel more deeply the thrusts and jibes of his fellowmen." This same author quoted another moneylender who said he had discovered in this business "romance and the spirit of humanity." For him, the intimacy of the work—hearing so much about the "inner life" of his customers— was like nothing so much as "constantly living in many varicolored novels."[16] Similar arguments are made today. Several years ago the chairman of one the country's largest check-cashing companies argued that critics who attack such businesses for turning a profit in low-income communities had it all wrong. "We're the George Baileys here," he insisted.[17]

The early twentieth-century moneylending business, while profitable, may not have been quite as lucrative as reformers' exposés and historical accounts usually suggest. First of all, borrowers often defaulted on their loans. Moreover, running a loan-sharking operation required advertising, thorough investigation of applicants' credit history, and substantial paperwork, which was meant to underscore the seriousness of the lenders and the transactions in question. Even a $6 loan required personal references and a twenty-four-hour wait.[18] And there were legal costs to consider because loan sharks were occasionally prosecuted for usury. Even at the time, one investigative journalist, Charles Rogers, rejected some of the more sensationalistic claims against loan sharks. In a 1911 *Atlantic Monthly* article, Rogers reported that after factoring in expenses and losses, the profit from a $10,000 investment amounted to no more than $2,600 a year.[19] Even squeezing out that amount of profit was hard work, Rogers argued, which is why loan sharks were so often extremely efficient and maximally enterprising.

In fact, the difficulty of running a successful small moneylending operation with reasonable rates for borrowers was made emphatically clear when semi-philanthropic remedial loan companies, set up in the early 1900s as alternatives to loan sharks, reluctantly concluded that they would have to abandon their affordable rates. There were just too many customers skipping out on repayment. As a consequence, reformers in the 1910s began to push for the creation of the Uniform Small Loan Law, which permitted small loan businesses to charge simple annual rates of 42 percent, together with a brokerage fee.[20] By 1932, twenty-five states had enacted a version of the Uniform Small Loan Law.[21]

If loan sharking was not as lucrative as commonly believed, apparently neither were all small moneylenders always as relentlessly cutthroat as we might think. That same *Atlantic Monthly* journalist found that loan sharks could be more flexible in their dealings with borrowers than popular stereotypes suggested. Ruthlessness was bad business if practiced indiscriminately, he argued. Although a loan shark would not want to be seen as soft and malleable, neither would he want to be perceived as coldhearted to one and all. One can see the logic of this, and why someone like my grandfather, in contrast to many moneylenders today, did his best to avoid lending to those who were obviously bad risks.[22]

In my grandfather's time, loan sharking was considered a low-down, disreputable business—a fact underscored by the dingy, poorly lit offices where loan sharks typically worked. This was not a line of work for respectable men, except for those such as Denver's Stratton, whose business was so big and spanned so many states that he was no longer involved in its day-to-day operations. Despite being a disreputable line of work, loan sharking was, curiously, a place in which women regularly worked. In contrast to today's male-dominated world of fringe financing, loan sharks of yesteryear relied heavily upon female labor. Female employees were not only cheaper but also less likely to be assaulted by angry borrowers, which is why they were often sent out on a "bawlerout," which involved trapping a delinquent borrower and browbeating him as a "deadbeat" in front of family, friends, and fellow workers. I cannot determine when my grandmother became a stay-at-home wife, but it is plausible that she was still working by her husband's side when he entered the moneylending business. If so, she likely handled the masses of paperwork generated by such a business.[23]

Being a loan shark had its frustrations, beginning with the long hours spent chasing down "slows" and "skips." That's probably why my grandfather always carried a cane, and it may be how he acquired a very visible scar on his hand. Moreover, it was not so profitable that his wife could stay at home with their daughter—a key metric of the respectability he craved. Perhaps more than anything, he too often felt at the mercy of his borrowers. After all, his was a realm of old-school debt. He had not figured out how to make money—real money—off other people's lack of it.

Yet one would never know from his studio photographs that Walter Davis felt vulnerable or insecure about his standing. In those photographs he looks ruthless, his lips settled into a near sneer and with a stare best described as predatory. He also made a point of being tight-lipped, just as the big-time capitalists claimed they were. "Silence Is the Trait of Money Kings" was one of several such articles in his scrapbook, and it notes that J.P. Morgan hardly ever talked, and that other Wall Street figures also kept their "lips locked" on business matters. "No one ever made a mistake by not talking" was Wall Street financier George F. Baker's advice. Their taciturnity, their "cloaks of silence," had everything to do with the fact that the money business, claimed this journalist, was "a precise science" that could be fatally undone by something as seemingly trivial as a misplaced comma.[24] Like Wall Street titans, loan sharks also emphasized playing things close to the chest, and this became my grandfather's mode as well.[25] Years later the chauffeur who drove my grandfather between Colorado Springs and Denver reported that his boss remained silent throughout the entire journey. But even at this juncture, as he tracked down "skips" and "slows," the photographs suggest he was doing his best to provide visual evidence of his bloody-minded determination to have his way with the world.

A "near banker" was how the Colorado Springs police chief described Walter Davis after he went on the lam in 1932.[26] In the years before the stock market crash America was loaded with near bankers. By 1929 there were 25,000 banks operating under fifty-two different regulatory regimes—the result of President

Andrew Jackson's war on central banking a century earlier. Until the Great Depression forced its reorganization, America's banking system was an incoherent muddle. For example, while national banks were required to join the Federal Reserve, which was created in 1913, state-chartered banks were under no obligation to join, and few did. With the economy roaring, those in charge of state banks brushed aside the notion that they might need a backup source of liquidity. What this meant was that if a financial panic hit, the majority of American banks, and their depositors, were unprotected and on their own. Haphazard, undercapitalized, and unevenly regulated, the banking system imparted dangerous elasticity to the term "bank." Many were little better than pawnshops run by "little corner grocery-men calling themselves bankers," as Senator Carter Glass, one of the key men in the establishment of the Federal Reserve System, noted.[27]

In the lead-up to the Depression, plenty of B&L men, including my grandfather, masqueraded as bankers. However, when building and loan associations first migrated to America from England there was nothing banklike about them. They were self-help societies organized by the working classes—people not served by the country's national banks. Operating as nonprofits, they kept no physical offices and had no salaried officers. Very often they rented space for their monthly meetings in churches, community halls, or taverns. In bigger cities they were often organized along ethnic lines, and sometimes consisted of people who had lived together in the same neighborhoods in Europe. Building and loans at this stage owed their success to the fact that they were mutually owned, which meant that association members had a stake in their safe and sound operation.[28]

B&Ls had a specific aim: to foster homeownership among the working classes through the practice of thrift.[29] They developed distinctively in different regions and states, and over time they came to look less and less like self-help societies, which complicates efforts to generalize about their methods of operation. But in many places in this period they operated as follows: A prospective home-buyer would invest his savings in shares of a building and loan association. He would then borrow against these shares to finance his house at a low rate of interest. A borrower was usually required to subscribe for an amount of association stock that was equal to the loan he hoped to borrow. Along with a membership fee and premium paid on the loan, which was determined by auction, the borrower made monthly payments on the loan, which carried an annual interest rate of 6 percent, and monthly installment pay-ments on the shares. During the term of the loan, the association's officers would distribute any ensuing profits as dividends to the membership. When the shares were paid up, the loan was effec-tively liquidated.

Historian Lendol Calder explains the way the process worked on the ground, through the example of a borrower desiring a $1,400 house loan. The borrower would buy ten shares in an association of his choice, at one dollar each. As a member of the association, he would be allowed to bid for the privilege of receiving a loan for $2,000, which typically could be obtained at a 30 percent pre-mium. He would then receive an actual loan of $1,400 to pay his contractor to put up the house. For security, the house and the borrower's shares were mortgaged to the association. Repayment of the loan occurred gradually as the new homeowner paid monthly dues on his ten shares and interest on the loan to the association. After eight or nine years of payments the debt would be declared paid and the mortgage would be released.

Even an influential official and booster of the thrift industry ad-mitted that the building and loan contract was "crude and very few people understood it."[30] But B&L home financing had real advan-tages over other methods of home financing. Until the thrift indus-try changed the landscape of home finance, the preferred method of homeownership involved saving money until one could build—a prohibitively expensive option for all but a sliver of the population. Even many white-collar workers, who on average earned $1,000 a year, found themselves priced out of a housing market that required substantial money up front. With houses for low- and moderate-income families ranging in price from $1,000 to $4,500 in the late nineteenth century, accumulating the money for one's house could take as long as fifteen years.[31] As a consequence, for many people owning a home happened late in life, with the result that homeownership was of little help in building assets. For those with resources, methods of financing included savings banks, relatives, and the many small investors operating through mortgage dealers. But for those of modest means, the B&L method was a godsend because it did not require a substantial down payment and it enabled interest and principal to be paid off in monthly payments in an amortized home mortgage.[32]

Building and loan associations grew slowly and spread unevenly, taking root first in the East, particularly in New Jersey, Massachusetts, Maryland, New York, and Pennsylvania. Between 1880 and 1893 B&Ls really took off as more than five thousand new associations formed. (Philadelphia became known as the "City of Homes" because of its more than nine hundred building and loans.) By 1893 there were 5,838 B&Ls operating in every state and territory, with 1.4 million members. Their assets came to $473 million, and they held mortgages of half a billion dollars. After private lenders and savings banks, building and loans were the third-biggest home mortgage lenders.[33]

The appeal of building and loan associations owed a lot to the fact that they were local, small, and democratically run. The average B&L had assets of no more than $90,000; sixty percent of all associations had fewer than two hundred members, most of them of modest means. In this period, real estate mortgages made up roughly 90 percent of the assets of the average thrift.[34] They practiced a kind of participatory democracy, with frequent meetings in which each shareholder, no matter how great the number of his shares, had one vote only, even when it came to electing association officers.

The people organizing B&Ls saw these "poor men's banks" as part of a movement, a larger cooperative movement promoting mutuality and reciprocity, values they deemed increasingly vital (and under siege) in a world of industrial capitalism whose guiding principle seemed cutthroat competition. By the 1890s the culture of building and loans included America's first important labor organization, the Knights of Labor, and the Farmers' Alliance, which spawned the anti-monopoly People's Party, as well as the Women's Christian Temperance Union. The Knights of Labor, in particular, generated thousands of cooperatives across the country. This ethos of mutuality, the working classes' pushback against the ruthlessness of industrial capitalism, was for a short time an antidote to the ideal of rugged individualism.[35]

Mutuality and cooperation reportedly defined the early building and loan movement, but those ideals began to lose traction as the popularity of B&Ls led to the first effort to subvert their original purpose. In the late 1880s businessmen began forming what were called "national" building and loan associations, which had headquarters in a city and a network of local branches, often in other states entirely. In contrast to traditional B&Ls, the new nationals were for-profit businesses that often were formed and run by wealthy industrialists and bankers. Whereas the traditional B&L had generally operated without salaried officers, the new nationals frequently paid out large salaries to organizers and officers, as well as to the promoters or agents who sold stock in places far from the national office. Gone, too, were the days of one-shareholder-one-vote democracy, as ordinary members were rendered effectively powerless.

These new-style B&Ls proved popular, in no small part because they advertised a dividend rate three to four times higher than what was on offer from other financial institutions, including traditional B&Ls. For people looking to make fast money, the nationals were seductive. As for the operators of the new nationals, much of their money came from the hefty fees and fines they imposed on members and from payment requirements that were much more likely to result in borrowers' foreclosure.[36] By 1893 there were approximately 240 national associations with 400,000 members.[37]

However, the nationals' practices were so egregious that the courts, state officials, journalists, and old-style B&Ls began to weigh in against them. In one New York case of 1897 the judge, who ruled in favor of the aggrieved borrower, noted that the bloated expenses and large salaries of national associations meant that they functioned like "investment corporations pure and simple" rather than like old-fashioned associations that were meant to benefit their members. The state superintendent of banks was even blunter, saying that national companies were "in practice responsible to nobody, under the sole control of their organizers and officers and managed for their advantage." He drew a stark contrast between the nationals and local associations, which met their few expenses with their profits and made sure that every dollar the subscriber paid in went toward his interest or reduced his principal. The *New York Times* article on the case emphasized the "vivid contrast" between local and national associations when it came to their methods, conduct, and costs to borrowers.[38]

The depression of 1893, which reduced the numbers of new members and borrowers and also led to a collapse in real estate prices, proved to be the downfall of the nationals. Between 1893 and 1897, more than half of all nationals closed their doors, and by 1910 virtually every national association had folded. As a consequence, many of their working-class members lost their savings. One estimate puts the losses at a quarter of a billion dollars. For a few years the fallout from this first B&L crisis damaged the reputation of even traditional, local associations. In Colorado the B&L

industry remained volatile for some time, with three new associations forming and thirteen dissolving between 1916 and 1918.[39] One thrift leader declared that the "schemers" who ran these "bogus concerns" had so sullied the reputation of the industry that it would take years before genuine building and loans could operate successfully in some parts of the country.[40]

In order to regain people's trust, B&L heads renewed their commitment to the ideals of thrift and homeownership. They also took some steps toward self-regulation. Yet despite the enormous size of the nationals' failure, the B&L industry successfully resisted any and all federal oversight.[41] The laws governing B&Ls varied widely from state to state, and provided the skimpiest of regulations. Twenty-five states set no minimum for the amount of capital required of B&L organizers. Those states that did establish a minimum capital requirement more often than not set that amount in shares, not in dollars, or in a dollar sum that was negligible.[42] B&L operators' fateful decision to press for toothless regulations rather than push for effective and uniform regulation paved the way for the collapse of the industry some thirty years later.

The late 1880s marked a turning point in the history of B&Ls, and not just because the nationals provided a road map for financial dubiousness down the line. It was during this period that the B&L ethos of cooperation began to fade. We know that nationals failed at an alarming rate, but did those small, democratically run associations go down with them or had they already begun to wither away when the nationals, with their lucrative dividend offers, appeared? Or is their decline attributable to the fading of the cooperative movement? Existing histories do not explain this shift, but from this point on the earlier B&L model seems to have been in decline. One measure is the creation in 1892 of a national trade organization, the United States League of Local Building and Loan Associations, which set about aggressively advancing the interests of what was now an industry rather than a movement. Increasingly, building and loan men were enmeshed in a web of business interests with title specialists, contractors, insurance agents, surveyors, lawyers, and suppliers of building material. These entanglements would introduce serious conflicts of interest.[43]

The B&L league would become one of the country's strongest and most influential trade groups. It became a public relations juggernaut, cranking out upbeat news stories about the surging thrift business.[44] It lobbied Congress with great success. In 1894 it deployed old-school B&L rhetoric to win the thrift industry an exemption from a proposed national tax on corporations. A federal tax on what were effectively "semi-charitable" institutions was, the trade league argued, nothing short of an "injustice to the workingman."[45] And as states began to establish agencies charged with monitoring the thrift business, the League took to cozying up to the officials charged with regulating it.[46]

The League also urged associations to put more effort into advertising and into cultivating a more professional image. It urged operators, who had traditionally rented unadorned, upper-floor space in bank buildings, to narrow the architectural distance between their businesses and banks. Buy your own space, the League urged, deploy classical architectural styles, dress it up with marble and brass fixtures, and install a teller's cage. All of this was intended to convey financial solidity.[47] It was also meant to fudge the difference between building and loan associations and banks.

The effort to sell B&Ls as banks took many forms and further shifted the experience and meaning of homeownership for the working classes. According to the original B&L ethos, buying a home was not a private, individual matter; it was a community enterprise. Remember the famous bank run scene in It's a Wonderful Life when George Bailey, besieged by desperate depositors, explains the way a B&L works: "Your money isn't on the premises, it's in each other's houses. . . . You're lending them the money to build and they're going to pay it back to you as best they can. What

Developer S.E. Gross's 1891 advertisement suggests that his new subdivision is located in tree-lined suburbia when it was actually just beyond the gates of Chicago's stockyards. (Image courtesy of the Chicago History Museum, ICHi-003656)

are you going to do?" he asks. "Foreclose on them?" Bailey Brothers Building and Loan is several steps away from a Knights of Labor building and loan, but the screenwriters made sure that it retained vestiges of the older model of mutuality and reciprocity whereby self-advancement is community advancement. Yet by the 1890s homeownership was becoming more of a private enterprise even if it was achieved through a building and loan association.

This shift in the experience and meaning of homeownership— from a more collectivist orientation to a more individualistic one— is crucial to understanding the relationship between capitalism, class, and conservatism. Long before the disastrous bursting of the housing bubble in 2008 and the ideology and policies behind the "ownership society" that helped to fuel that bubble, home-ownership was the key element of the American dream. From the earliest days of the republic the idea took hold that what made America distinct from Europe, that is, what enabled "American exceptionalism," was the independence and self-sufficiency of its people. A nation of property-owning yeoman farmers was, for the founding fathers, vital to the success of the new republic. In their view, nothing would be more corrosive to the fragile republic than the development of a class whose dependence upon landlords or employers made its members politically malleable and easily ma-nipulated. The elevation of homeownership and its rendering as quintessentially "American" united people across the political spectrum—from Walt Whitman, who wrote "a man is not really a whole and complete man until he owns his home," to the Baptist minister and writer Russell Conwell, whose popular lecture "Acres of Diamonds" drew on the poet's language.[48]

By the time Conwell was delivering that lecture, America was no longer a country dominated by yeoman farmers. With industrializa-tion came the pushbacks against it, first with the culture of cooper-ation advanced by the Knights of Labor, Populists, social reformers, and building and loans, and later, by the twentieth century, with the increasing number of adherents won by socialism.[49] In response to the spread of radicalism, politicians, pundits, and real estate developers provided a different spin on white working-class home-ownership. Once understood as promoting mutuality and collectivity in ways that put a brake on capitalism, it was now promoted as a way to save capitalism. What better way to defeat radicalism than through a property-owning working class? "Men who have roofs of their own do not go about scattering firebrands," claimed the developers of one Los Angeles white working-class suburb.[50]

In the early 1920s Herbert Hoover was among the country's most effective evangelists for homeownership. As secretary of commerce, he created the government's "Own Your Own Home Campaign." Hoover's enthusiasm for homeownership never slackened, even in the Depression, when he spoke at some length about the virtues of owning your own home. Drawing a distinction between homes and housing, he opined, "Those immortal ballads, 'Home, Sweet Home,' 'My Old Kentucky Home' and 'The Little Gray Home in the West' were not written about tenements or apartments." For Hoover, these songs were nothing short of "expressions of racial longings" that reflected "a sentiment deep in the heart of our race and of American life." Hoover did acknowledge the unfortunate fact that, even in the best of times, homeownership was out of reach for many Americans. Nonetheless, he maintained, "To own one's own home is a physical expression of individualism, of enterprise, of independence, and of freedom of spirit." The evidence? Americans, he said, "never sing songs about a pile of rent receipts."[51]

Hoover's language—its emphasis on the "American race," whose core values he identified as individualism, enterprise, independence, and freedom of spirit—spoke to many whites of the working classes. That it did suggests how much older values of mutuality, reciprocity, and collectivism had lost ground among these Americans. That they lost ground owes something to the decline in traditional building and loan associations. Real estate developers, such as those in Sinclair's *The Jungle*, sold homeownership as the (white) "working-man's reward," a phrase that suggested that they might be compensated for their "dismal labor" with "pleasant leisure."[52] And in America, where race and class are such deeply enfolded categories, race brought some privileges for the white working classes, including homeownership.[53] It is worth noting that despite innumerable obstacles to owning (and holding on to) their own homes, African Americans did pursue homeownership, and sometimes through black-owned building and loan associations.[54] However, for people of color living in early twentieth-century America, a period of intense segregation and racist violence, values of rugged individualism and self-sufficiency may have made less sense than those values of community, congregation, and collectivism that had once been bedrock in some white working-class communities, too.

The Loan Man acquired the City Savings Building and Loan Association sometime in 1914. Formed in 1911 by three Colorado Springs businessmen, including Merton Stubbs, the clerk at the county court downtown, the City was a tiny association. At the time that Walter Davis acquired it, it had fewer than thirty shares in force, and a reserve fund of $1.[55] Its prospects seemed unpromising, particularly because Colorado Springs already had an established and respected association, Assurance Savings and Loan. Yet within just a few years the City was the leading B&L in Colorado Springs. By 1923 Walter had moved the business out of his third-story office and into a new ground-level space at the covetable corner of Cascade and Kiowa. He made sure it was designed to resemble a bank.

The quickness with which he turned the City around suggests that Walter came to it with ideas about how to make it lucrative. Certainly the B&L business had its attractions. For one, Colorado Springs had never known a truly member-run building and loan of the sort that had operated in big cities such as Philadelphia. For another, loan sharks were coming under increasing attack, both nationally and locally. About the time he acquired the B&L, a group of businessmen in Colorado Springs formed the Farm Loan Company in order to extend credit at a reasonable rate to local farmers. They did so in order to prevent any more farmers from falling into the clutches of loan sharks. In testimony before Congress, one Colorado Springs businessman explained that although they had managed to pass laws against usury, local loan sharks had succeeded in evading them by refashioning their businesses as banks, which were explicitly not covered by the new law.[56]

Tellingly, Harry Leven, who appears to have been the best-known and most cutthroat loan shark in Colorado Springs, went into the B&L business around the same time as my grandfather. Leven's association failed after a few short years, perhaps because his reputation for ruthlessness preceded him. Nonetheless, both he and my grandfather likely calculated that they could evade prosecution by reorganizing their loan offices as B&Ls. They surely realized that much of what they were already doing could be done almost as easily under the cover of a building and loan because B&Ls operated largely outside of any state regulatory regime. Colorado did not even have a law on the books pertaining to the B&L business until 1897, and even then established no real mechanisms for supervision. According to that 1897 law, no reserves were required, and officers and directors were not prohibited from receiving commissions. The original statute presumed that all associations would be of the "mutual" type, that is, an old-style building and loan, which meant the statute was of no use when it came to businesses that called themselves B&Ls but departed from their standard practices.[57] One auditor, stunned to discover that some associations were engaged in the business of chattel loans, pointed out that this was scandalously out of step with the purpose and intent

of building and loan associations.[58] Maybe that auditor had Harry
Leven in mind. In 1915 Leven Savings, Building and Loan Association had only $350 loaned on real estate and $4,037 in chattel
mortgages.[59]

The state made no effort to regulate the industry until 1907
when it established a Bureau of Building and Loan Associations
in the state auditor's office. From the beginning, the state auditor's
biennial reports to the governor on the building and loan industry called for legislative action to develop an effective regulatory
regimen. Reports routinely cited the lack of authority and the in-
sufficiency of funds accorded to the B&L inspector. By the end of
1920, the salaries and expenses allotted to the state bank commissioner's office amounted to $30,693, far outstripping the measly
$4,997 appropriated for the B&L inspector's office.[60] Given the
growth in building and loans in the state—by 1931 the aggregate
assets of B&Ls were over 30 percent more than those of banks in
Colorado—the disparity in funding made no sense. In most other
states the office regulating building and loans relied almost exclu-
sively upon field examinations to ascertain the actual condition of
associations. But in Colorado the lack of money and the absence of
trained officials meant that only a fraction of the state's B&Ls were
actually ever subjected to a field exam. Eventually the legislature
did allot more money, but without qualified and motivated examiners, it made little difference.

Also undermining state regulation was the coziness between
building and loan officers and the men whose businesses they were
meant to regulate. Colorado's first commissioner of building and
loan associations, Eli Gross, took direction from an unofficial cabi-
net of B&L men that included Walter Davis and other sharp operators. Gross's predecessor actually received a $6,000 loan from my
grandfather, who, uncharacteristically, requested no security for
the loan. Moreover, there was sometimes a revolving door between
B&L regulators and B&L operators. (In California Andrew E.

Falch and John Franklin Johnson, respectively the state's former building and loan commissioner and former superintendent of banks, together established a large building and loan association in the late 1920s.)[61] Despite the fact that virtually every biennial report to the governor of Colorado cited numerous defects in the law, nothing changed.[62]

Lax regulation characterized the B&L business in much of the country, especially the West. And as we shall see, the tendency to treat building and loans as self-regulating entities encouraged businessmen to once again take advantage of the state's hands-off approach. In the case of my grandfather's association there were few remnants of the old-style B&L about it. Walter appointed himself the president and treasurer and made his wife, Lula, the secretary of the association. An attorney with whom he had conducted business was the only non–family member on the association's three-person board of directors. According to the bylaws, only two members of the board needed to be present for a meeting to have the necessary majority.[63] The bylaws further mandated that for withdrawals of less than $100, members would have to file written requests thirty days in advance. For larger sums, sixty days' written notice was required, just as it was at Bailey Brothers. The association could simply turn down requests for withdrawal if the demands of withdrawing shareholders amounted to more than one-half of the monthly receipts of the association. These were standard bylaws that were actually rooted in the cooperative character of the earliest B&Ls, and they stood in contrast to the rules governing commercial banks, whose depositors were legally able to demand immediate withdrawal of their deposited money.

The City's policies regarding withdrawals were B&L boilerplate, but its policies toward lending were not. There was nothing of the loan shark business about early building and loans. Chattel loans were understood to be completely at odds with the mission of B&Ls. However, at both Leven's association and at the City moneylending was a key part of the business, and the terms were not advantageous to the borrower. At the City the borrower absorbed all expenses associated with the transaction. Even applying for a loan cost the applicant $10 (using 1916 as baseline, that would come to $220 today), and failure to pay on time was penalized. If the borrower failed to make payments over a three-month period the Board of Trustees could declare the loan due and payable and require payment of the interest and principal. And although B&Ls stressed that members' money was backed by first mortgages only, the City's bylaws allowed its Board of Trustees to invest pretty much where it pleased, not just in first mortgages.

When propertied borrowers did business with the City they typically secured the promissory note with a deed of trust to a property that they would forfeit should they default on their payments. For example, when P.J. Hecox, a self-employed gardener who sold vegetables and fruit from his yard, borrowed $1,500 from my grandfather in 1924, he signed an agreement that stipulated:

> In case of any default, whereby the right of foreclosure occurs hereunder, the second party or the holder of the said note, shall at once become entitled to the possession, use and enjoyment of the property aforesaid, and to the rents, issues, and profits thereof, from the accruing of such right and during the pendency of foreclosure proceeding and the period of redemption, if any there be; and such possession, etc., shall at once be delivered to the second party, or the holder of said note on request, and on refusal the delivery of such possession may be enforced by the second party, or the note-holder by any appropriate civil suit or proceeding including action or actions in ejectment, or forcible entry, or unlawful detainer.

In 1928, after apparently making no payments on his loan, Hecox, by now seventy-eight years old, lost possession of his ramshackle home on East Yampa Street because he had secured his loan with the deed to his property. He ended up renting a space behind a shoe repair shop, where he raised hens. My grandfather waited nearly four years before going after Hecox.[64] He sometimes waited a few years before going after delinquent borrowers who owned property, perhaps to make his portfolio of loans appear more attractive and to detract attention from any bad loans he had made. The bottom line was that when borrowers defaulted, the City could legally take over their property and rent it out or sell it. Foreclosure was one way the City acquired so much property.

According to histories of the thrift industry their biggest problem at this stage in their history was the amateurism of too many of their operators. But that didn't describe the City or many of the other B&Ls that would go belly up during the Depression. These were, like the nationals, for-profit corporations designed to be maximally lucrative to their operators. Making them profitable involved misrepresenting them to the public. B&L men like my grandfather regularly ran advertisements that deliberately fudged the difference between their businesses and banks. "Come, deposit your money with us," they beckoned. "You can withdraw it whenever you like."[65] Even though my grandfather eventually abided by the wishes of bankers and stopped advertising his business as a bank, in face-to-face encounters he described the City as a bank. Court records show that on at least one occasion he claimed that his banking business was separate from his B&L.[66] The case involved an eighty-one-year-old chiropractor, Dr. Woody, who in 1929 had "loaned" Walter $15,000 at 6 percent interest. Disturbed by talk that the City wasn't really a bank, Woody went to Walter's office and confronted him. My grandfather proved persuasive. The next day Woody loaned him another $2,000. Four years later, Woody's estate was in court suing the City for $17,500.

B&L men further confounded the distinction between B&Ls and banks by handing out passbooks to customers who, unsurprisingly,

No._____

THE
City
Savings
BUILDING AND LOAN
ASSOCIATION
COLORADO SPRINGS

STATE SUPERVISED
SAVINGS INSTITUTION

_____

_____

TAKE CARE OF THIS BOOK
IT MUST BE PRESENTED WHEN MONEY IS
DEPOSITED OR WITHDRAWN. IF LOST OR
STOLEN, NOTIFY THE ASSOCIATION AT ONCE

The front cover of a passbook for the City Savings Building and Loan. (Author's archive) understood themselves as depositors, not investors. Remember Tom, the pushy depositor during the bank run in *It's a Wonderful Life*? Tom is the one who demands his money on the spot, and is incredulous and indignant when George replies that withdrawal require paperwork and a wait of sixty days.

Lax regulation and definitional haziness about banks versus B&Ls would have made the building and loan business appealing to my grandfather. Moreover, as long as he remained a loan shark, which carried with it predatory associations, my grandfather's dream of refashioning himself as an affluent professional would remain out of reach. As one *New York Times* writer noted, "men who wanted the approval of society" would not find it by making their living as a small lender.[67]

Business must have been good because in February 1916, two years after acquiring the City, Walter moved his family from their modest house on East Willamette to one in the fashionable North End of town, adjacent to Colorado College. With four bedrooms and two and a half bathrooms, the twenty-year-old Victorian was nearly three thousand square feet. He made improvements over the years, among them turning the one-car garage into one that accommodated two cars. Like Harry Leven, he made sure the house at 1628 North Tejon was in his wife's name.

As my grandfather's business practices indicate, building and loan associations, formed in the interest of the common good, were once again changing. Hijacked by operators whose goal was lining their own pockets, they became concerns where a loan shark like my grandfather could make himself comfortably at home. As early as the 1910s an economist, someone sympathetic to the thrift industry, admitted that some building and loan associations were no better than loan shark outfits.[68]

Button-down types, wheeler-dealers, scam artists, speculators, and usurious moneylenders—by the early twentieth century the building and loan industry was filling up with them. The

permeability between the respectable and illicit was even acknowledged in some of the early scripts for *It's a Wonderful Life*. At
least two scripts (one by left-winger Clifford Odets) called for two
Georges—the original man on the bridge who wants to commit
suicide and the other George, the rich philanderer he could have
become. When George embarks on his angel-assisted journey, he
finds not a desolate and corrupt world without him, but a world
with a bad George. As we shall see, these discarded scripts capture
better than Capra's movie the culture of building and loan associations in some American towns and cities.[69]

3

Racketeers and Suckers

"A decade of debauchery" was how Franklin Delano Roosevelt summed up the 1920s. To economist John Kenneth Galbraith, writing some thirty years later, the decade ushered in a period of shameful speculation in which getting rich became the new normal. Galbraith pointed his finger at ordinary Americans who had succumbed to the lure of easy money. According to this view, the twenties represented the tipping point, when the mass consumption of mass culture corroded America's core values. Hard work and self-denial were the victims of this new consumerism, in which hedonistic individualism reigned supreme. It was only during the Great Depression that America sobered up, came to its senses, and was finally redeemed.

Through most of the last century U.S. historians often shared this censorious opinion of the Jazz Age, but more recently historians have shown that mass culture and mass consumption did not always play out in predictable ways. For one, scholars have demonstrated that the surge in unionism in the 1930s was at least partly due to the participation of the working classes in mass culture. Going to the movies, listening to the radio, and shopping in chain stores had the effect of breaking down parochial ethnic enclaves

and of homogenizing the American working class—a precondition
for the development of class-based solidarity, a sense of "we-ness"
that facilitated unionism. Historians of gender and race have also
shown that sites of mass consumption could play out in ways that
increased autonomy and freedom.[1] We cannot really grasp the era
if we don't also acknowledge the profound and sometimes empow-
ering newness of the period. Imagine the thrill of sitting behind
the wheel of an affordable automobile for the first time or the
wonder of watching a movie with so many strangers in a darkened
movie palace. Think of George Bailey's excitement as he prepares
to set out to travel, before his plans are upended by his father's
stroke. Who can't identify with his desire to avoid his father's fate
of unrelenting hard work and self-sacrifice?

That said, by decade's end income inequality had never been
greater, and Americans had developed a different relationship to
money as mass culture reached more deeply into American society. It was a time of technological innovation that featured radios,
movies, and automobiles, and the eye-catching advertising used to
market them. Underwriting the go-go twenties was debt. Particularly striking is the unprecedented extent to which personal debt
was becoming, in the words of historian Louis Hyman, "commer-
cially profitable, institutionally resellable, and legally available."[2]
This change was aided by the passage in many states of uniform
small loan laws and the phenomenal expansion during the interwar
years of installment credit. By 1930 installment credit financed the
sale of between 80 and 90 percent of all furniture, and between 60
and 75 percent of automobiles. In fact, General Motors succeeded
in pulling ahead of the Ford Motor Company by offering customers
financing. Consumers would discover that usury laws offered them
no protection from deceptive and predatory installment lenders,
including GMAC.[3]

Nevertheless, loans for consumer purchases doubled during
the 1920s, from $3.3 billion to $7.6 billion. In another signal that

times were changing, some banks began moving into the area of personal loans, although they limited their lending to white-collar professional men. In this period, American capitalism executed a turnabout as the ideals of hard work, discipline, and self-denial began to give way to the virtues of spending and the pleasures of consumption. Being in debt, once considered shameful, was becoming a way of life for Americans.[4]

People, even the working classes, caught the investment bug. Why let your money gather dust when you could invest it? After World War I some Americans fell for the pitch of Charles Ponzi, who promised to pay investors 50 percent on their money. Ponzi's pyramid scheme of paying off old investors with the money of newer investors soon collapsed, but that wouldn't stop others from using his methods. And soon enough other opportunities beckoned—in oil, real estate, mining, utilities, and building and loan associations, some of which began to offer depositors inflated rates of interest.

Indeed, the building and loan industry is a good barometer of the shift in attitude toward money. It had been established during the old regime; it was called the "thrift" industry, after all. However, by the early twenties many B&L operators were offering interest rates so lucrative that they blurred the distinction between savings and investment. Walter Davis was offering as much as 6 percent interest, a full 2 percent more than the Assurance, the town's oldest B&L, or any of the town's banks. Soon enough in Colorado Springs and elsewhere the rates would go even higher, with the result that B&Ls began to attract greater numbers of middle-class depositors. One measure of the thrift industry's growing appeal is that by 1925 the *Magazine of Wall Street*, a leading personal finance and investment weekly, was carrying regular stories on building and loans.[5]

Blurring this distinction between savings and investment proved profitable, and it played a role in the massive expansion of the B&L industry in the twenties. Between 1920 and 1924 the number of building and loan associations in the United States grew from

8,633 to 11,844.[6] By the fall of 1929 the *New York Herald Tribune*, citing an industry source, reported that the number of building and loan associations had grown 70 percent since World War I.[7] Growth was especially strong in the West, but in many parts of the country the thrift industry took off. Take Manhattan, which by 1925 reportedly had two B&Ls with combined assets of $30 million.[8] By 1930, building and loan associations held nearly 50 percent of the country's institutionally held mortgage debt on one- to four-family houses.[9]

The expansion of the B&L industry was also attributable to the explosion in home construction, which soared in the twenties because wartime restrictions on building had produced a serious housing shortage.[10] Nationwide, hundreds of associations formed in order to take advantage of the overheated real estate market. Many of these newer associations offered members very low down payments and second mortgage financing, which was far riskier for the lender than first mortgage financing. Over time, such lenient financing would play out very badly, just as it did during our own recent subprime mortgage crisis.[11]

The breakneck speed with which the thrift industry grew stemmed as well from the proliferation of for-profit stock concerns masquerading as building and loans. In many respects the new "permanent" or "guarantee" associations followed the nationals' business model—the seductively high interest rates along with the extra fees, the penalties borne by shareholders, and terms that disguised their actual position as investors. They also featured two different classes of stock, an arrangement all too typical today of public companies and investment consortiums. The holders of one class of stock—a minority—held the exclusive right to hold annual meetings, elect the directors, make the bylaws, manage the business, and control its assets. Those that held the other, inferior class of stock—both investors and borrowers—had few rights. They could share in the profits, but only according to the less-than-favorable terms named in their contracts. Forget share-holder democracy. Upon signing up, members were required to authorize one or more association officers to vote their proxy at stockholders' meetings. A culture of freewheeling, unregulated finance took hold, with officers routinely advancing loans to themselves. When Colorado's B&L law was amended in 1927, it actually benefited for-profit operators. And the "reform" B&L bill of 1931 duplicated many of the worst provisions of the 1927 act.[12] The legislators who served on the governor's special committee investigating Colorado's thrift industry would blame its collapse in 1932 on the growing numbers of these new-style B&Ls.[13]

Finally, key to the growth of the building and loan business were Liberty Bonds. In Colorado Springs the two associations that formed in the twenties announced their arrival with a pitch involving war bonds. In fact, Dollar Building and Loan Association, Home Building and Loan Association, and the City all competed for customers holding issues of Liberty Bonds and War Savings Stamps that would stop paying interest—of roughly 4 percent—after December 15, 1922. One big ad for Dollar urged readers to present their bonds and stamps so that the association could either collect the principal and interest for the customer or assist them in converting them into the association's 7 percent tax-free building and loan certificates. Home also advertised a 7 percent rate, while the City's ads offered 6 percent on savings accounts for those converting Victory War Bonds. Colorado Springs had been a heavy subscriber to these bonds, and studies show that people who had taken the plunge and invested were inclined to do so again. Nationally, 22 million Americans, many of modest means, purchased Liberty Bonds. One survey of six hundred mothers (almost all of them foreign-born) working in unskilled positions in Chicago packinghouses showed that a full 84 percent of their families owned Liberty Bonds.[14]

For many, buying war bonds made the world of investment feel

U.S. Treasury Secretary William McAdoo saw the Liberty Bond campaign as a critical part of the "powerful stream of romanticism" he believed necessary to mobilize Americans behind the war effort. (Courtesy of the Prints and Photographs Division, Library of Congress, cph 3c07238)

less risky. Lots of people who had believed the best place for their money was in their own house or backyard now turned to small banks, building and loan associations, and a range of investment companies—everything from local opportunities to Wall Street securities.[15] During and immediately following World War I, a number of factors—Liberty Bond campaigns, employee stock ownership plans, and the elimination of the cruder sort of "bucket shops," betting parlors that constituted a shadow world of securities exchange—dramatically increased the numbers of Americans, including working people, who were participating in the world of investments. Before long slick stock promoters were taking advantage of these novices. They often targeted farmers, offering them stock, which would turn out to be worthless, in exchange for their Liberty Bonds. The extent of swindling was such that the movement for a national blue-sky law, meant to protect consumers from securities fraud, gained momentum in these years.[16]

In Colorado Springs a speculative culture was already well established, with all kinds of people, including laborers, trading in stocks and futures.[17] After all, this was a town whose 1906 city directory included more than six pages of small-print listings devoted to mining companies whose stock was sold throughout the country. My grandfather was just one of many townspeople who owned a few mining stocks. By the twenties, with the downturn of mining in Cripple Creek and all those Liberty Bonds coming due, there were plenty of businessmen eager to invest townspeople's money.[18] In other communities, such as Youngstown, Ohio, unscrupulous businessmen even opened up shop as "Liberty Bond scalpers" and bought war bonds at a steep discount from investors who had no idea how to go about selling their bonds.[19] There is, of course, an irony in the way that Liberty Bonds, which were originally promoted as furthering both thrift and the common good, became yet another example of the individualistic, acquisitive culture of the twenties.

One local case that illuminates some features of America's new financial landscape involves the former Springs building and loan man Merton Stubbs. The son of Colorado Springs pioneers, Stubbs was one of the men who sold the City Building and Loan Association to my grandfather. He was also the town's court reporter. A man known to all the judges, he was someone whom you would have thought that even a sharp businessman would refrain from scamming.

In the summer of 1922, Stubbs, like many Americans, was looking for a lucrative way to invest his money. He had invested in Liberty Bonds, which would soon stop paying interest. He had $5,000 ($71,430 in 2016 terms) that he hoped to invest in order to pay for his children's college education. Stubbs explained this casually one evening to a man at the Elks Lodge. Perhaps Stubbs initiated the conversation knowing that the man worked at a local investment and real estate company and might have some thoughts on the subject. The salesman claimed that the company had just the ticket for him, and several days later Stubbs stopped by the office for a more formal conversation. The company had a number of loans on its books, any of which Stubbs was assured would provide a handsome return. Stubbs would earn 7 percent, and the company would earn 1 percent for administering the loan, that is, for making sure the taxes and insurance were paid and that the interest was sent to Stubbs. Stubbs chose to buy the loan of a farmer, but not a local farmer. This was a farmer in Cedar Rapids, Iowa, a man who was said to have excellent credit and good land.

For three years Stubbs had no reason to believe he had made anything other than a smart investment. Indeed, he was sufficiently pleased with the company that he made other investments with it and steered his friends there. All that changed in 1926 when Stubbs stopped receiving payments. It later came out in court that the Iowan had been in arrears on his taxes when the Springs investment firm sold Stubbs the loan. And although the real estate company had paid Stubbs the interest for nearly four years, the farmer had stopped paying the company soon after Stubbs bought his loan. The farmer's problems turned out not to be his Cedar Rapids farm but instead a failed Wisconsin land deal. By the time Stubbs was informed of how wrong everything had gone—the farmer was a staggering $50,000 in debt—the Iowa farm had been sold for taxes.

When pressed in court about why the company had not informed Stubbs, the firm's president insisted it was company policy in such instances to try to "work things out" in order to avoid causing the client any "distress."[20] The case is instructive in several ways. First, we see that even in the 1920s there was a business in debt, with ordinary Americans buying the debt of other individuals, and doing so at some geographical distance. Second, we can see the lure of investment for ordinary Americans. Most interesting of all, the men running the investment and real estate company had no compunction about cheating Stubbs, a well-positioned member of the community and a fellow Elk who had known the company president for twenty-five years. This was how business was sometimes transacted on Main Street USA. And yet if there was a wink and a nod accompanying the transactions of many Springs businessmen, including the B&L men I write about in this chapter, that was not the case with Merton Stubbs, who, like many people, never got the message that it was all a game of suckers and racketeers.[21]

There is no reason to think that this game was conducted with particular ruthlessness in Colorado Springs. However, for men trying to get ahead—men including my grandfather and the area's three other building and loan operators—the city presented distinct challenges. By the twenties Colorado Springs, a city that had grown cocky about the region's mineral wealth, began to entertain the previously unmentionable—that a gold-based economy might not be sustainable.[22] In his 1921 address to the General Assembly, Colorado governor Oliver Shoup, a longtime Springs resident and booster, argued that the state needed to confront the possible "passing of the prospector." Shoup was an anti-statist politician who usually made a point of disparaging the federal government, but on this occasion he called on the federal government to help the state address this grave problem.[23]

By this point even some local mine owners had come to realize that Cripple Creek would not keep producing.[24] They started looking for the next big thing and turned to sugar beets, oil, and, of course, other minerals—all of them extractive industries. With the slowly dawning realization that mining might not always be the town's economic engine, Colorado Springs itself began to search, sometimes anxiously, for what might take the place of gold.[25] Some, including Spencer Penrose, bet on tourism. Penrose made millions from mining copper in Utah, but he was among those who banked on tourism as the saving grace of Colorado Springs. He financed the Pikes Peak Highway, the Broadmoor Hotel, and the Cheyenne Lodge. One group plotted to turn Monument Valley Park into a world-famous spa.[26] In nearby Manitou the "golden dream" had long been the discovery of hot mineral water that would permit the resort town to operate on a year-round basis. In 1930 a Texas oil magnate, who had vowed to find Manitou's hot water by drilling 1,500 feet deep or deeper, became one of many who promised (and failed) to deliver.[27] A year later, businessman Merrill Shoup, son of the former governor, argued that the city should exploit the region's "coal wealth" until a "new Cripple Creek is discovered."[28]

Colorado Springs did its best to turn itself into a commodity. City leaders promoted it as "the City of Sunshine" and "the gateway to the roofgarden of America." In an apparent effort to cover all bases, they even marketed it as both "the Playground of the Nation" and "the City of Churches."[29] Tourism had long been an essential part of the town's economy, but with the downturn in mining, its economy became almost entirely dependent on tourism. By contrast,

Los Angeles, the city that sold itself better than any other, could boast by the twenties that it had the movies, real estate, tourism, and the beginnings of industry.[30] Tourism produces service-sector jobs, and the Springs became so well known as a city of such jobs that people joked that the place was made up of three classes: a leisure class revolving around society and sports, another class of tourists, and everyone else whose job it was to serve those groups.[31] I mention it here because it captures something of what Colorado Springs was like for ambitious men who were not already part of the city's leisure-class elite. They had arrived in the Springs when the lure of gold was still alive, but only the most delusional could continue to hold on to that fantasy. More and more Americans thought they might make it in the twenties, a time when a full four million were trying their hand at the stock market and when radio, newspapers, and women's magazines ran stories on how to strike it rich on stock "tips."[32] Those hopes lived on in Colorado Springs,

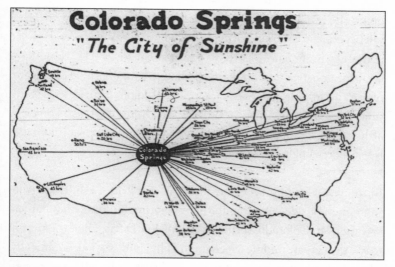

In 1923 Colorado Springs was selling itself as "the City of Sunshine," beckoning tourists from other parts of the country. (*Gazette*)

too, but the jobs on offer there were increasingly service-sector jobs, only some of which were lucrative.

The 1920s have the reputation of having been a boom time, and they were, particularly for urban elites. Take the changes in the tax code, which created "windfalls for the wealthy" and spurred speculation among the affluent.[33] However, for the middle class, participating in the consumer revolution meant assuming more debt and trying their hand at investing. For the men who ran the B&L business in Colorado Springs it must have been an especially frustrating time because the Springs was characterized by an unrivaled concentration of wealth. Moreover, at this juncture Colorado Springs was a small city with distinct limits, very unlike Los Angeles, which even in the early twentieth century was characterized by both sprawl and a "private, fragmented urbanism."[34] By contrast, even Millionaires' Row was a part of the North End; its residents were visible, not cloistered. This would shift with the housing development in Broadmoor, where more affluent residents began to settle, particularly from the late 1920s onward. But up until that point the wealthy tended to live in relative proximity to other townspeople. My grandfather would have seen Spencer Penrose and other millionaires as they moved about town. He would have seen the construction on Penrose's house—an enormous garage to house the mining magnate's four canary-colored Lozier cars, for a time the most expensive car built in the United States.[35] The city's affluence was palpable, but in a context of limited upward mobility it felt increasingly out of reach.

In the years leading up to the building and loan crash, there were three men besides my grandfather operating building and loan associations in Colorado Springs. Like Walter Davis, all of them were from the great middle—geographically and socioeconomically. Their early years were spent in the Midwest, in families positioned somewhere in that baggy territory that extends imprecisely from the lower middle class downward. Their backgrounds were similar, but each of them lived and failed in ways that were distinctly their own.

There was Willis Sims, a staunch Republican who made his name in a successful credit reporting business he ran with his brother Robert.[36] Credit bureaus began forming in the years before the Civil War, and they helped to bring about a sea change in American society by judging and rating men according to their creditworthiness. Those who fell short of "character, capital and capacity" would have their disappointments catalogued and tracked, much like "damaged or unclaimed freight."[37]

Knowing the gossip and the rumors with which to fill up these reports required being a part of the town's lodges and clubs. Sims was active in the Knights of Pythias, the Elks Club, and the Masons. He wasn't your run-of-the-mill Mason; he was a Master Mason. A founding member of the town's Rotary Club, he was also active in the town's conservative Chamber of Commerce, and for one term served El Paso County in the state legislature. During World War I he was the chairman of El Paso County's Four-Minute Men, a national effort to drum up patriotic support for the war and the purchase of Liberty Bonds through rapidly delivered four-minute speeches.[38]

In 1916 Sims acquired a controlling interest in the town's very first building and loan association, the Assurance Savings and Loan.[39] His association grew despite the fact that he did not offer bloated interest rates on savings accounts. In the summer of 1918 he also began working at the State Savings Bank in Colorado Springs as the cashier, which in those days was the crucial stepping-stone to the presidency. The State Savings Bank was far from a banking powerhouse. However, Sims was an establishment businessman and it was his bank where the city of Colorado Springs and El Paso County kept their money.

Sims seems to have run these businesses conservatively, but he was not immune to the get-ahead sensibility of those times. As in much of the nation, the Springs was awash in new housing construction, and in 1921 Sims became involved with the former mayor of Manitou in an ambitious deal to develop a big parcel of land right by the doorstep of the Garden of the Gods.[40] The eighty-two-acre residential townsite, Lennon Park, was due north of Adams Crossing, an area between Colorado Springs and Manitou.[41]

There was just one problem going forward: Sims had no money of his own to invest. Unable to resist this surefire opportunity, he began embezzling. Legally, an embezzler is someone who misappropriates money or property that was placed in his or her care, and that's what Sims set about doing. Like many embezzlers, he was doubtless full of good intentions about returning the money.[42] However, sales of Lennon Park lots proved sluggish, and that led Sims to take some of the unsold lots and develop them himself, not into homes, but into a deluxe auto lodge. Maybe his brother Robert, who was by this point also working as the secretary for the local Automobile Dealers Credit Association, encouraged him to get in on this growing industry. After all, the Springs was a tourist destination and some people were looking for an alternative to camping by the side of the road, a practice that municipalities were increasingly outlawing. At Sims's Buffalo Lodge tourists would find themselves within feet of the entrance to the Garden of the Gods, with its stunning red rock formations. How could it fail? According to court records, Sims financed its construction and outfitting by embezzling nearly $30,000 from his B&L and taking out a $10,000 loan from his own bank. But by the time construction began on his lodge it was 1930, just months after the stock market crash. As the Depression set in and the tourist industry withered, Sims scrambled to pay back the loan to his own bank, to keep the shortfall in his B&L hidden, and to keep his handsome auto lodge going. Over the next months he used his good name to borrow another $25,000 from individuals and local banks.

Why did Sims become an embezzler? Perhaps as he approached middle age he despaired of ever being able to provide for his wife and children as well as he would have liked. He had been the golden boy of the Republican elite, yet it was his younger brother who just bought a home in the new upmarket Broadmoor development. Meanwhile, even though he labored at three jobs his family lived modestly in a house in the business district, an area already of diminished desirability. He may have wondered whether he would end up like those men he had judged so harshly: society's "unclaimed freight."

In contrast to Sims, who was part of the Colorado Springs establishment, Fred Bentall was an outsider. In a town dominated by Protestant Republicans who opposed the Ku Klux Klan, Bentall was a Democrat, a deacon of his Baptist church, and a leader of the local Klan.[43] Born and raised in Minnesota by his Swedish immigrant parents, the twenty-six-year-old Bentall showed up around 1908 in Colorado Springs. He secured employment as a clerk in an attorney's office and studied the law. In 1912 he listed his line of work in the city directory as "notary public" and "loans," and a year later he was admitted to the bar.

Bentall later claimed that it was Walter Davis who had encouraged him to open his own association. However, it is unlikely Bentall needed any encouragement to get into the B&L business; he had spent much of the past decade working as a moneylender, which supplemented whatever income he earned as a lawyer. The Home Building and Loan Association opened right before Thanksgiving 1922. Within weeks of its opening, the association was running ads that screamed "7% interest" and promised that money could be withdrawn as needed, which was not, of course, true. Despite offering inflated rates of interest, the Home remained a small and amateurish concern, and at least one lawsuit suggests that Bentall sometimes took advantage of his more vulnerable working-class customers.[44] It's also possible that potential customers were put off

All the town's building and loans ran advertisements in the local dailies. From the time it opened its doors in 1922, the Home, like the Dollar, offered 7 percent interest, and sometimes, as here, with promises of interest compounded monthly. This ad ran in April 1930. (*Colorado Springs Gazette & Telegraph*)

by the association's disheveled office and Bentall's uncertain handle on the details of people's accounts. It was later revealed that his bookkeeping sometimes amounted to nothing more than notations on scraps of paper stuffed into the pigeonholes of his desk. Bentall did not use his depositors' money to buy a flashy car or a more expensive home, which might have caused comment. Rather, he acquired equity in an Oklahoma property and bought a ranch outside of town, which he stocked with cattle and outfitted with $2,000 worth of farm machinery.

Edward C. Sharer, the other building and loan man at the heart of this saga, came to the business after a long career in the employ of some of the most powerful capitalists in Colorado Springs. After finishing law school in Chicago, he moved to the Springs to be the private secretary for James R. McKinnie, a mining contractor who struck it rich in Cripple Creek. McKinnie's network included his business partner Robert P. Davie, the legendary mining man Verner Z. Reed, and Reed's private secretary, Oliver H. Shoup, the future Colorado governor. All of these men were national capitalists who made fortunes in mining, oil, and what many regarded as the "new gold," sugar beets.

McKinnie and Davie were land speculators who bought up promising land, sank some wells, pumped some water, and then moved on, having sold the land to someone with the money to properly develop it.[45] They were, as one newspaper put it, "hustlers," men who made their money by transforming the West's "waste places."[46] Sharer worked alongside these hustlers, and even followed them to Los Angeles, where he tried to make his fortune as a real estate developer. Despite his proximity to power, the forty-one-year-old Sharer returned to the Springs in 1916 after three years in L.A. with little to show for it. Shoup, a millionaire, provided him a soft landing, appointing him president of the Manitou Mineral Water Company. Ginger Champagne, a nonalcoholic beverage, was the company's big seller. (Ed Sharer was possibly the man my mother regarded as her father's nemesis, the mysterious "Bubbles.")[47] Back in the Springs Sharer resumed his role as a community pillar, serving as the secretary of Liberty Bond drives, heading up financial campaigns for the Red Cross, and directing the Sunday school program at the First Presbyterian Church. He was active in the Republican Party and the Chamber of Commerce.

Sharer was among the men who formed the Dollar Building and Loan Association, which opened for business in April 1922. Just as the Home did several months later, it announced its arrival with advertisements promising rates of 7 percent interest on deposits. Sharer used his position at the Dollar to further his ambitions as a land developer, and in the process his personal business grew entangled with that of the B&L. The Dollar was so haplessly managed that in 1927 a concerned employee contacted board member Shoup, who then alerted the state's building and loan commissioner to its condition. An audit revealed the association was operating with a $32,000 shortfall (more than $441,000 today) and a $40,000 impairment of its assets. When the accountant handling the audit confronted Sharer with his finding, the B&L man implored him, "Think of my wife and children."[48]

This wasn't a trivial matter caused by an absentminded staffer, as with *It's a Wonderful Life*'s Uncle Billy misplacing $8,000 of depositors' money. Indeed, the commissioner judged what had happened at the Dollar a "serious malfeasance." Yet the authorities chose not to prosecute Sharer or to warn the public of its precarious condition.[49] The state's unwillingness to pursue the matter reflected its long-standing reluctance to regulate the industry it was charged with supervising as well as the influence enjoyed by the former governor, who offered to put the association on sounder footing before quietly resigning from the association's board of directors. Whatever arrangements were made in 1927—and they were never entirely explained—Sharer went unpunished.

As these thumbnail sketches show, the culture of building and loan associations in Colorado Springs was not one of selfless operators committed to helping ordinary working people. Yet the assumption that the B&L industry was just that is rarely challenged. Take one reliable book about the catastrophic savings and loan crisis of the 1980s, which notes that if Hollywood did a remake of Capra's movie, George Bailey's speech during the bank run would require a complete overhaul. "The money's not here," Bailey would have to say. "Why, your money's in racehorses, a bordello in Nevada, a share in the Dallas Cowboys . . . vacant shopping malls, unneeded condominiums, Rolls-Royces, golf courses, prostitutes to pay off regulators, credit cards."[50] It's an amusing passage, but it reinforces the same naive view of thrifts that informs Capra's movie.

Whether depositors' money was in racehorses or cattle, unneeded condos or deluxe auto lodges, it wasn't where it was meant to be. The point is that this is what capitalism sometimes looked like on the ground on Main Street, and it flies in the face of long-standing, nearly baked-in assumptions that when capitalism goes awry, distance is the culprit. What existed in Colorado Springs was face-to-face contact, with those crucial "social checks of personal obligation" in place, and yet they provided absolutely no protection from financial dubiousness, even embezzlement.[51]

Embezzlement, in contrast to other forms of larceny, is character-ized by what the economist John Kenneth Galbraith called a "time parameter." Years may pass between the time the embezzlement occurred and its discovery. During this period, the person whose funds have been embezzled not only feels no sense of loss, he or she experiences a "net increase in psychic wealth." And that psy-chic wealth makes a discovery of defalcation much less likely. So it is that in flush times the frequency of embezzlement increases and during lean times it falls off, as surpluses disappear and auditing becomes more exacting.[52]

Well in advance of the Depression, many building and loans were headed toward insolvency. Several years later when B&Ls began "crashing," journalists and the authorities spoke of their "shortfalls." What they meant was that these businesses had come up short—they were in the red and unable to meet their financial obligations. They could no longer pay their depositors or, for that matter, cover the taxes and insurance on mortgages now in default. There are shortfalls and shortfalls. Some are temporary and can be solved with short-term loans. Businesses and organizations can de-velop shortfalls for reasons beyond their control.[53] However, what was happening in the twenties in the building and loan industry in Colorado Springs and elsewhere were shortfalls that stemmed from a variety of causes, including mismanagement, high interest rates on deposits, real estate speculation, lax regulation, poor account-ing, financial irregularities, and embezzlement.

I cannot say with any certainty what led these three men to steal

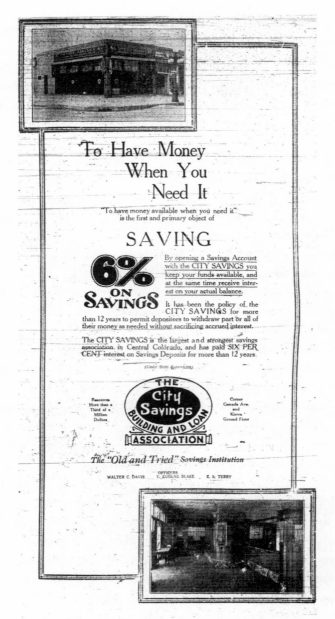

This ad from March 2, 1924, is the most lavish of the newspaper ads for Davis's City Savings Building and Loan. (*Gazette*)

from their neighbors, to rip off their fellow parishioners, lodge brothers, or klavern members. Had they internalized what historian Scott Sandage claims was a key cultural imperative for white-collar men by the turn of the last century: the avoidance of averageness? If so, they would have shared with Walter Davis the determination to avoid a "plodding, listless life."[54] In my grandfather's case, however, the existence of a substantial family archive allows me to know something more about the personal circumstances driving his embezzlement.

During the early years of the twenties the Davis family lived well, but their lifestyle was not extravagant. By 1921 my grandfather had started paying out more in interest—up to 6 percent—to depositors than he could afford. However disastrous this pyramid scheme would prove in the long term, what it meant in the shorter term was that he began to attract more middle-class people, most of whom owned their own homes. Should they default, well, there would be property to go after. At this juncture the City was not in jeopardy, but in 1923 things started to shift as he began to take bigger risks. Perhaps he was fearful of losing ground to his new competitors, Ed Sharer and Fred Bentall. Then there was his brother's growing prominence as a Republican politician and a civic leader.[55] In 1923 Roy Davis's election as the president of the local Rotary Club was the lead article one day in the dailies.

One way white-collar men such as my grandfather could claim "manly success" when more conventional measures of professional achievement eluded them was through sex, often with female subordinates in their workplace. I can't prove that my grandfather's relationship with his twenty-three-year-old stenographer had anything to do with shoring up his masculinity. However, Walter's relationship with Eva Terry seems to have started in 1923, when he had reason to feel anxious about being overtaken by his competitors and overshadowed by his brother. What I do know is that in becoming her lover as well as her boss Walter Davis became a

cliché. In the world of white-collar work, relationships between female stenographers and their bosses were so common as to be the
stuff of cartoons.[56]

Whether or not he had affairs with other women, there's no
doubt that Walter found the pretty redhead in his employ compel-
ling, perhaps because she reminded him of a younger version of his
wife. Both women were resourceful and high-maintenance, pragmatic and fiery, and their personal histories were also uncannily
similar. Eva, who was born in a small town on the other side of the
San Juan National Forest from Durango, was orphaned soon after
she was born. She and her six siblings were farmed out to relatives
of both parents. In the shuffle, Eva landed in Costilla County with
her uncle Warren, a struggling real estate agent, his second wife,
Harriet, and three children. About 1912 the Terry family moved to
Colorado Springs, where Warren continued to work in real estate.
They ended up settling in the working-class neighborhood of Ivywild. By 1924 he became the proprietor of Tent City Pikes Peak, an
automobile campground on the same grounds as the once-famous
and lavish zoo. It may have been a "First Class Ground for First
Class People," as it was advertised, but its facilities were minimal,
offering only tents. By 1925 Eva's uncle had moved his business to
the outskirts of town, and although it now featured actual cottages
(and a so-called free zoo), it was too close to a poultry yard and a
dairy to be the most desirable of such outfits.[57]

Walter's infatuation with Eva gave the Terry family its best
chance for upward mobility. Warren Terry's eldest son had married and relocated to Denver, where he drove a taxi while his wife
worked as a waitress. Their daughter Pearl also moved to Denver,
where she worked as a nurse. Their youngest son was killed in
1913 during southern Colorado's bloody coal wars, in which miners
went out against the Colorado Fuel & Iron Company, which was
largely a Rockefeller concern. Luke Terry was behind the wheel in
an open-topped motor wagon when striking miners ambushed and

In 1941 the newspaper published photographs of a stretch of buildings along South Nevada slated for demolition. Among the businesses affected by the widening of the road was the auto camp owned by Eva's uncle. This photo gives some sense of working-class Ivywild, where Eva lived with her family. (*Gazette*)

murdered him and three mine guards he was transporting. Their deaths were part of the run-up to the infamous massacre in nearby Ludlow six months later when the Colorado National Guard executed several miners and set fire to the striking miners' tent city. (Among those killed during the Ludlow massacre were 11 children and 2 women who suffocated to death during the fire in a dirt bunker built for safety.) In the pages of the anti-union *Gazette*, Luke Terry became a symbol of the miners' murderous lawlessness.[58] But it would take more than twenty years for the socially negligible Terry family to register once again in the local press.

My grandfather was preoccupied with social rank, but he seems to have been untroubled by Eva's lack of standing. Whatever it was about Eva—her good looks, style, smarts—it seems to have largely nullified her working-class background for him. Of course, there was also Eva's youth, which was perhaps the decisive factor given that it was a quality forty-one-year-old Lula did not possess. It is possible that Lula had not enjoyed Walter's undivided attention during their seventeen years of marriage, but she was used to being admired for her looks and her charm. My mother was not infrequently in the awkward position of looking on as fathers of her friends fell over themselves to win Lula's attention. She remained a looker well into middle age.

Other men's continued interest in her did nothing to blunt Lula's disappointment at being supplanted by Eva. Walter's affair tormented her. On more than one occasion she gathered up her daughter—who at the start of all this was no more than fourteen— hurried her into the Packard, and drove downtown to a spot across the street from the hotel where Walter and Eva often liaised. There Lula and Dorothy would sit in the car and wait for a glimpse of each one. These stakeouts did more than confirm Lula's worst suspicions about her husband. They permitted her to practice her own unique method of retaliation. Lula knew that Walter was picking out Eva's outfits on shopping trips. Once upon a time he had chosen her clothes, too. Every time she spotted Eva in a new outfit Lula would hunt down its duplicate, purchase it, and make a point of wearing it in his presence. In my mother's telling, this was not a desperate effort to win Walter back. Eva was nearly twenty years Lula's junior and had a fashionably boylike build—a flapper's shape. Instead, Lula was letting her husband know that there was no pulling the wool over her eyes. She wasn't having any of it—his excuses, deflections, lies, or blandishments.

Lula surveilled, she harangued, and day in and day out she "gave him hell." Walter responded by becoming scarcer and scarcer. There were the missed dinners—always unavoidable—and then there were weekend trips to Denver. When he had more money at his disposal, he hired a driver to take him to Denver's finest hotel, the Brown Palace, where he would stay the full weekend. He claimed that opening a branch office of the City required he be there. Even when Lula wasn't on the lookout for Walter and his mistress, there was no escaping their affair. In Colorado Springs, a town that was both claustrophobically small and obsessed with propriety, it's very likely that a good number of people did know about his affair. Even if waiters and salesclerks were not exchanging knowing looks when

My mother's memory of life with her parents was that there was no escaping their drama. That could be true even here, that is, several years before Eva entered the picture. (Author's archive)

Lula entered the restaurants and stores where they worked, one can imagine how easy it would have been, given the circumstances, to think they were.

Over time Lula became convinced that Walter intended to leave her for Eva. Maybe Lula believed that he would ditch everything—family and business—just as George Hurstwood, the saloon manager in *Sister Carrie,* left behind everything in pursuit of the desirable Carrie Meeber. Or maybe she imagined that he would divorce her and the alimony would prove inadequate.[59] If she fretted over divorce, he apparently did as well.[60] Divorce was still semi-disreputable, especially for a family that was not part of Springs society, and the stigma that attached to it is very likely part of my grandparents' story.[61]

Feeling her husband's distractibility and her own vulnerability, Lula resolved to do whatever she could to avoid landing in the poverty she had known as a child. Over the course of nearly a decade, she took $100 bills and stashed them inside hatboxes and stuffed them inside socks and gloves. From her time working at the Indianapolis tailor, she had a good working knowledge of the way fur coats were put together. Eventually she took to sewing money into the lining of her own fur coats. My mother never told me if Lula squirreled away part of her allowance from Walter or how she came by this money, but the house on North Tejon Street became my grandmother's bank.

Lula did more than stockpile money. A couple of years into Walter's affair, she decided that if her husband could make himself scarce, she could as well. In the summer of 1925 she and Dorothy traveled by train to Los Angeles, where they lived for a month just a few blocks from the beach in Santa Monica. The distance between Colorado and California briefly rekindled Walter's interest in his wife, but it also cost him $350 or nearly $5,000 in 2016 dollars. I know the figures, roughly speaking, because my grandparents conducted their relationship in this period through telegrams, which sometimes detailed the cost of lodging and travel.

The trip to California was just the beginning of Lula's attempt to renegotiate her marriage and construct a life of semi-independence. The telegraphic record of their communication suggests that she never stopped loving him. Years later from Florida she telegraphed, "Baked in sun all day. Blistered neck. Real summer. Florida moon. Band and everything but you." Lula remained in love with Walter, but as long as her husband continued his affair with Eva, she stayed away, usually with her daughter in tow. For her part, my mother was never able to occupy neutral territory with her feuding parents.[62] Lula was "very morose about the situation" and just went on and on about it. "When life was a tragedy with her," my mother recalled, "it was a *tragedy*." As she developed into a teenager Dorothy grew convinced that her father's reputation as a philanderer was causing friends to keep their distance from her. As a consequence, she developed what she called, in the jargon of the day, "an inferiority complex." One solution was to go away to school, and beginning in the fall of 1926 Dorothy enrolled in a boarding school in upstate New York. Walter tried to keep his daughter in the Springs, with promises of a fur coat and her very own roadster, but she chose the Knox School for Girls in Cooperstown, about seventy-five miles from Albany. Quite possibly Lula played a role in her daughter's decision to attend Knox because it gave Lula an excuse for prolonged stays in Manhattan.

No doubt my mother could have found a way to take classes in French, English-style horseback riding, and golf in the Springs. But there was no way she could have enacted "being somebody" in her hometown. It was one thing for her father to finance Knox, but quite another to gain the family entry into what Lula called the town's "charmed inner circle."[63] These were the people who belonged to the Cheyenne Mountain Country Club, which accepted

Will Return for Holidays

MISS DOROTHY ALLEN DAVIS
Daughter of Mr. and Mrs. Walter Davis of 1628 North Tejon street, who is attending Knox school at Cooperstown, N. Y., and is returning soon to spend the Christmas holidays with her parents.

Wealthy residents of the Springs had their comings and goings detailed in the local dailies, often accompanied by a picture. This picture of Dorothy is one of the few that appeared in the *Gazette* before her father's scandal. (Author's archive)

no more than one hundred local members and was in no hurry to fill those slots.[64] The *Gazette* did publish two pictures of Dorothy while she was at Knox, but she was never asked to "come out" into society. This was not simply a question of wealth, because Roy's daughter was a debutante. As long as she remained in the Springs Dorothy Davis would be the daughter of the man who tried to fool people into thinking he was a legitimate banker. By contrast, at Knox my mother was not only able to learn the etiquette, habits, and skills of the upper class but was also able to pass, so much so that when Lula met up with her daughter after her first term there, she telegraphed Walter, "Dorothy looks natural, but speaks a foreign language."

Lula may not have known Jazz Age slang, but she, too, was interested in refashioning herself as a member of the moneyed class, which the Knox School and its connections made possible. Before long, Lula and Dorothy were no longer staying at the Hotel Pennsylvania, choosing instead the more luxurious Savoy and the new Waldorf Astoria. And when Lula and Dorothy made their first trip to Europe, they didn't travel like most Americans. They paid for Dorothy's French teacher, an accomplished woman and White Russian émigré, to serve as their tour guide. They traveled first class, stayed in four-star hotels, and returned home with pricey clothes made by a Parisian dressmaker. Stateside, the Davis family chose models and brands that would most effectively signal their elevated class position. In the twenties, American mass culture threw up "virtually infinite distinctions" among commodities, which permitted Americans to situate (and differentiate) themselves from others on the class ladder. In his bestselling 1922 novel, *Babbitt*, Sinclair Lewis suggested that it was a family's automobile that provided the definitive measure of its social rank.[65]

What happened in this period, classwise, within families remains largely unexplored. What was the emotional fallout as some family members pulled ahead and others were left behind, as some drove Packards and others made do with Model T's? The Davis family was certainly no stranger to such class cleavages. For my mother, the distance separating her from her uncle Willard, someone with whom she had played as a youngster but who now pumped gas at the local Conoco station, congealed into nothing less than a class difference. After a family dinner celebrating her twentieth birthday, my mother had this to say about her uncle: "Of course Willard had to intrude—greedy, sat and waited—enormous appetite." His coarseness annoyed her, all the more because he was her kin and all of Colorado Springs knew it.

Walter and Lula's marital arrangement—his philandering and her refusal to play the good wife—was something of a class marker

Making It. (Author's archive)

as well, more typical of wealthy cosmopolitans than Rotary Club members and their wives. Taking a mistress may have originally been about disproving his averageness, but Walter's inability to end the affair may suggest he was genuinely in love with both Lula and Eva. However, it's worth considering some pragmatic reasons for his prevarication. Throughout this period there existed what were known as "heart balm" laws, whereby a woman could sue for breach of promise a man who had reneged on his promise to marry her.[66] Perhaps Eva threatened him with such a suit, although she likely would not have succeeded given that she knew Walter was married. It's also possible that Eva, who rose from the association's stenographer to become its secretary-treasurer, threatened to expose his dodgy business practices. As for Lula, their home was in her name, and had she filed for divorce she would have sought substantial alimony. Divorce would have opened up Walter's bank accounts and financial records to scrutiny. He may have figured that anything short of chronic equivocation would have revealed the state of his finances. Unwilling or unable to commit to one

Willard, the youngest of Walter's brothers, worked for years as a gas station attendant, and then turned to raising poultry in his backyard. Eventually he got a job as a conductor for the Pikes Peak Cog Railway. When my family visited Colorado Springs in the mid-fifties we visited Willard and his wife, who lived in a rickety house on West Colorado. (Author's archive)

woman, Walter saw only one remedy for his emotional shortfalls: spending his way into their hearts.

Lula and Eva may have understood this. Lula's hard-nosed strategy of absenting herself always brought Walter around, at least for a while. And Eva's willingness to play hardball worked as well. In the summer of 1928, after Walter decided impulsively to meet up with his family in Europe, Eva sent him a telegram while he was on an ocean liner. He had charged her with sending him telegrams

Left: This photograph of Dorothy was likely taken in 1927, after a year spent at boarding school. (Author's archive). *Right:* A flapper-like Dorothy, post-boarding school. (Author's archive)

about each day's deposits and withdrawals at the City, and one day she sent him this terse wire: "Forty Seven and Twenty Eight. Leaving Fifteenth Job. Terry." When he returned her desk was indeed empty.

For a while during this Eva-less period Walter showered Lula with gifts, including a Model 640 Packard Deluxe Coupe. But then Walter insinuated himself into Eva's life again. Eva had moved to Denver, where she was working as a stenographer. He discovered she was living in the Washington Arms Apartments, just a short walk from the Brown Palace, where he now kept an apartment year round. Walter insisted she quit her job. To dissuade her from being a working girl in anybody else's office he began depositing $350 each month into her bank account. Maybe this was when he went on a spending spree, buying Eva an automobile as well as furniture, a baby grand piano, and Oriental rugs—perhaps the cousins of our very own rugs—with which to outfit her apartment. In May 1929, three weeks before he and Lula would head east for their daughter's graduation, he composed a brief note to Eva in advance of what he promised would be a proper letter. "It isn't too good to be true," he wrote. *"It is true. I am going through with it."* With Lula and Dorothy in Europe that summer he could have run off with Eva. Instead, he presented Eva with a $1,300 diamond ring. True to form, Walter was soon sending Lula ingratiating telegrams, on this occasion to see

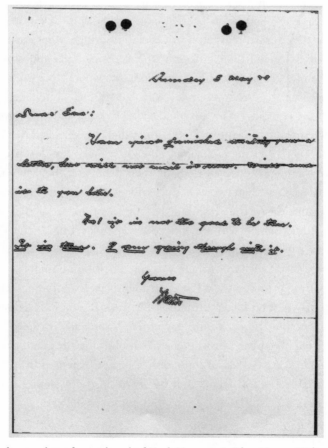

According to a letter from police chief Hugh Harper to J. Edgar Hoover, Walter never sent this letter to Eva. (Photostat copy, Bureau of Investigation File 62-27247; author's archive)

if she wanted him to get the wheels on her new Packard nickeled. Once again he met up with his family in Europe. When the Davises returned home that October Lula's Packard had been nickeled and there was a brand-new Cadillac sitting in front of their house.

Ten days after the Davises returned to the Colorado Springs, Black Tuesday, the most devastating of the late October stock market crashes, happened. In those parts of the West that became the Dust Bowl—the Springs was just outside it—the downturn in the economy happened before Wall Street cratered. Still, the October 1929 stock market crash registered in Colorado Springs, where agonized investors badgered their brokers with telephone calls and crowded into their brokerage offices.[67] Throughout the nation, stock exchanges the day after the crash were filled with "perspiring, white-faced people." Just as quickly, many people decided the market crash signaled only a temporary downturn. The Springs dailies even joked that local investors got a kick out of bragging about how much they lost because it gave them an excuse for dodging their debts and their charitable obligations. Less than two weeks after Black Tuesday the big news in the Springs wasn't the crash but the imminent arrival of Alexander Film Studio, which had announced it was relocating to the Pikes Peak area, where it anticipated having an annual payroll of $60,000.[68]

Inside the Davis family there was some belt-tightening, but Walter continued to deposit $350 each month in Eva's bank account and to pay rent on his apartment at Denver's Brown Palace hotel.

Even before the economic downturn, Walter had to have been concerned about the outsized costs of mollifying the three women in his life. A partial list of some of his biggest expenses from 1926 through 1929 reveals that what he spent on them alone came to more than $33,000, that is, $463,170 in today's dollars:

3 years at Knox School: $8,100 ($113,687)
2 European trips, 1928: $6,000 ($84,213)

2 European trips, 1929: $5,000 ($70,177)

1929 Packard coupe (after trade-in and with nickeled wheels):
    $2,826 (nearly $40,000)

1930 Cadillac: $3,000 ($42,115)

Outfitting Eva, 1929: $4,000 ($56,456)

Eva's maintenance for one year: $4,200 ($56,142)

One hedge against the precariousness that these expenditures introduced into his life was life insurance. Beginning in the 1910s Walter had started to buy premium policies that offered "universal" coverage, that is, they paid out no matter the circumstances of death. The earliest records I have go back to 1918. Over the course of the next three years he took out a $5,000 policy each year, which seems prudent. However, from the mid-twenties onward he seemingly could not buy enough insurance. By 1930, he had accumulated more than a half million dollars' worth of life insurance, with an annual premium cost of about $6,000. That year the *Denver Post* carried an article entitled "Rich Coloradans Carrying Millions in Life Insurance." In a state that could claim many a millionaire, including Spencer Penrose, Bert Carlton, and Oliver Shoup, the *Post* reported that Walter Davis was tied for second place on the list of the most-insured men in Colorado. He shared that spot with another North End resident of the Springs, a Texas-born oil man whose family enjoyed the services of two maids, one servant, and a nurse. Charles Tutt II came in two positions below them, at number four.

For Lula and Dorothy the *Post* story must have felt vindicating, as if it proved that it was only the stuffiness of Springs society that kept them from being part of the town's fashionable set. Would Lula have kept this clipping folded neatly inside one of her diaries had she not been proud of her husband? For at least some of the area's working people, his heaps of life insurance likely seemed further proof of Walter Davis's financial acumen and solidity. After all, he was a self-made man who had become enviably rich. Yet surely there were other people—members of the town's elite—who were brought up short by this news item. Why was it, they must have wondered, that the head of a local building and loan association, even one with 3,600 depositors, was carrying more than a half million dollars' worth of life insurance?[69] But if the story did give them pause, it was likely short-lived because, after all, Walter Davis was not their banker.

Part Two

4

Slipping Through Your Fingers

By the time the local building and loan business began to implode in December 1931 the country had been in a depression for over two years. Its effects were everywhere as banks failed, factories turned idle, shops were shuttered, houses were abandoned, and more and more shantytowns began to dot the landscape. Individual experience varied enormously, as some people got by with careful budgeting while others got by through eating every other day, wearing clothes that turned to rags and shoes with makeshift cardboard soles. Some people, of course, did not get by at all. Despite real differences in circumstances between working people and professionals, few people were entirely immune to worry, especially as they came to realize that the economy was broken, frozen.

In September 1931, U.S. Steel announced a wage cut of 10 percent, and not long thereafter General Motors, Bethlehem Steel, and U.S. Rubber followed suit. Henry Ford had already fired 75 percent of his company's workforce, but he, too, slashed wages. By 1932 American factories were producing less than they had in 1913. Automobile production was only a quarter of what it had been before the Depression. Steel factories were operating at 11 percent of their capacity. By the end of 1931 nearly 2,300 banks had shut their doors.

Herbert Hoover, who had been elected president in 1928 with widespread support, had a stellar record in humanitarian relief in Belgium and France during World War I. But now that he was president and there was talk of starving Americans, he turned belligerently defensive, denying that any Americans were going hungry. As for all those men selling apples on the corners of American cities, it didn't mean that the economy was tanking. They were there, he said, because selling apples proved to be more profitable than their previous jobs. Hoover believed in voluntarism, not government solutions. Rather than devising ways to fix the system, he took to applauding the superiority of free enterprise over communism. Meanwhile, as Hoover celebrated the American way, the United States was shedding jobs, so much so that when the Soviet Union, the one country not in depression, advertised six thousand job openings, one hundred thousand Americans applied.[1]

Even formerly well-heeled professional men—doctors, dentists, and lawyers—found they had to tap their depleted savings to pay for necessities. As professionals, they discovered that when it was a choice, say, between groceries or a trip to the doctor most people felt there was really no choice. Take the case of the doctor in Youngstown, Ohio, whose income one week was a one-dollar bill. A friend of his, a lawyer and an astute chronicler of the Depression, recalled watching him carefully smooth the bill out on his desk. And there was the lawyer's dentist, who begged the lawyer to keep sending his family in for visits, even if he could not immediately pay for them. As for salesclerks, it was not unusual for them to learn that their pay would be solely based upon sales commissions.[2]

As elsewhere, merchants in the Springs, scrambling to pay rent, slashed prices on their merchandise. With property values in El Paso County plunging, those who worked in the building trades and in real estate found themselves sidelined, with many workless days. Even in Colorado Springs the inventory of vacant houses increased, and many were in such a state of disrepair that real estate agents despaired of ever being able to move them.[3] The collapse of the real estate market was a national problem, and it was especially tough on building and loan associations, whose assets were meant to be primarily in real estate. When it came to police and schoolteachers, they counted themselves lucky if the worst that happened to them was a reduction in pay; but some were laid off and joined the already swollen ranks of the unemployed. A local Springs group calling itself the Organization of the Unemployed sought to relieve joblessness with its "Give a Job" campaign. You might imagine that in a town such as Colorado Springs, with so many wealthy families, this campaign might have had an impact. However, in January 1931 the group's secretary reported that wealthy families had rarely made use of their registry of 821 unemployed men. Middle-income and even poor families were the ones, he claimed, who hired their men.[4]

America's agricultural sector had been in a slump since the end of the war. If the twenties had been boom years for some Americans, for plenty of farmers they had been lean years. Toward the end of the twenties, Colorado's growers, who raised everything from sugar beets and cantaloupes to cauliflower and beans, rebounded. But the recovery was short-lived and soon the combination of drought and the global collapse in the price of agricultural goods made for desperate times. In the more rural parts of El Paso County, only a hundred miles from the dust bowl, officials noted evidence of both starvation and what they termed "comparative nakedness."[5]

In the wake of the Wall Street crash of October 1929 people who had invested heavily in the stock market discovered that their net worth was a fraction of its former value. If residents of Colorado Springs needed a lesson in this, they got it on Christmas Day 1931 with the news that the estate of Bert Carlton, once valued at several million dollars, was now worth only $991,069. The onetime "King of Cripple Creek" had been a heavy investor in the stock market, and by late 1931 fifty separate stocks in his portfolio had absolutely no value and many others were close to worthless. Carlton's case was not unusual, as the ranks of the wealthy plummeted. Colorado, the home of 181 millionaires in 1929, could boast only 29 by 1932.[6]

By 1931 faith that recovery was just around the corner had worn thin. And yet if you lived in those parts of the country that, like the Springs, leaned Republican, you had grown accustomed to journalistic appraisals of the economy that parroted the view of President Hoover, which was that the worst had already passed. Newspaper columnist Heywood Broun captured the cynicism felt by some when he said that the GOP "seems to want to solve unemployment by keeping it a secret."[7] The ongoing depression forced even Hoover to make an about-face of sorts. By December 1931, faced with an economy that was inert, enervated, and unresponsive, he dropped the cheery predictions of recovery and began pushing for an expanded role for the federal government in fighting the Depression.

Hoover waited far too long and his Democratic opponent in the 1932 race, Franklin Delano Roosevelt, won in a landslide. During the waning days of the campaign the once-popular Hoover looked so broken, his face so ashen, that he resembled a "walking corpse."[8] In contrast to Hoover's voluntarist interventions, Roosevelt advanced collectivist, big-government solutions to the Depression. FDR's New Deal created America's welfare state by vastly expanding both the power and the reach of the federal government. Critics have characterized the New Deal as "improvisational, inconsistent, almost half-hearted." True enough, but it did help many Americans who were in need of relief, facing foreclosure, and looking to more equitable relations between labor and capital at the workplace. And Social Security, once it finally took effect, proved enormously significant.[9] That said, in the end the New Deal was more successful at generating a right-wing backlash than in pulling the country out of the Depression. It would take World War II to decisively change

America's fortunes. What that meant, as we shall see, is that suffering continued for many Americans during the entire decade.

As the economy worsened, every week seemed to bring fresh news of a financial scandal. In the fall of 1931 lawyer and diarist Benjamin Roth noted that his local paper wrote of bank closings in Philadelphia, Detroit, and Pittsburgh. He knew that these closings, many of which he blamed on outright fraud, would have a knock-on effect on surrounding communities. "The whole banking fraternity is in public disfavor," he wrote, "and many face prison." In his history of the Great Depression, economist John Kenneth Galbraith claimed that the most spectacular scandal of all was the much-publicized looting of the Union Industrial Bank of Flint, Michigan. The men behind that swindle—twelve in all—were found guilty of embezzling $3.5 million and drew prison sentences totaling 240 years. They were, predictably, pillars of their community—Sunday school teachers, family men, and Boy Scout supporters. Each one of the bankers had been embezzling individually when adversity—losses on the stock market—led them to band together. From that point on, they engaged in carefully coordinated looting. They not only kept the bank's books in perfect order but for months had lookouts standing by at Flint hotels to warn them whenever a bank examiner arrived in town.[10]

However, the embezzlement of the Union Industrial, big and complicated though it was, turns out to have not been the biggest embezzlement in the country. That honor belongs to one of the largest building and loan associations in California, which crashed just days after news of the Union Industrial scheme hit the papers. With 24,000 depositors, some of them big-draw movie stars, the Hollywood Guaranty Building and Loan Association seemed too big to fail. And it would have been had it not been for its president, Gilbert H. Beesemyer. The forty-five-year-old businessman was a fraternal society leader, a layman in the Presbyterian Church, and a big-time Hollywood booster. Investigators discovered a jaw-dropping shortfall of $8 million after noticing discrepancies in the accounts of the Bank of Hollywood, another Beesemyer institution. After initially claiming his innocence, the Hollywood native came clean. During Christmas week he admitted there was "a lot more wrong with the books than you imagine." He didn't stop there, stunning friends and colleagues in a crowded courtroom by confessing that he was "a dirty crook." Southern California real estate had been the start of Beesemyer's undoing. He had tried to lure a department store to Hollywood in order to increase property values and attract other businesses to Hollywood Boulevard—a quixotic project, one that continues to animate developers to this day. When that failed, he devised a system of "honoring his own overdrafts with depositors' money," as the *New York Times* put it. His next move—investing in oil wells—proved much more disastrous.[11]

Other thrifts would be thrown into receivership as California's once booming real estate market sagged. Perhaps it was the overheated quality of real estate there, but California boasted behemoth associations, quite a few of which, including Pacific States, would sustain losses during the Depression. The *Los Angeles Times* was reticent in its coverage of building and loan impairments, receiverships, and liquidations. Still, the crisis in California was serious enough that the state's much-disliked B&L commissioner became the object of bomb threats and was forced to temporarily vacate the family home.[12] By August 1933, the state of California had moved its overburdened building and loan department to a larger building to accommodate the seventy-two staffers hard at work on liquidating eleven associations.[13]

There were problem B&Ls throughout the country, including in Pittsburgh, where in June 1932 two building and loan men were sentenced to long prison terms for having embezzled $96,000 from the city's Modern Building and Loan Company. A month later in Philadelphia forty building and loan and bank officials were charged with embezzlement, fraudulent conversion, and misappropriation of more than $1 million from four separate associations. Plenty of small-fry operators also stood accused of malfeasance as well. The secretary of a Newark, New Jersey, B&L killed himself in November 1929 shortly after being accused of embezzlement.[14]

Closer to home, Coloradans learned in early December 1931 that the president of a building and loan association in Golden, Colorado, had tendered his resignation. Over the years, John Vivian, a prominent Republican Party operative, held many political appointments in the state. That fall he was fired from one of them—the post of regional administrator for Prohibition—when investigators uncovered numerous irregularities in his administration. Now, as the head of the Golden association, he stood accused of mishandling two estates, one of which was his very own aunt's.[15] And just before the New Year the *Denver Post* carried an article about a banker in eastern Colorado whose $86,000 embezzlement earned him a sentence of eight to fifteen years in the state penitentiary. However, none of these stories prepared the residents of Colorado Springs for the saga that began to unfold there in the closing days of 1931.

Three nights after Christmas, on December 28, 1931, O.S. Sutherland was making his rounds on Pikes Peak Avenue, right by the Mining Exchange in downtown Colorado Springs. Sutherland worked as a night watchman for a business that provided local shop owners with what were called merchant police. His boss had only recently bought this route, and Sutherland had been working it for just a few months. Still, he knew whom he could count on seeing, and Willis Sims was not among them. However, that night the president of the State Savings Bank was at his desk. At about 1:30 a.m. Sutherland stopped by his office and chatted with him. An hour later the night watchman returned. The State Bank building, as it was known, contained several businesses besides the bank, including Sims's Assurance Savings & Loan Association and the State Realty Company, all of which were loosely connected through their directors. As he entered the building Sutherland noticed someone sitting on a bench that was located about halfway down the long corridor. He was slumped over. As the watchman approached, he realized it was Sims. With a .22 caliber revolver in his hand and a bullet in his head, Sims was unconscious, with only a faint pulse perceptible. Efforts to revive him proved futile.

The local dailies treated Willis Sims's suicide as the most baffling of mysteries. In this respect, they appeared to be taking their cue from the tight-lipped way that New York papers just weeks earlier had handled the suicide of the prominent banker and Democratic Party operative J.J. Riordan.[16] According to the "Daily Twins," everyone who knew Willis Sims was at a loss to explain what might have led him to end his life. Bank customers reported that he had seemed especially jolly that day. And Sims's widow reported that he had seemed in good spirits that evening. After supper with her and their two teenage sons, he had retired to the living room where he read a magazine leisurely for an hour or two. At about nine he had asked her to drive him to the bank. He told her he had paperwork to tackle in preparation for the New Year. Whatever he did over the next five hours did not include penning a suicide note.

According to the *Gazette* and the *Evening Telegraph*, Sims's suicide left his friends and business associates feeling as blindsided and dismayed as his widow. Sims had been a tireless booster of the country, the town, his businesses, and the building and loan industry. Just four years earlier at a meeting of the state's thrift trade group he had declared that a building and loan association, if properly managed, was failproof.[17] Reporters and editors at the local dailies furnished readers with nothing by way of a motive, but they were confident that Sims's suicide was unrelated to his business affairs. They made much of the fact that on the very day of Sims's death Colorado's state banking commissioner, Grant McFerson, declared that he had examined the bank's books and

WILLIS V. SIMS,
Banker and leader of civic affairs
at Colorado Springs, Colo., who
died early Tuesday a short time
after he was found shot in the
head in a room of the State Savings bank, of which he was president.

SPRINGS BANK HEAD ENDS HIS LIFE WITH GUN

Night Watchman Finds Former State Legislator in Rear Room of Bank, Revolver in Hand; Left Home After Midnight.

Willis Sims, B&L Man. Springs' District Attorney Clyde Starrett said of the state's B&L commissioner Eli Gross, "When Willis Sims fired the shot that ended his life, a man exercising due caution would have walked into every building and loan office in Colorado Springs and ascertained just what cash and bonds it had." (*Gazette*) had discovered no shortages. As for the Assurance Saving and Loan association, readers were advised that the affairs of that concern were not believed to be in any way involved in Sims's suicide. When it came to banking failures in their own backyards, local newspapers tended to be sanguine. When Missouri-based Farm and Home, a $50 million institution and the nation's third-largest building and loan, applied for receivership in June 1932, the local press reported that the organization's board of directors promised that it was a "friendly receivership" in which depositors "would not lose a dollar." [18]

In Colorado Springs some residents doubted whether Sims's suicide could be completely unrelated to his business. The *Denver Post*, which had its share of subscribers in nearby El Paso County, noted in its coverage that Sims's friends believed that his personal finances were a factor in his decision to take his life. A little more than a month after Sims's death, the state building and loan commissioner, Eli Gross, revealed that he had read the report on the Assurance but had decided against commenting on it. "I do not believe the situation would be helped," he told the press, "by an announcement at this time." Gross's non-explanation, which the *Gazette* buried on page ten of the paper, proved what all the skeptics had feared—that the institution was seriously in the red. [19] Three weeks later, at a meeting of association stockholders, it was announced that the Assurance was insolvent, with liabilities of $179,000. It took the local press another week to make the association's insolvency public. The directors of Sims's savings and loan were able to reorganize and liquidate the business rather than have the courts mandate that it go into receivership. [20]

It took six months before the town's newspapers revealed that the original pronouncement about the State Savings Bank was too sanguine. In mid-June 1932 it was disclosed that Sims had caused the bank a loss of $23,158, and that the former credit watchdog had died with his own personal account withdrawn by $34. This was the one truly unflattering article about Sims to appear in the local dallies, but it was damaging. It was also reported that Colorado's banking commissioner had slapped a $15,000 lawsuit against Sims's estate and the bond company insuring his bank. The local representative of the bond company was court reporter Merton Stubbs, who was also on the board of directors of the Assurance, in which he was heavily invested. Depositors of the State Savings Bank would receive their final dividend payment seven years later, at the beginning of 1939. They were paid a total of 87 percent of their claims. As for the depositors in the Assurance, a little more than a year after Sims's suicide they learned that the shortfall there totaled nearly $180,000 and that they would receive only 20 percent of the money they had on deposit there. As late as September 1936 depositors had yet to receive a penny.[21]

In the months that followed Sims's suicide the local papers dutifully covered the latest developments as they affected his depositors. However, the story of how Sims had gotten himself in such a fix was not one that any Colorado newspaper pursued. When depositors of the Assurance got the bad news about their money, the association's sorry condition was tied to heavy losses in assets, a sharp depreciation in its remaining assets, and what were discreetly called unexpected liabilities.

As with the Hollywood embezzler Gilbert Beesemyer, Willis Sims's troubles began with real estate. His biggest problem was the Lennon Park development, which never took off. Sims embezzled and he took out loans. Unable to pay back anything but a fraction of this money, he proceeded to take out more loans. In the months before his suicide he was frantically moving money between his bank and his building and loan association. Banking commissioner McFerson later claimed that in 1931 Sims took $6,000 that a retired schoolteacher had deposited at his bank and applied it to his own personal account. I cannot prove that the $6,000 loss forced the woman to come out of retirement to take a job as a librarian, but it seems plausible. He allegedly tampered with the funds of other depositors, including those of his mother. According to court records, Sims also audaciously removed $100 from the account of his own brother's brokerage firm in order to make good on the $100 that his brother had loaned him. As late as December 28, 1931— the day before his suicide—Sims was juggling money, "borrowing" $543 of State Savings funds in order to pay his building and loan customers the money that would be owed them on their certificates of deposit come the New Year.

One imagines that Sims believed that his auto lodge would eventually prove profitable and that he would be able to begin paying back his debts. But 1931 was hardly a banner year for tourism, even in the Springs. What these court records reveal is that by December Sims had to know that all his artful juggling was for naught and that within months he and his family would be out of their home.[22]

While the collapse of the local tourist industry in 1930 and tumbling real estate values contributed to Sims's money woes, there's no getting around the fact that his bad personal investments were made using other people's money. And yet aside from that one mid-June article, the press gave Sims a pass. His character went unquestioned, even as the lawsuits revealed his ethical shortcomings. His connections to the Republican establishment, his position as an esteemed Master Mason, and his patriotic activities help to explain the press's reluctance to probe his character. Also working in his favor was that he had not personally benefited in any obvious way from his embezzlement. At the time of his death, his sole material possessions were reportedly a $40 radio and a three-and-a-half-year-old Chrysler Model 65 with more than forty thousand miles on its odometer. After making the needed repairs and outfitting it with new tires, the automobile dealership estimated that it could pay his widow $75 for it. Anna Belle Sims resorted to petitioning the court for a widow's allowance. Over a year later, and after waiting a year for some payment, she asked the court if she might be permitted to keep the Chrysler in lieu of the allowance.

The modesty of Sims's estate and the unwillingness of the press to pillory him kept his family from being shunned. Three months after Sims's suicide, the *Evening Telegraph*, perhaps in an effort to ensure that the Sims family did not feel like social outcasts, published a brief mention of a party that one of the Sims boys had attended. But people must have gossiped, perhaps particularly about why it was that Willis and Robert Sims had dissolved their partnership in 1924. Did people whisper about what Robert might have known about his brother Willis's finances? Available records suggest that Robert Sims emerged from his brother's tragedy with his own reputation intact. His brokerage firm was successful enough that even through the worst years of the Depression the family was able to continue living in their $13,000 Broadmoor home. The family remained part of the congregation at Grace Church, whose minister trusted Robert enough to have him serve as its treasurer. His wife, Margaret, continued to play golf at the Broadmoor with other members of the town's "social contingent" such as Mrs. Miriam Shoup and Mrs. Francis Drexel Smith.[23]

Robert was a successful businessman who enjoyed the trust of his community. Yet in February 1940, a shocking turn of events revealed that all was not well in his life. One Friday afternoon Robert arranged for his wife to meet him at work. However, as Margaret waited patiently for him downtown, Robert made his way back to Broadmoor. After leaving a note for her in their home, he headed out for a hike. It was a mild day and he walked some distance until he reached a wooded area. Quite possibly he knew these woods from the days before the Broadmoor was developed. He stopped there directly behind the house owned by longtime Springs lawyer P.M. Kistler. Perhaps he took in the beauty of the place, but sometime that afternoon he also removed a gun from his pocket, put it to his head, and pulled the trigger.

BUFFALO LODGE, MANITOU BLVD. AT 37TH STREET, COLORADO SPRINGS, COLO.

THE MOST UP-TO-DATE COTTAGE CITY IN COLORADO

Willis Sims's ill-fated Buffalo Lodge, which featured a handsome central lodge of four thousand square feet, was an expensive undertaking. It has recently been made over into a bicycle-themed hotel. (Courtesy the Postcard Collection, the Pikes Peak Library District, 208-9295)

Robert Sims's body was found Saturday morning by one of the Boy Scouts who had been dispatched to search for the missing broker. The local press emphasized that the fifty-six-year-old was ill, and he may have been.[24] Then again, this could have been a case of journalistic spin. Whether his decision to end his life was in some way related to his brother's suicide cannot be known. Not long after his brother's death in 1931, the liquidating committee for the Assurance had sold the lodge to a local man, who further developed it. About the same time, the State Savings Bank Building was also sold and converted into a movie theater. In the intervening period the Buffalo Lodge must have begun to do a pretty fair business, because in late November 1939, nearly a decade after Willis Sims's suicide, the operators of a Denver hotel bought it for $99,000.[25]

What did Robert Sims feel when he learned that the business whose insolvency had so figured in his brother's suicide was now worth almost $100,000? Did the article, which appeared ten weeks before he ended his life, start him brooding about his brother? Did the lodge's stunning sale price vindicate Willis's conviction that the lodge would, in the longer term, prove to be a winning proposition? And had Willis felt that his younger, wealthier brother should have loaned him more money to help him keep his businesses afloat? The evidence here is slender but telling. Willis's decision to defraud his brother's company in order to give the appearance of repaying him suggests more than desperation. After all, why hadn't he defrauded someone else? Stealing from his brother and not really repaying him, which he had to have known Robert would discover, may signal that Willis felt his brother should have done more for him. And did all of this come back to haunt Robert Sims ten years later?

When Willis Sims killed himself in December 1931 he set in motion a process that no one could stop. To many people in the Springs, Sims's suicide told them all they thought they needed to know about the condition of the region's B&L industry. Association members' fears were confirmed when they waited in long lines outside their B&L and discovered that no amount of haggling or pleading or threatening would produce their money. Time and again, depositors were sent away empty-handed, no matter how desperate their circumstances. Evidence suggests that the City Savings Building and Loan did its best to honor some depositors' requests through the spring by allowing partial withdrawals.[26] My grandfather's willingness to bend the rules probably wasn't George Bailey–like generosity on his part. Rather, I imagine he figured that outright refusal, while an association's legal right, would only provoke a bigger panic.

B&Ls were attacked for refusing depositors' withdrawal requests, but again, the bottom line was that they were within their right to deny on-demand withdrawals. Associations required either thirty or sixty days' notice for all withdrawals, and they could deny any request that would result in the association paying out more than one-half (and in some cases more than one-third) of its stock in any one month. These stipulations—along with others about the fees and penalties associated with withdrawals—were in the by-laws of every association. But when they faced a tsunami of withdrawal requests from their members, many of whom could not pay back their own loans, my grandfather and his staff were eventually forced to say no, just as the town's remaining B&L operators, Ed Sharer and Fred Bentall, were doing. To members who had believed their associations' advertising and directors' smooth talk and assumed that money was available on demand, the enforcement of these basic B&L rules proved that the entire industry was a racket.

Fueling customers' aggrieved feelings was a small-circulation newspaper called *Common Sense Weekly*. The *Denver Post* covered the B&L scandals in the Springs and Pueblo, but in the months following Willis Sims's death, this small westside weekly was the one local paper that did not ignore the people crowding anxiously into the town's building and loan associations as they tried to pull their money. Newspaper readers in much of the country were more apt to find boosterish articles about the B&L industry, planted by the industry trade group, rather than honest accounts of failing and frozen B&Ls.[27] *Common Sense* was published by the husband-and-wife-team of J. Herbert Pratt and Clara Pratt, recent arrivals to the Springs. Herbert Pratt presented himself as a pragmatist committed to what he called "hard-headed business, men of good judgment, foresight and common sense."[28] He tried to use the paper to launch his career as a tax-slashing politician. One of the few businesses in the Springs where unions enjoyed any semblance of power was the print trade, and almost immediately the Pratts, who ran their own print shop, butted heads with the local Allied Printing Trade Council. The Pratts railed against labor unions in the pages of their paper, and they helped to pioneer one particular line of attack that in the future would prove very effective on the national stage. They accused union officials of being "racketeers," linking them in the process with headline-grabbing mobsters. Several years later this argument eventually eroded public support for the New Deal, which in many ways was supportive of labor unions.[29] The Pratts' coverage of the B&L scandal was sensationalistic, which won the paper many readers, but it ratcheted up the panic and the anger.[30]

Ed Sharer got the lion's share of negative publicity as the scandal unfolded that spring. Readers of the local dailies learned something of Sharer's legal troubles as early as March 1932, when hoisting engineer Joseph Borah sued him and Sharer's Texas business partner on grounds of fraud and unlawful deceit. Borah, who had several thousand dollars in Sharer's association, claimed that the B&L head had induced him to purchase an oil lease in Texas with $1,000 of this money, and later lured him into making a $2,000 loan to his Texas partner. Borah, asking for exemplary damages, sued for $8,000. On April 11, 1932, a month after a jury found the B&L head guilty of willful deceit, Sharer's request for a new trial was denied. The judge in the case told Sharer he had five days to come up with the $3,000 bond or arrange a further stay of execution. On April 15, the day before he was meant to post bond, Ed Sharer, with his wife, Myrtle, by his side, fled Colorado for a town just across the state's southern border—Raton, New Mexico. Sharer reportedly skipped town on borrowed funds and left behind a slew of bad checks and several lawsuits in the making.

Sharer did not have the $3,000, but that wasn't the only reason he opted to make himself scarce. He knew the Dollar Building and Loan Association was insolvent. From Raton, Sharer mailed his letter of resignation as president of the association to the state building and loan commissioner, Eli Gross. It was not until May 8, three weeks after Ed and Myrtle Sharer had left the Springs, that the local dailies reported on the association's insolvency. Whereas the *Gazette's* article, entitled "Plan Liquidation Loan Association," was discreetly tucked away inside the newspaper, the *Denver Post* went into great and alarming detail about the looming financial scandal, which it said "threatens to shake Colorado Springs to the core." The *Post*, which ran the story (and an accompanying picture of Sharer) on its front page, noted that the accountant examining the association's books estimated that the Dollar's shortfall would likely come to $140,000. Even determining that wasn't easy, the *Post* revealed, because proper credits and debits had not been entered into the company's books. Furthermore, it looked as if the Dollar had no legal officers or directors. Neither its president, Ed Sharer, Ruth Smith, its secretary, or its board members, Smith and Mr. and Mrs. Sharer, seemed to own any association stock, which most people assumed (wrongly, it turned out) was a requirement for all directors.[31]

The state B&L commissioner could not yet determine if criminal liability was involved in the Dollar's collapse, but he traced its current problems back to 1927, when the association had suffered that $32,000 shortfall and $40,000 impairment of its assets. Local authorities were divided on the question of Sharer's guilt. However, he certainly aroused suspicion by traveling with his wife from Raton to Los Angeles rather than returning to the Springs and helping the auditor sort out the association's books. On May 9, Colorado attorney general Clarence Ireland announced his intention to move forward. "Sharer might be able to tell us who owns the association stock," he said, "but we don't know where he is. So apparently there's nothing left to do but apply for a receiver." Depositors—or some of them—preferred to see the company liquidated rather than put into receivership. However, two weeks later the press reported that such a move required the cooperation of the Sharers, who initially had refused it. All this time, Sharer was on the lam somewhere in Los Angeles. According to the El Paso

County sheriff whose task it was to find him, the fugitive banker went to considerable lengths to thwart efforts to locate him.

While Sharer was at large several lawsuits against him went forward.[32] On June 1 a coal mining engineer, John A. Shields, appeared in court as the plaintiff in a $2,500 lawsuit against the former B&L president. In 1924 Shields had loaned $3,000 to the Dollar association. He had received in writing the assurance that what he had negotiated with the association was a 7 percent certificate, and that repayment (with interest) was his with thirty days' advance notice. Shields signed that agreement, but he told the court that Sharer had verbally assured him that he could get his money any time he needed it, that the usual requirement was the giving of thirty or sixty days' notice but that the association did not go by that. Sharer emphasized that he would give Shields 7 percent and would make the loan payable on demand. Shields had received regular interest payments and had succeeded in withdrawing $500 as recently as November 1931. Yet on December 5, 1931, when Shields served notice that he intended to withdraw the remaining $2,500 due him, the association refused him on the grounds that he was actually a stockholder. Shields maintained that he knew nothing about this thing called "stock." What was a stockholder? he demanded. His lawyers argued that Shields was, in fact, a creditor of the association, and the association his debtor. Sharer later maintained that whatever he told Shields in that conversation, it wasn't legally binding.[33]

Five days later, seventy-three-year-old George Oswald filed suit, claiming that in July 1931 the Sharers (and their employee Mrs. R.M. Smith) had induced him to loan the Dollar $5,000 at 7 percent interest. Oswald, a retired rail conductor, said he had agreed to the loan largely because the Dollar's officers had persuaded him that the association was solvent and secure. But when he went to pull out his money on January 2, 1932, just four days after Sims's suicide, he had been turned away, as had Shields a month earlier, on the same grounds—that he was a stockholder in the association and would have to abide by its rules.

A little more than two months after Oswald won his case, Sharer was slapped with another lawsuit, this one for an alleged 1927 forgery involving local house painter, Fred Forbes, who had been involved with Sharer in a complicated Black Forest land deal.[34] When asked at the September trial if he thought that Sharer had tried to forge his signature, Forbes replied, "He did the best he could, I'll say that." Forbes's response elicited such an outburst of laughter from the spectators in the crowded courtroom that the bailiff had to loudly rap his gavel to establish order. Just as damaging was the testimony of Pueblo auditor George W. Purcell, to whom Sharer had admitted his dishonesty. By the time the forgery cases went to trial in September, Sharer was incarcerated in the county jail, where he had been since the El Paso County sheriff had nabbed him in Los Angeles in late June. In addition to the multiple lawsuits against him, the district attorney charged Sharer with falsifying reports about the condition of the Dollar. Throughout, Sharer maintained his innocence and blamed all of his problems on Walter Davis, whom he claimed controlled the Dollar.[35] Sharer's wife and two daughters must have boarded with friends because in the couple's absence both their house on North Tejon and the furniture inside it had been seized to satisfy the mortgage.

Life for the Sharers changed dramatically during the weeks the couple were gone. Since the couple's departure in April, conditions in the state and in the town had also worsened. The sugar processing company, Great Western Sugar Company, suffered a $1 million deficit in 1932. The Colorado Fuel & Iron Company, which produced 30 percent of the state's coal and 2 percent of all American steel, saw its earnings drop, and it responded by slashing the pay of some of its workers. By 1933 the corporation would declare

FORMER LOAN ASSOCIATION OFFICER HELD

WARRANT IS ISSUED THURSDAY; NABBED IN LOS ANGELES

Sheriff Jackson Leaves Today to Bring Back E. C. Sharer

Charged in a fugitive warrant with falsifying his report of the condition of the Dollar Building and Loan association, E. C. Sharer, who was president of the now defunct organization, is under arrest in Los Angeles and should be back in Colorado Springs Thursday or Friday. He was taken into custody yesterday morning on a warrant issued here secretly last Thursday on application of John M. Meikle, district attorney, and given to Sheriff Robert M. Jackson for service. He is charged in the warrant with making false statements regarding the assets of the association to the extent of $153,259.

Sheriff Jackson said last night he plans to leave this afternoon for California to return Sharer. A requisition for the tradition of the former Colorado Springs business man was issued in Denver yesterday by Gov. W. H. Adams.

Information from California to the effect that Sharer will not oppose his extradition was received last night by Sheriff Jackson and The Gazette and Telegraph. Los Angeles police telegraphed the sheriff that Sharer had signed an extradition waiver and accordingly it is not expected that any difficulties will be encountered in that connection.

Authorities here express the opinion that Sharer's role in the tragedy of the Dollar Building and Loan collapse was to a considerable extent that of henchman to Walter Clyde Davis, missing president and director of the defunct City Saving and Loan association. Investigation of the records of the Dollar Building and Loan association since the organization went into receivership has disclosed, it is said, that the affairs of the association were in a hopeless tangle for some time and that the opinion now is entertained

(Continued on Page Six—Col. One)

MAN KILLS WIFE, SON.

ROOSEV

Nothing to Fear, Sharer Announces

E. C. SHARER
Former president of the Dollar Building and Loan association, who is under arrest in Los Angeles, in connection with irregularities in the affairs of the association, who told newspaper men there yesterday he will waive extradition and return to Colorado Springs at once.

SPONSORS OF BILL ASSAIL PRESIDENT

Little Hope Seen for Relief Legislation in Garner and Wagner Attack

By NATHAN ROBERTSON
Associated Press Staff Writer

WASHINGTON, June 25 (AP) — The possibility of revising the huge $2,300,000,000 unemployment relief bill to meet President Hoover's wishes almost vanished today as its sponsors shot back hot retorts to the chief executive's charge of "pork-barrel" legislation.

The bill was vigorously defended

Ed Sharer, once on the fringes of the Springs capitalist class, stood accused of fraud and forgery. (*Gazette*)

bankruptcy. Farmers in the state who had earned $213 million in 1929 were earning only $82 million three years later.

By mid-1932 Little London could not claim immunity from the Depression even if the Golden Cycle Company boasted that conditions for gold mining had never been better. Even Spencer Penrose's luxury hotel, the Broadmoor, was in trouble. By August 1932 it would be in bankruptcy, although it did reorganize and survive. While high-end traffic to the Broadmoor hotel slowed, the number of transients passing through Colorado Springs tripled from the previous year. Twenty thousand men passed through Colorado Springs during the month of April alone. In the first half of 1932, 10,974 transients sought a "flop" at its municipal shelter. During only one week of April the Salvation Army served 2,780 meals to the destitute.[36] There was an "implied code between the city and the drifters," according to the local papers: "'Colorado Springs will give you a warm and comfortable place to sleep and a solid, wholesome meal, and then you must go your way.'" Transients were housed for the night in a heated building the city had remodeled for drifters. The facility resembled an army barracks and featured two rows of double-deck bunks covered with soft mattresses. Before bed and once again in the morning drifters received a hot meal. The shelter had many names, including Hoboes' Rest, Hotel Del Gink, and Hotel de Harper, after the police chief.[37]

The Great Depression soon altered Colorado Springs in other ways as well. Indeed, the very sounds of the city were changing as the familiar rumble and grind of its little trolley cars, once the pride of the Springs, forever ended on May 1, the day modern buses were introduced. The junking of its streetcar system, which covered forty-one miles and, much like the system in Los Angeles, had taken passengers virtually everywhere, reflected residents' greater reliance on the automobile. It was also a part of the city's belt-tightening regime.

By mid-1932 it seemed to some that even the weather was

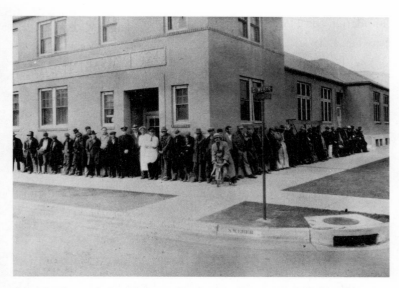

A crowd gathers at the local Salvation Army in 1932. During one week of April that year, the organization served 2,780 meals to the destitute. (Courtesy of the Margaretta M. Boas Photograph Collection, the Pikes Peak Library District, 001-720)

turning strange. On June 10 a tornado appeared east of the city. After jumping over the city's business district, it sheared a path a block wide and a half mile long through the west side of town. For residents of the west side the tornado literalized the pain of the escalating building and loan crisis, which grew scarier and scarier that summer. Middle-class people were hurt by the crisis, and much more than the news coverage ever suggested, but nowhere was the dread of loss more profound than on the west side of town in the former Colorado City.[38]

That fear played itself out in the offices of the town's remaining building and loan associations. Sometime that spring Fred Bentall called the police after an angry depositor entered his Home Building and Loan Association, pulled out a gun, and demanded his money. On June 21 the fifty-one-year-old Bentall disclosed that he would be conferring with Commissioner Gross about voluntarily liquidating the Home. Association members, who numbered only between sixty and seventy, had no reason to be concerned, he said. "Our little association was going along nicely," he said soothingly, and there was "absolutely no reason for any of our depositors to become worried." Worried! Bentall's depositors, like those at the other building and loans, were consumed with fear and anger and worry as the bills piled up and the one source for paying them lay out of reach, perhaps forever.

They grew more despairing after one of the Home's more afflu-ent depositors, a forty-nine-year-old man who ran a plumbing busi-ness, filed an $8,000 suit against Bentall.[39] Within a week Bentall phoned B&L commissioner Eli Gross to request a receivership. Bentall met with reporters and explained that throwing the Home into receivership meant losing everything that he had accumulated over a lifetime of work. He also admitted that the shortage in his association was far larger than he had let on and that it would be almost impossible to liquidate securities now for anything close to their onetime value. The upshot was that his association would be unable to make its July 1 interest payments. Whatever his current circumstances, however, Bentall cheerfully promised to make good on his debts. "I'm going to see to it that none of the depositors who have trusted me loses money," he claimed. "If, when the whole thing is over, they are not repaid in full, I'll give them my personal notes and I'll devote myself to paying them back, no matter how long it takes."

Within days the district attorney took decisive action and ar-rested Bentall on embezzlement charges. Bentall came clean, con-fessing to authorities that he had juggled funds for years, with the result that his association now faced a $65,000 shortfall. He admit-ted that he had used the stolen money to purchase property in the Springs and equity in an Oklahoma property. He also purchased cattle and $2,000 worth of machinery, which were on his ranch. He claimed that the property was worth no more than $12,000,

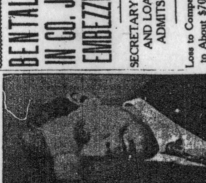

KIDNAPING PLOT AGAINST DOROTHY DAVIS, TO FORCE RETURN OF FATHER, REVEALED

Admits Theft of B. & L. Funds

Police Establish Guard at Home of Missing Head of Defunct City Savings Building and Loan Association; Question Group of Depositors

Persistent rumors of an alleged plot by a group of depositors of the defunct City Savings Building and Loan association to kidnap Miss Dorothy Davis, pretty 23-year-old daughter of Walter C. Davis, former president of the association, and hold her captive in an effort to force Davis' surrender, resulted last night in the establishment of a police guard at the Davis home, 1633 North Tejon street.

Chief Hugh D. Harper of the police department admitted that the kidnaping threats, vaguely rumored for about a week, had crystallized yesterday into definite reports that prompted him to take steps to guard Miss Dorothy Davis and Mrs. Lola Davis, wife of the missing loan man. Last night Officer Hugh Higgins was assigned to the first detail in a 24-hour police guard of the Davis home, which will remain in effect for the time being at least.

The identity of the men comprising the alleged group of conspiratory seeking to kidnap Miss Davis was not revealed by Chief Harper, who, in fact, indicated that the investigation into the reports was not far enough along to result in definite information.

BENTALL HELD IN CO. JAIL FOR EMBEZZLEMENT

SECRETARY BUILDING AND LOAN ASSN. ADMITS GUILT

Loss to Company Will Run to About $70,000; Name Barron Receiver

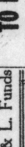

FRED N. BENTALL.
Secretary of the Home Savings, Building and Loan association, who is in the county jail facing embezzlement charges.

Fred N. Bentall, secretary of the Home Savings Building and Loan association, was charged with embezzlement late yesterday afternoon in a justice court warrant following an investigation which Colorado

In the June 30, 1932, issue of the *Gazette*, the B&L scandal dominated the paper with news of Bentall's jailing and a thwarted kidnapping of Dorothy Davis. (*Gazette*)

although the paper noted that it was unclear if that pertained to all the property he had purchased with association funds. From the county jail a contrite Bentall declared, "I'm ready to take my medicine," as Los Angeles B&L man Gilbert Beesemyer had said eighteen months earlier. He also promised to pay back his defrauded depositors.

However, a week later G.W. Barron, the court-appointed receiver of the Home, declared that the association was in far worse shape than Bentall had admitted. "Every day the shortfall increases by between $6,000 and $7,000, and we have no idea when the end will come." Barron was horrified to discover thirty-five accounts totaling $66,198.90 that were nowhere listed on the association's books. And then there was the "appalling condition" of the books. Moreover, the president of the Home had lied about having $1,600 of his own money invested in the association. It turned out he actually owed it between $5,000 and $6,000. Receiver Barron estimated the shortfall would reach $100,000. Bentall took offense at this, and insisted that the receiver must have miscalculated: "It is difficult to understand how that much could slip through your fingers without your receiving something for it." All he really had taken was "a few hundred here and a few thousand there to meet demands for money similarly disposed of," he said. His own life had been simple, he contended. Making off with the association's funds was about "staving off financial disaster," not about "luxurious living."[40]

During the summer of 1932 Ed Sharer and Fred Bentall both occupied space in the county jail, but they were not treated equally there. In contrast to Sharer, who had been part of the town's establishment, Bentall was an outsider whose time in the KKK had not endeared him to the authorities. Was this why the police took mug shots of Bentall, which were then distributed to the press, while Sharer escaped this indignity? That was the view of *Common Sense*, and it seems plausible. The press treated Bentall's mug shot, in which he appeared "haggard and old," as visual evidence of his guilt. Why else would he have aged so if he weren't guilty? The dailies made much of the fact that Bentall swayed side to side in his cell, his heads in his hands, moaning to himself, while Sharer kept a "bold, almost defiant front" in his cell, where he played cards by himself.[41]

Bentall pleaded guilty to embezzlement at his August 25 sentencing. As best as could be determined, he had caused a deficit of $92,000. As he stood before the court, sobbing, he repeatedly clenched and unclenched his fists. Conspicuously absent were his wife and his thirteen-year-old son. Clyde Starrett, a former district court judge and, like Bentall, a Democrat, argued for leniency, but the district attorney, John Meikle, was having none of it. He pointed out that Bentall had used other people's money to buy houses in Colorado Springs, a ranch on the fringes of town, and a 160-acre farm in Oklahoma. And he emphasized that Bentall had embezzled from poor people concerned about their old age and about having enough money to tide them over in times of financial adversity. Meikle also noted that Bentall had actually asked him if he needed to charge him on so many counts, especially after he had cooperated and pled guilty. "It was unintentional even if it may not look that way" were his final words of defense. Judge Cornforth sentenced him to between sixteen and thirty-five years in the state penitentiary. On his way to the state pen he confided in the sheriff that he thought his sentence was fair, but harsher than what he had expected. According to the local press, Bentall's wife was "nearly prostrated" after he was hauled off to prison. A year into her husband's prison sentence fifty-three-year-old Selma Bentall died.[42]

Excess—playboy mayors, channel swimmers, yachting parties, Wall Street brokers and holding companies—went a long way toward defining America in the twenties.[43] Now Americans were faced with something else entirely. With thousands of banks and

B&Ls shuttered, payrolls slashed, and rents, mortgages, and taxes unpaid, you could say the whole country was coming up short. There was a money drought in the United States so severe that by spring 1933 there were 150 barter or script systems operating in thirty states.[44]

"Shortfall" usually refers to a financial deficit, but there were other kinds of deficits during the Depression. There was the weather, which threw the Plains into a drought for nearly a decade. And there was something else just as disorienting as the bizarre weather. It was the deficit of character that was now so manifest. Most Americans before the crash were not so cynical as to believe the world consisted of suckers and racketeers. In Colorado Springs Bentall, Sharer, and Sims had been respected leaders within their own communities. And while Walter Davis had never been a pillar of the community, he was considered financially shrewd. Indeed, when his business crashed, one of Walter's employees admitted to a reporter that the news had flattened him. It was not only that his own money was invested in the City, it was also, he said, just "an awful smash . . . to see a man he trusted in such a position." For depositors these failures reverberated emotionally as they confronted the shortcomings of men they had once trusted. If you are searching for a metaphor for these Depression years, try "shortfall."

5

Sowing Grief

It would be easy enough to mistake Walter Davis for the sort of careless person who turns up so frequently in F. Scott Fitzgerald's writing about the period he dubbed the Jazz Age. Still, even when you factor in his womanizing, he was not cut from the same cloth as Tom and Daisy Buchanan, the couple whose recklessness proves to be the final undoing of Jay Gatsby in Fitzgerald's famous novel. My grandfather certainly knew something about being rich—where to shop, what to drive, and where to stay—but the feeling of immunity that undergirds the carelessness of the Buchanans was not a feeling with which he would have been familiar. Like Gatsby, what Walter knew was the fear of being exposed as a fraud—the cabin boy strutting about in a captain's uniform. Think about the man's meticulousness—his preoccupation with the daily ledger of deposits and withdrawals at his association. Consider the steady flow of flowers and candy to his wife and his daughter—and all those telegrams. He was a man who gambled, but not without doing his best to hedge his bets.

For at least a decade his gambling had not tripped him up. In this he was helped by his considerable shrewdness. Walter carried out his financial dubiousness in a more sophisticated fashion than his competitors. He did not forge people's signatures to big checks or embezzle directly from customers' accounts. Even his critics admitted that he had made some canny, if sharp, moves. First there was his decision to establish a holding company as a wholly owned subsidiary of the City. A holding company allowed him greater leeway in his financial dealings, and in setting up Fleming and Company he was perhaps following what was being done in Los Angeles's building and loan business. Over the years he acquired property through foreclosure, typically when an association borrower defaulted on a loan that had been secured with a trust deed on his or her property. That property would then become part of the assets of Fleming and Company. In Walter's hands, it became a way of siphoning off profitable properties from the City and of keeping bad debts off his associations' books. He named the company after Jim Fleming, whom he also made an officer of the company. Fleming, the man who had been so crushed by his boss's failure, was a carpenter and Walter's handyman, or, as Fleming later put it to the press, his "hired hand."[1]

Through foreclosure, a number of very modest bungalows in the Springs and Pueblo and a few large ranches in El Paso, Kiowa, and Elbert counties, fell into my grandfather's hands. These foreclosures enabled him to broaden his reach beyond working-class neighborhoods and to invest in some of the most valuable property in downtown Colorado Springs. Fleming and Company owned the prized corner of Tejon and Bijou, which Walter had acquired for $30,000; he spent another $26,000 developing it. He expanded into the North End as well. In December 1928 an established real estate firm approached him on behalf of one its clients, a doctor who was interested in pursuing a possible swap with him. Would Walter consider trading a lot he owned on Wood Avenue—Millionaires' Row—for the doctor's residence on North Cascade? By the time of his fall he owned, through his holding company, thirty houses and commercial buildings in the Springs, fifteen houses and an apartment building in Pueblo, and an apartment building and a dozen houses in Denver. It was all made possible by his ruthlessness in capitalizing on other people's tragedies.[2]

In normal times, all that property would have cushioned him against financial downturns of the expectable sort. He could always make good on his association's dividend payments by selling off a few of the valuable properties he had acquired over the years. In certain respects he was, as Eva later observed, a conservative businessman. He had not tried to make a killing on the stock market; he invested in Liberty Bonds and U.S. Treasury bonds instead. He hadn't bet the bank on a motor lodge and a development in an unproven part of town, as Willis Sims had. He hadn't bamboozled people into investing in shady land deals, the way that Ed Sharer had. In contrast to Fred Bentall, he was a fastidious record keeper; money didn't just slip through his fingers.

But if Walter's business practices were less reckless than those of his local competitors, his living-large lifestyle set him apart from them. Then Pueblo's Railway Savings B&L, the largest association in the state, began advertising in the local press, in an effort to compete with the City on its own home turf. Walter retaliated by hiring a Pueblo representative for his firm.[3] In October 1931, in a move to stave off financial disaster, Walter arranged for Fleming and Company to execute two promissory notes—one to himself for $60,000 and another to Lula for $35,000. He subsequently repaid the loans by selling properties belonging to Fleming and Company.

Maybe some of that $60,000 went to prop up the City, which, like all the other building and loans in the area, was operating in the red. For most of this period he was paying his depositors somewhere between 5 percent and 6 percent on money that some of the time was not even earning him 4 percent. Several years earlier he likely had believed he could make up that difference through his real estate investments. It was later revealed that from 1920 until 1932 my grandfather had paid his depositors almost $450,000 more in interest than their money had actually earned.[4] He had not promised customers 50 percent interest within forty-five days, as the famous swindler Charles Ponzi had, but the same principle applied. He was "robbing Peter to pay Paul," as the *Gazette* put it.[5]

Ponzi schemes are bound to collapse during hard times. With unemployment and underemployment people lacked the money to open savings accounts or to make payments on their loans. And then there was all the foreclosed property that Walter was now stuck with, some of it close to worthless. By 1932 the City owed a whopping $30,000 in back taxes on its properties.[6]

Walter could see how the story was unfolding, which is doubtless why he made sure that his wife and daughter were nowhere near Colorado Springs as the building and loan business unraveled. Within three weeks of Sims's suicide they were on a train, on their way to New Orleans. For two months they vacationed there, as well as in Havana and Miami, before heading to their usual destination, New York City. Dorothy soon returned to Boulder, where she was studying law at the University of Colorado. Lula remained in New York at the luxurious Waldorf Astoria Hotel. Lula's telegrams to Walter make it clear that she was taking her travel cues from him. "You know best" was her refrain. As for Eva, she was already out of town, living in Denver. But just two weeks after Sims's death she rented a safety deposit box in which she put an expensive diamond ring and three $1,000 bills, which were among Walter's many gifts to her.

As for his own depositors, Walter tried to allay their fears. He advertised aggressively in the local papers (even in the Pratts' weekly), although he had lowered his interest rate on savings accounts to 5 percent—two points below his local competitors' rate. He tried to compensate by emphasizing the safety of his association. And then, during the first week of January, just days after members of Sims's association learned that all those rosy prognostications about the condition of the Assurance were misplaced, he

'Bar Maids' of a different sort from those of the preprohibition era are these three coeds at the University of Colorado in Boulder, who are studycase books and Blackstone in preparation for law careers. They are, left to right—Helen Arthur, Boulder; Dorothy Allen Davis, Colorado Springs, and Gweneth Winters of Custer, S. D.

Dorothy was one of only three women studying law at the University of Colorado in 1932. (*Denver Post*)

began to selectively enforce the City's sixty-day withdrawal policy. We know he did so selectively because court records show that the first depositor to sue him was able to make withdrawals from her savings throughout most of the spring. It wasn't until late May that the plaintiff in that suit was turned back by employees of the City when she tried to withdraw the $1,314 remaining in her account. A divorced bookkeeper, she had both an eleven-year-old son and a mother to support. Her example suggests that for much of that spring he continued to honor at least some of his customers' requests in the hope that his flexibility would counter the public's growing apprehensions about building and loan associations.[7]

As conditions deteriorated, Walter continued to plot and scheme to ensure that his association would be the one left standing. Retaliating against Railway Savings Building and Loan for muscling in on his territory, he circulated a flyer attacking its operators' dubious business practices.[8] My grandfather played all the angles, but circumstances that spring were beyond his control. Late one afternoon toward the end of May, he found himself accosted by a depositor, later identified as an Italian American woman. As he was locking the door to his office, she came up behind him and demanded that he give her all the money she had on deposit. When he refused, explaining that he did not have the money to pay her, she didn't back off. Instead, she tried to hustle him into a nearby automobile. When he saw that her husband was behind the wheel, Walter coughed up some cash. Having gotten at least some of her money, she relented and let him go. These depositors were hardly the only angry customers of the City that winter and spring. My grandfather would later tell his family that during his last weeks in Colorado Springs he often feared for his life, as depositors grew increasingly fierce.[9]

Instrumental in provoking depositors' fury was the Pratts' *Common Sense Weekly*. Week after week the paper denounced the town's B&L men as "money demons" and "human vultures," men who would "rob a home of sunshine and sow grief or anguish in their wake." Worst of all was "Double Dynamite Davis." Should the Pratts try to expose him, people warned them, he would use his "far-reaching power" to crush them. He was the "henchman" behind all of the local associations, and working to enhance his power was his brother, Roy Davis, the state senator. In the June 3 edition of their paper, the Pratts predicted that despite demands that something be done about these B&L swindlers, depositors would find that justice would prove as elusive as the proverbial "ship that never comes home."[10]

The very day that this edition of *Common Sense* arrived on subscribers' doorsteps, the man the Pratts called Double Dynamite Davis was on his way out of town. He traveled by train to Denver and headed for his room at the Brown Palace Hotel. He visited Eva, who was in St. Joseph's Hospital recovering, the papers later reported, from two successive abdominal surgeries. Walter also met with his lawyer, Bernard Seeman, and separately with Eli Gross, Colorado's B&L commissioner. (It later emerged that my grandfather, Eli Gross, and the B&L men at Pueblo's Railway Savings all shared the same lawyer: Bernard Seeman.)[11] He told both men that he was traveling to Washington, D.C., where he planned to meet with officials at the newly formed federal agency, the Reconstruction Finance Corporation. The RFC was established to make government credit available to banks and other financial institutions, and he said he hoped people there might help him in sorting out the affairs at his association.[12]

Rather than traveling to Washington, Walter took the train to New York City. He arrived in Manhattan on June 6 and headed straight for the Waldorf Astoria. Lula was apparently unaware of her husband's imminent arrival because on June 5, while he was traveling, she sent him a telegram in Colorado Springs thanking him for his most recent gift of roses and candy. On June 9 the couple registered at the more modest Gramercy Park Hotel and paid for a month's rent on a room there.[13]

On Sunday, June 19, just under two weeks after arriving in New York, Walter placed a long-distance telephone call to his Denver lawyer. He was resigning as president of the City, he said, and he told Seeman that the association needed to be put immediately into receivership. He said he would be returning to Colorado Springs shortly. When interviewed by the press several days later, Seeman ventured that the Springs banker had been so "harassed" by one particular local publication that his "nerves were on the ragged edge and could stand it no longer." The lawyer made it clear that his client was no quitter. "If they let me alone," Davis told Seeman, "I can pull out!" Seeman explained that the public's distrust of building and loans and Davis's inability to meet the City's July 1 dividend payments to depositors left the banker with no choice but to throw his business into receivership.[14]

Even before news of the City's receivership hit the dailies on June 21, Colorado Springs had grown ugly with fear. By this point word had gotten out that Walter was in New York City with his wife. The City had 3,600 depositors, most of whom lived in the area. Unable to withdraw their money for several weeks, depositors were feeling some combination of anxious and furious. A group of them, described by the police as "working people," hatched a plan that they were convinced would force Walter to return home, and with no choice but to pony up. Their plan was to kidnap his daughter, Dorothy, whom they knew was a student in nearby Boulder. Somehow my mother got wind of the plot, and she decided to lie low and out of sight in her father's room at the Brown Palace. Protecting her there were her boyfriend and his fraternity brother. Her parents knew she was staying at the Brown Palace because on June 20 Lula (or perhaps Walter posing as Lula) wired her there. The telegram managed to slip past the authorities.

COME ANY TIME BEFORE JUNE TWENTY NINTH TAKE BURLINGTON FROM DENVER FOUR IN AFTERNOON CHICAGO NEXT EVENING LEAVE NINE MICHIGAN CENTRAL LAKE SHORE LIMITED CHANGE STATION IN CHICAGO CHECK TRUNKS THRU ALL RIGHT TO GO DOWN THERE AND DO AS I SAID NEED NOT BREAK LOCK ENJOY YOURSELF

LOVE MOTHER

The telegram's emphatic precision about trains, combined with its opacity about Colorado Springs—rendered as "down there"—and its reference to a prior conversation about checking trunks and not breaking a lock indicate that whoever wrote the wire knew something about the unraveling situation back home. And why was it necessary that Dorothy arrive in New York before June 29? Had Lula and Walter cooked up some scheme whereby the family would travel abroad before Walter's passport expired on July 11? Did they

REQUESTED TO FAVOR THE COMPANY BY CRITICISM AND SUGGESTION CONCERNING ITS SERVICE   1201-8

WESTERN
UNION

NEWCOMB CARLTON, PRESIDENT   J. C. WILLEVER, FIRST VICE-PRESIDENT

SIGNS

DL = Day Letter
NM = Night Message
NL = Night Letter
LCO = Deferred Cable
NLT = Cable Night Letter
WLT = Week-End Letter

The filing time as shown in the date line on full-rate telegrams and day letters, and the time of receipt at destination as shown on all messages, is STANDARD TIME.
Received at 915-919 Seventeenth Street, Denver, Colo.   Always Open   1932 JUN 20 PM 9 47

NB407 49 NL=WA NEWYORK NY 20

MISS DOROTHY DAVIS=

543 BROWN PL HOTEL DVR=

COME ANY TIME BEFORE JUNE TWENTY NINTH TAKE BURLINGTON
FROM DENVER FOUR IN AFTERNOON CHICAGO NEXT EVENING LEAVE
NINE MICHIGAN CENTRAL LAKE SHORE LIMITED CHANGE STATION
IN CHICAGO CHECK TRUNKS THRU ALL RIGHT TO GO DOWN THERE
AND DO AS I SAID NEED NOT BREAK LOCK ENJOY YOURSELF LOVE=

MOTHER.

MINUTES IN TRANSIT
FULL-RATE | DAY LETTER

On June 25, 1932, Receiver Fertig obtained a court order allowing him to subpoena the records of the Mountain States Telephone & Telegraph Company as they pertained to the Davises. Lula's lawyer Horace Hawkins presumably requested a copy of the transcript, which he must have given to the Davises once the threat of prosecution had passed. This telegram appears to have escaped the authorities' attention, perhaps because it was sent from the Waldorf Astoria Hotel to the Brown Plaza Hotel, where my mother had gone to thwart her kidnappers. It's not known whether the plan was for Dorothy and Lula to spend the summer in the east, as Lula claimed, or if it was for the family to escape to Europe or Cuba while Walter's passport was still valid. (Author's archive) somehow imagine that the family could weather the storm in Europe or Cuba or Mexico?

A day later, on Tuesday, June 21, 1932, a brief mention of the City's receivership and likely insolvency appeared in the *Colorado Springs Evening Telegraph*. The next day the *Gazette* reported that Walter Davis had departed to "undetermined places," and that the City's safety deposit box at the Exchange National Bank would be opened that morning. The paper claimed that news of the receivership came as "a complete surprise to the city." And yet it also noted that while the authorities hoped to find somewhere between $300,000 and $400,000 in Liberty Bonds inside the box, they had not ruled out the possibility that the association's assets had been looted.

It turned out that even getting into the association's box that Wednesday proved to be a drama. First of all, the bank's lawyer, P.M. Kistler, objected to the wording of the court order. After that was resolved there was still the matter of physically getting into the box because Walter had left town with its key. It took another thirty-five minutes for an expert to drill open the City's box. It was one of the bank's larger boxes, and the authorities assumed that a box that big would likely be crammed full of bonds. Instead what they discovered were seven lapsed life insurance policies, a letter from a life insurance company, a 1921 notice on the sale of a hundred shares in Portland Gold Mining, three empty security envelopes, one empty expanding mailing envelope, and $3,700 worth of Liberty Bonds. Bank authorities also revealed that Davis, who had rented the box for ten years, had rarely visited it, at least in the recent past. Charles Fertig, an insurance broker whom the courts had just appointed receiver of the City, must have looked stricken, for at that precise moment he had to have realized how much tougher his job had just become.

"Walter Davis and $1,000,000 Are Missing" was the *Gazette*'s extra-large headline on Thursday, June 23. It was a figure that

Within days the papers put the shortfall at $1.25 million. (*Gazette*)

only got bigger with time. Meanwhile, with the help of an auditor, Charles Fertig was trying to sort out the association's books. He explained to the press that the City had more than seven thousand accounts, whose total deposits amounted to just over $2 million. Offsetting liabilities were the $3,700 of Liberty Bonds that had been found the day before, $3,000 in the association's vaults, $8,000 in cash in various banks of the city, real estate loans that were once worth approximately $692,000, and the real estate assets of his holding company, Fleming & Co, which were once valued at $500,000. Denver lawyer Seeman would subsequently provide the receiver with an additional $24,320 that employees of the City had been directed by Walter to hand over to him. The figures suggest that the association had a deficit, which would have amounted to nearly $770,000 if the real estate market had been solid. But with a cratered real estate market, the shortfall was much larger, closer to $1.25 million, which became the agreed-upon figure. A day later Colorado authorities issued a warrant for my grandfather's arrest. He was charged with filing false claims about the condition of his business to the state's B&L commissioner. Other charges would follow.[15]

From that moment on, my grandfather—his apparent swindle, his whereabouts, his intimates, and his character—became the leading story in the Springs. The latest news of his scandal was always presented as authoritative, that is, until a day or two or a week or two later when a new account based on yet another impeccable source would emerge. These were some of the stories circulating in the press: in early June Davis had been spotted in Denver with valuable securities bulging out of his pockets; before leaving town he taken out a promissory note on one of his holding company's priciest properties for $100,000 and he had deposited $70,000 of that money into his wife's New York City bank account; a million dollars of depositors' money was sitting in one of Davis's bank accounts or safety deposit boxes back east or possibly in Europe.

And then the press reported that there was no money because the banker had spent it all in his many years of "riotous living." At some point, all of these claims were treated as the truth until suddenly and inexplicably they weren't. Still, some facts of the case were undisputed: Walter Davis was undeniably missing and so were almost all of his association's liquid assets.[16]

From the point of view of many Coloradans, the one bit of good news to emerge during that first week concerned Walter's insurance policies.[17] Bernard Seeman revealed that his client had given him power of attorney and further instructed him to alter the beneficiary status for most of his policies, which totaled, it was said, $541,0000. Lula had always been the beneficiary of all of his life insurance. However, he now ordered Seeman to designate her the beneficiary of only $100,000 and to assign the remaining $441,000 to his holding company, Fleming & Company. "If anything happens to me," Walter reportedly said, "the insurance can be applied to association assets."[18] It was an unusual move—what one lawyer characterized to me as "preemptive restitution."[19]

Even if the City's assets received an infusion of his insurance money, the authorities were still looking at a terrible wreck. Efforts to locate assets in four more of my grandfather's safety deposit boxes yielded so little one wonders if Walter was engaged in some elaborate tease or taunt. At one bank, three of the four boxes were entirely empty, and the fourth held two silver dollars, a Grant half dollar, and a one-dollar gold coin. The City had so many depositors, many of them with multiple accounts, and they were now clamoring for their money or at least some evidence that any of it still existed. Fertig made it clear that he would not fold in the face of obstacles, and that he would not tolerate any "pussyfooting" in the case. Whatever his investigation uncovered, he promised to make it public. To prove his seriousness he asked for and obtained a court order allowing him to search all the records of the Mountain States Telephone and Telegraph Company pertaining to Walter and Lula

Davis. Eventually the receiver had access to every telegram that passed between my grandparents and an accounting of at least some of their phone calls.

In fact, the authorities had carte blanche when it came to investigating the Davises, who were not in town and had no lawyer protecting them from prosecutorial overreach. After searching the office of the City, Fertig conducted what he described as a thorough search for assets at the Davis home on June 24. There is no indication that he obtained a court order for any of these searches. What Fertig turned up at their house, whose address the newspapers always printed, were some telegrams, which turned out to be regular banking transactions, and some canceled checks, drawn by my grandfather between 1927 and 1928 for amounts ranging from $5 to $32,000. The FBI file suggests that Fertig also got his hands on some family correspondence. The only other person in the North Tejon house that Wednesday was the family's African American housekeeper, who, when questioned by the press the previous day, had refused to give up any information about her employers. Perhaps she called Dorothy after her encounter with reporters or after Fertig departed, because later that evening my mother reportedly stopped by the house briefly.[20]

With Walter on the lam, the authorities and the press might have turned their attention to the officers and employees of the City. Yet they showed no interest in the vice president of the association despite the fact that Vertal Eugene Blake, a former salesman at the local J.C. Penney store, had worked for the City for nearly a decade. The same was true of Howard Claus and Jim Fleming, but officials' indifference to them makes more sense because Claus was a clerk and Fleming a handyman. Instead the authorities and the press focused their attention on the women in Walter Davis's life.

By 1932 the idea of female innocence was pretty tattered. For one, suffragists and flappers had done in the notion that women were an entirely different species who always deserved a pass. In the weeks ahead both Lula and Eva's actions would confirm this more realistic view of women. Lula should have had the advantage over Eva of being all the way across the country, but then Lula had the disadvantage of having Roy Davis as her brother-in-law. Roy counted among his many friends the men who ran the local police force, whom he helpfully tipped off as to Lula's whereabouts.[21] They then gladly passed on Lula's address at the Waldorf Astoria to the New York City reporters who were harassing them for information. Lula did herself no favors in her first phone interview with the press. She admitted that she was from Colorado Springs, but claimed that to the best of her knowledge her husband was not the head of the City Savings Building & Loan. Yes, he had departed for D.C., but not because he was in any financial trouble. She gave the impression she hadn't seen him for several days, although bank records subsequently showed that she and Walter had withdrawn the contents of a safety deposit box on June 23, and in a way that had aroused that attention of one bank employee. As for Eva Terry, whose name was by this point all over the newspapers back home, Lula claimed to have never heard of her.[22]

By this juncture Eva Terry must have wished that she could disappear just as Walter had. It was much too late for that, though. Eva had to have known something was amiss almost two weeks before the story of the crash broke. She was accustomed to having two checks land in her checking account each month, one on the first and another on the tenth of the month. That June, when she discovered that the second check had not been deposited, she called Walter's office in Colorado Springs. She reached an employee who presumably told her that Walter was out of town on business. Walter, who had visited her at the hospital just days before, had shared with her neither his travel plans nor his shortfall and what it would mean for her. Nearly two weeks later, on June 23, when the *Denver Post* reported that the police wanted to question the thirty-one-year-old former employee of the City Savings, she understood the seriousness of her situation. When an enterprising journalist, eager to beat the police to her fashionable apartment building, knocked on Eva's door, there was no response, just the sound of her chirping pet canary. The journalist spoke with her neighbors, who observed that Eva rarely went out except for outings in her expensive car. They also noted that Walter Davis was a frequent visitor to her apartment, but that he usually stayed at the Brown Palace hotel. As for Eva, she was hiding out at the home of a friend whose husband worked as a journalist at the *Rocky Mountain News*. It was this reporter who set up a meeting between Eva and the Denver police.[23]

The meeting between Eva and the police did not go well. Sassy and belligerent was how the police characterized her. Eva freely admitted that Walter had showered her with gifts and had been supporting her. When a detective asked her point blank if there was another woman in Walter Davis's life, she replied, "I suppose that would be me." After the Denver police had quizzed Eva for more than two hours, Colorado Springs detective Irving Bruce took over. He told her to get ready for a car ride to the Springs, at which point Eva tried to summon a doctor to verify that she should not be forced to travel because of her recent abdominal surgeries. (The newspapers mentioned these surgeries more than once, perhaps because in this period they could signal something unseemly.)[24] The detective was in a hurry, and in any case promised Eva that he would see to it that she was put up in a hotel, albeit one with a guard posted at her door. However, during the trip she proved so "sullen and sarcastic" and so uncooperative he decided she could do with a night in jail.[25]

Eva Terry would spend more than one night at the county jail. In fact, at one point that summer Eva Terry, Ed Sharer, and Fred Bentall were all incarcerated there. Throughout, Eva maintained she knew nothing about the missing money. She acknowledged that she enjoyed a "strong friendship" with her former boss, but she also

CITY SAVINGS RECEIVER QUIZZES EVA TERRY

From left to right, attorney for the receiver T.C. Turner, the receiver Charles T. Fertig, Eva Terry, and District Attorney John Meikle. Eva is smiling here, but she does not yet know that the police will insist on keeping her in jail, where she will spend a full week before her uncle meets the $10,000 bond required for her release. (*Gazette*)

claimed that their affair had ended in 1929. Their feelings for each other had "softened," she said. They had stopped corresponding with each other and had restricted themselves to visits, as though this was somehow less incriminating.

What Eva seems not to have bargained on was that for many people, including her interrogators, her complete lack of shame (her pride, even) about being the "other woman" suggested that her moral compass was disastrously misaligned. Convinced that she knew more about the business affairs of her "warm friend" than she was letting on, investigators searched her apartment for incriminating evidence. A small clock with the initials "WCD" engraved on it was all they turned up. During the weeks ahead, the authorities tried (and failed) to get the IRS to prosecute her for tax evasion on the grounds that she had not claimed as income Walter's many gifts to her. They opened up her Denver safety deposit box and seized its contents. And they fed information to the press, including scandalous snippets from the "mass of papers" they had seized from Walter's office and home. Readers learned, for example, that the couple had rhapsodized about the house-hunting pleasures that awaited them once Walter divorced Lula.[26]

The *Evening Telegraph* observed that as she languished behind bars, Eva had to "imagine the hum of avid comment about her as the latest details of the case are eagerly devoured." The hum certainly got to her family. Her brother defended her as a "thrifty girl," who he had believed was socking away money from her real estate job in Denver. Her aunt begged the press to stop playing up Eva's affair with Walter, but her efforts to support her niece went somewhat awry when she said that Eva was living "as clean and decent a life as anyone could expect."[27]

After almost a week in jail Eva grew even more defiant and demanded her release. But it was one thing to be Ed Sharer and assume a posture of defiance. This played well in the press, which seemed to take it as proof of his innocence. By contrast, Eva's defiance only made her seem more culpable to the reporters covering the scandal. As for the police, their response to her demand was to file formal charges against her. She and Walter were jointly charged with having conspired on June 4, 1932, to maliciously and feloniously defraud the depositors of the City. Bond was set at $10,000. Eva continued to stick to her guns, claiming she knew nothing about the money. She restated her conviction that Walter Davis was a fine man. Even if she did know his whereabouts, she made it clear that she would be keeping that information to herself.[28]

Eva was still cooling her heels in the county jail on Sunday, June 26, when Lula's train pulled into the station at nearby Falcon. Waiting for her as she disembarked were receiver Charles Fertig, police chief Hugh Harper, and Mr. and Mrs. Roy Davis. The story of her husband's million-dollar-plus shortfall had been in the news only four days, and yet everything had changed—for the depositors, the authorities, Eva, the Davis family, and, of course, Lula. Along with thousands of newspaper readers, she now knew that her husband had deceived her yet again. She discovered that in the wake of Sims's suicide, while she was out of town, he had spent many weekends in Denver with Eva.

The humiliation was so awful that one wonders why she didn't betray her husband. And now she had to contend with Roy, who assumed a stance even more insufferable than usual. Roy, who had long distrusted his older brother, knew what Walter's shortfall meant for him. In late March, just two and a half weeks before the Sharers left the Springs, he informed the press that he had no intention of running again for the state senate. Perhaps he meant to signal his interest in running for the governorship, not his permanent exit from politics. He did hold on to newspaper clippings suggesting that the Republican Party groom him for that position.[29] But now, three months later, he knew his political career was finished, and he must have worried about whether even his typewriter shop would survive. As rumors of his collusion with his brother spread, Roy did everything to dispel them, mostly by very publicly cooperating with the authorities. Lula shared her husband's view of Roy—that he was a pompous, self-regarding know-it-all. Years later, it took Roy well over a month of visiting Lula in the hospital when she was close to death to talk about anything other than himself. "I guess Roy realizes I'm sick at last" was how Lula put it to my mother the day before she died.

That afternoon as they drove to Colorado Springs, Roy pushed Lula to tell the truth about her husband. What came out instead were uncontrollable sobs and unstoppable tears. When she did take a stab at answering questions, she was hopelessly, frustratingly, and worryingly vague. After three to four hours of fairly unproductive questioning at Roy's house, the authorities decided that being in her own home might have a calming influence upon Lula. But as she walked into the foyer of her home the first thing that caught her eye was a large photograph of Walter, and she once again burst into "hysterical sobbing." Finally her doctor was called in. I imagine he administered a tranquilizer. "Hysterical during police quiz" was how the newspaper characterized Lula the following day. The paper noted that Roy promised the authorities they would have the "hearty cooperation" of the entire Davis family.[30]

In the days ahead Lula seems to have satisfied her interrogators that she was truly doing her best to aid them. She reportedly told Chief Harper that she thought her husband would either return to the Springs voluntarily or surrender to authorities, wherever he might be. "She cannot believe," declared Harper, "that he would desert his wife and daughter and his business." Believing that Lula was cooperating, the authorities began to roll back their original story. They now claimed that there was no evidence that Walter Davis had deposited $70,000 in his wife's account. As for the mountain of Liberty Bonds he was supposed to have made off with, they now doubted that, too. They reasoned that he would have needed to cash in the bonds periodically to meet his extraordinary personal expenses. They also revealed that it had been two or three years since the association had reported any interest on its bonds. And soon it came out that no one had actually seen the Liberty Bonds, just the records that had been submitted, which included the numbers of the bonds.

Within just a few days the authorities' efforts to reverse themselves took on a new urgency when the police determined that the plot to kidnap Dorothy Davis was a serious one. My mother had already gone into hiding once out of fear she might be kidnapped, but this was a week later. Kidnapping in America had become sufficiently common that just that March the *Gazette* had called it a "vicious racket." The 1930s witnessed an epidemic of "ransom kidnapping" of wealthy businessmen or their relatives, often by crime gangs. This sort of extortion-for-profit scheme characterized the recent kidnapping and murder of the Lindbergh baby, whose body had been discovered in mid-May 1932. Many Coloradans also knew about the recent near kidnapping of "millionaire capitalist" Verner Z. Reed Jr., the grown son of the onetime mining magnate. Of course, the effort to kidnap my mother was not a ransom kidnapping per se, but the police took the threat seriously. By June 30 there was a twenty-four-hour police detail on the Davises' home. The police also did a strategic about-face on the "Davis women," declaring them practically destitute. Harper emphasized that kidnapping Dorothy Davis would accomplish nothing if the looted money had been spent, which he said he now believed to be the case. Irrespective of what Harper put out to the press, "rabid talk" about the Davis family continued unabated.[31]

Depositors figured that kidnapping his daughter was a surefire way of forcing Walter Davis back to Colorado Springs. Had they succeeded, he might well have returned. But as things now stood it was all but certain that he would remain a fugitive, no matter what his wife told the police. Why would Walter, a man who insisted on his own innocence, return to a place where sentiment ran in favor of throwing him in jail or worse? Judging from one letter to Lula later seized by the authorities, he believed that the townspeople of Colorado Springs had lost their bearings, perhaps even gone mad. As long as his daughter's life wasn't on the line he was staying away until someone else's lawyer had proven in a court of law that most, if not all, of the charges leveled against building and loan heads were invalid. I suspect that this is what he at first imagined would happen. That conviction then turned to hope, which grew wobblier over time. One depositor expressed the feelings of many when he proclaimed that "fire or flood, tornado or earthquake" would have been less awful than what Walter Davis had done to the people of Colorado Springs.[32]

The press in the Springs and in Denver grew relentless in their criticism of him. A prominent handwriting expert maintained that his signature revealed a man who was a "bold, eccentric swindler."[33] A Sunday feature article on him claimed he had a "money complex." As evidence it cited the observations of people who had spied him alone in his office. There, with piles of bills on the table in front of him, he could be seen lifting the big bills and kissing them.[34] As if all of this wasn't bad enough, the press declared that his womanizing was so out of control he was a "polygamist."[35]

Critical to the hardening of public opinion against Walter were the depositors themselves, who wasted no time in getting organized. Between five thousand and six thousand residents were depositors in the town's four B&Ls. On July 1, only a little more than a week after news of the City's failure hit the headlines, two thousand of them showed up at a mass meeting to vent their anger about the looting of their B&Ls and the inadequacy of the official response to it. By meeting's end the group was calling itself the Depositors' Committee. They chose J. Herbert Pratt of *Common Sense Weekly* as the group's chair and Judge John E. Little as its attorney. The group immediately called for the arrest of state B&L commissioner Eli Gross, and threatened to go after district attorney John Meikle if he failed to file charges against Gross.[36]

Within weeks the Depositors' Committee filed a petition in district court demanding that B&L commissioner Gross be charged with conspiracy to defraud. Gross, a onetime official of the cigar makers union in Arkansas, had remained active in union politics after moving to Denver. A Democrat, he was appointed by Democratic governor Billy Adams to serve as a state factory inspector, a civil service position typically used as a form of political patronage. Gross had served on the state commission investigating the 1914 Ludlow massacre, and his pro-union stance likely made him a target of the Republican establishment. Moreover, Gross, whom the *Denver Post* derided as a "cigar maker," was not well qualified for the job.[37] Several years earlier he had held the position of deputy inspector of B&Ls; however, the new position of commissioner required passing an exam, which he had failed.

Skepticism about Gross grew when it came to light that his "advisory board" included both Walter Davis and Miles Saunders, one of the Railway B&L men (and a powerful Democrat who had served as Pueblo's district attorney). Nevertheless, Gross's critics ignored the state's miserly support of his office. He was never given adequate resources or qualified examiners. One of his two assistants, Byron Miller, the former deputy inspector, was so resentful about having been passed over for the new position that he shirked his duties. None of this mattered to the Depositors' Committee, which would only have been satisfied with Gross's head on a platter. As for Walter Davis, they were hoping to nab him with a widely circulated notice offering a $1,000 reward for his capture.[38]

It wasn't just Eli Gross and Walter Davis who came in for what one reporter called "scorching criticism." At a meeting of the Depositors' Committee late that summer the crowd also went after receiver Charles Fertig and his lawyer, Thomas C. Turner, who had shown up for the meeting. "How much is Fertig being paid?" people in the audience demanded. Turner responded that he had no idea because the City's receiver was actually an agent of the district court, which had set his pay. "You should know because you're our lawyer," someone yelled. The place grew a lot rowdier when Turner explained that he was technically representing Fertig, not them. As Turner tried to explain how a receivership actually worked, the place practically blew up. Turner became even less popular with this group when he told the press that people with money in building and loan associations misunderstood their relation to these businesses. They were investors, not depositors. Making matters

$1,000 REWARD

Wanted for Embezzlement—Absconded June, 1932

WALTER CLYDE DAVIS, aged 51 years, looks older; height 5 feet 10 inches; weight was 170 pounds, may have lost weight; face will no doubt look drawn and worried; complexion light sallow, gray-blue eyes, dark brown hair, bald in front, thin on top; has thick heavy neck, roll of fat extends over collar in back; bends body forward at hips when walking; has habit of moving lips several times before speaking, which is very noticeable; scar on top of index finger on one hand; well dressed; very neat; quiet mannered; carries cane; appears to be in deep study; very nervous; has habit holding arms bent at elbow. May have grown mustache and goatee. Chewed five Robert Burns panatela cigars each day, which he carries in a pasteboard box in pocket. Eats many apples. Will buy Colorado Springs or Denver newspaper each day if obtainable. Visits best nose and throat specialist frequently for sinus trouble. Always takes coat off in doctor's office and other places when possible. Wears muffler at all times when weather even slightly cool. Always carries stub lead pencil, which he holds almost flat when writing. Will live at good hotels or apartment houses. Will use bell boy to make most purchases.

Was president of a building and loan association and embezzled large sum of money, which may amount to one million dollars, from depositors consisting mostly of poor people. Is thought to have large sum of money in safety deposit boxes in this country and Europe. Had passport which expired July 11, 1932. Could have left country before expiration, but we believe he is still in North America. Has visited London and Paris.

The Receiver of the City Savings Building and Loan Association has been authorized by order of Court to pay ONE THOUSAND DOLLARS REWARD for information leading to and the arrest of Davis and his delivery to the proper officer of the State of Colorado; or, for information resulting in the identification of the body of Davis, if dead.

Check bodies of all persons found dead.

Please make every effort to assist us in apprehending this man in order to help his poor victims.

Wire any information you believe of interest to us at our expense.

September 7, 1932.

H. D. HARPER, Chief Police,
Colorado Springs, Colorado.

62-27247-11

The detail in this police circular about Walter Davis is exceedingly fine-grained, as it captures his odd gait—bending his body forward at his hips as he walks—and his habit of moving his lips before talking. (Bureau of Investigation File # 62-27247; author's archive) worse, most of their money was now tied up, he said, in a badly depreciated real estate market where properties were worth only somewhere between 50 and 75 percent of what the loans were for.[39]

The Depositors' Committee was comfortable inveighing against government officials, particularly Eli Gross, who presided over the agency mandated with supervising the thrift industry. Members of the committee were willing to use the power of the state to prosecute anyone they believed was a part of the scandal. And they were eager to indict all those who were cleaning up the mess— the receivers, lawyers, accountants, and secretaries—as insiders who were profiting from it.[40] Some of the group's members, such as those who plotted my mother's kidnapping, gravitated easily to vigilante justice. What they appear to have never contemplated was pushing their legislators to fight for a stiffer regulatory regime for building and loan associations.

The choices made by the Depositors' Committee should be understood as stemming, at least in part, from government's treatment of the "little people" who did business with building and loan associations. The thrift industry had successfully fought any effective regulation, leaving association members largely on their own in their dealings with their B&Ls. Some state legislatures and governors did take action during this crisis, although in Colorado it amounted to nothing more than a special committee appointed by the governor. And at the federal level the plight of building and loan members never received the attention or thought given to bank depositors, who mattered more than the working classes who comprised the ranks of B&L members.

One sees the privileging of bank customers over B&L members in the summer of 1932 when a congressional committee held hearings to discuss President Hoover's Home Loan Bank Bill. The discussion turned to the recently formed Reconstruction Finance Corporation (RFC). One congressman claimed the RFC had failed to meet the expectations of the great masses of people that the

RFC would help them. He had in mind B&L members who he said were "thronging the doors of these associations, trying to get the money they must have to buy bread and clothing, and they can not get it." Another congressman representing Philadelphia pointed out that B&Ls there were in a terrible mess because "they are loaded up to-day with properties that they are forced to take over, owing to the fact that payments cannot be made." Isn't it incumbent on the federal government, he asked, to help B&L depositors as well as better-situated bank depositors?

However, for opponents of government assistance, including a congressman from Missouri, it was not "the business of the United States Government to go into partnership with some private institution to help them realize on what perhaps turned out to be a bad investment." Just as the Colorado Springs lawyer T.C. Turner had argued, the Missourian noted that these people were not depositors, after all, but investors who chose badly by investing in poorly run businesses. When asked by another congressman about the recent closing of Missouri's own Farm and Home association, the third-largest in the country, he said, "I am not familiar with that situation."

Indeed, the hearings reveal just how little these congressmen knew about the building and loan business. To some extent their confusion reflects the hodgepodge quality of the thrift industry, whose practices and governance varied enormously from state to state. However, these hearings revealed that some congressmen didn't even know that B&Ls in many states paid dividends to depositors. Judging by these hearings, lawmakers paid attention to the leaders of the thrift industry trade organization. However, when it came to actual B&L members—the proverbial "little man" of the B&L world—well, they turned up in discussion, only to be forgotten. So if members of the Springs Depositors' Committee had little confidence in government to help them, one can perhaps understand why.[41]

Still, the way that the building and loan scandal played out in Colorado Springs was not the way events unfolded in every community where such scandals occurred. In California, depositors pressed the state to pass the Beesemyer Bill, named after the famously crooked B&L head, to provide compensation for their losses.[42] The situation played out very differently in Chicago, too. There, the building and loan industry was often organized along ethnic and racial lines. The men who ran these associations presided over them not because of their knowledge of banking and finance but rather, says historian Lizabeth Cohen, because of their "wealth and their prestige in the ethnic community." Investigations revealed that many of these Chicago operators had been financially irresponsible, which led their depositors to demand that they be treated like crooks. In Chicago, depositors' experiences disillusioned them about the "big men" in their communities, which in turn eroded the class harmony that had existed within the city's ethnic communities. Quite in contrast to depositors in Colorado Springs, Chicagoans came to see the federal government as their savior, and pressed for it to protect their savings and mortgages. When the Home Owners' Loan Corporation (HOLC), a New Deal agency, began to rescue homes from foreclosure, Chicago's workers reportedly took "tremendous comfort" in the government's new activist role.[43]

In contrast to their swindled counterparts in Chicago, the leaders of the Colorado Springs Depositors' Committee viewed the federal government warily and the local government as yet another swindler. In large measure the group's hostility toward the state stemmed from the fact that several of its most prominent leaders were veteran activists in the local anti-tax, anti-government movement. Westside newspaperman and conservative firebrand J. Herbert Pratt and two former KKKers, Judge John Little and Golden Cycle mill worker Arthur Elvis Walker, were already active in the El Paso County Taxpayers Association (EPCTA). Across America taxpayers' leagues such as the El Paso County group proliferated in the 1930s. These organizations mushroomed in the wake of sharp increases in local and state taxes, which were caused by a variety of factors. Across the nation, local taxes shot up from 5.4 percent of the national income in 1929 to an astonishing 11.7 percent in 1932. State taxes rose, too, from 1.9 percent in 1929 to 4.6 percent in 1932. As tax delinquencies grew so did the ranks of America's tax rebels. Tax revolts remain an understudied feature of the 1930s, but they were, as one well-known *New York Times* reporter put it in 1932, "the nearest thing to a political revolution in this country."[44]

The El Paso County group advocated, as did other such associations, scaling back the size and the power of local government, particularly its power to levy taxes.[45] Initially the local taxpayers association attracted homeowners who were somewhere between struggling and just barely comfortable. There were certainly many such people in Colorado Springs, where the rate of homeownership was 54 percent, and where 67 percent of all homes were valued at less than $5,000.[46] For wage earners of modest means living in small cottages, many of them on the west side, their homes represented the only economic safety net they had.[47] During the 1920s they had struggled to curtail what they viewed as a profligate city council and city manager. The city's leadership had long been pro-development, whether that meant constructing a small airport, building a public golf course, or repaving the city's key downtown streets with low-grade gold. To the taxpayers' group, whether it was street paving or schools (run by "theorists with no practical ideas"), it was all was frivolous spending. It also opposed the municipal ownership of utilities and was leery of workers on the government payroll, with the exception of the police.[48]

Some members of the taxpayers' association were, socioeconomically speaking, working class. Yet their allegiance was to their families and their homes, not to the class with which others might identify them. As memories of working-class solidarity receded further from residents' consciousness, it's not surprising that many such people identified first and foremost as homeowners. It's not as though unions, which might have kept alive such memories, had any clout in Colorado Springs. The upshot was that working people viewed with suspicion the gains of others, particularly public-sector workers whose salaries they paid for.[49] As the economy remained frozen, taxes became an even greater source of anxiety. The fear of coming up short, of falling, and of losing one's home through a tax sale loomed large for some members, which doubtless helps explain the fierceness of the group's rhetoric.[50] Particularly during the 1920s both the EPCTA's hostility to the development plans favored by the Republican elite and some of its own leaders' participation in the KKK had put it at odds with that elite and its favored politicians. In the thirties, however, class polarization between the taxpayers' association and the town's ruling elite became somewhat more muted as wealthier residents joined the taxpayers group.[51]

By 1931 Merrill Shoup, son of millionaire and former Colorado governor Oliver Shoup, had become the president of the group. Only thirty-two years old, Shoup, who held degrees in both law and business, would become chairman of the board of Holly Sugar and president of the Golden Cycle Corporation. Under Shoup's leadership the group attracted a number of affluent members. In fact, Mayor George Birdsall argued that the group's tax limitation plan, which looked to tap the resources of the city's municipally owned utilities, was actually an effort to shift the burden of taxation away from large property owners, including the Antlers Hotel, to small consumers. Colorado Springs had been embroiled in a decade-long fight over public utilities. Utilities there, after years of mismanagement by private corporations, were now city owned, but the debate continued to rage. In the mid-twenties former governor Oliver Shoup opposed municipal ownership of utilities on the grounds that "neither the community, nor state nor nation should engage in any enterprise which can be best conducted by private enterprise." To argue otherwise was "socialistic."[52] These debates didn't go away.

Colorado Springs was hardly the only city whose residents were divided on the question of utilities. The question of public ownership of utilities was so hotly debated that it made its way into Sinclair Lewis's *Babbitt*. Babbitt opposed it, of course.[53] And it remained a hot topic in the thirties. As the 1936 election approached and President Roosevelt tried to firm up his support among everyday Americans who opposed big business and "Wall Street," he went after utility companies. These companies were characterized by a pyramiding of holding companies atop actually operating utility firms, and they were among the most hated businesses in America. Utility holding companies were not themselves productive entities. Their only assets were stock in the lower companies, which they would issue more of and whose profits they made sure grew. They monopolized the country's private utility interests, with the result that there were "huge profits for speculators and grossly overpriced electricity for consumers." When Roosevelt targeted these utility companies big business cried socialism, just as Shoup had done a decade earlier, but this move cemented the president's support with many working people.[54]

What was happening in 1933 in Colorado Springs was part of a much larger conflict that would soon play out nationally, but here the class lines were blurred, as they so often were. Mayor Birdsall argued the taxpayers' plan would "transfer so large a portion of the tax burden to the utilities that they will falter under it, fall into bad repute because of it, and the one outstanding example of successful municipal ownership and the remaining sore thumb to the power interests will be wiped out and public ownership will have received its death blow."[55] Privatization would prevail. Although powerful interests would have benefited from the plan, the taxpayers' group maintained that working people were the true beneficiaries of their policies, and some of them apparently agreed. The group included both the president of the Antlers and City Coal Mines as well as the assistant engineer at the Antlers.[56]

In certain respects these taxpayer associations foreshadow our present-day Tea Party movement.[57] Judge Little believed the city of Colorado Springs should "emulate the example set by the public itself" and tighten its belt as ordinary citizens had. First on Little's chopping block was the minimum salary law for schoolteachers. He and other anti-tax activists routinely went after "high-powered educators," whom they accused of using the PTA to advance their "tax-spending programs." The group also attacked as wasteful the federal government's plan to build post offices throughout the country. Merrill Shoup argued that the biggest problem facing America was the expansion of government, which was overwhelming Americans with what he called "bureau after bureau and bureaucrat after bureaucrat." Here he was following in the footsteps of his old-line Republican father.

The taxpayers' association in El Paso County went so far as to push for passage of a bill in the state legislature that would have given such associations veto power over budgets. If a taxpayers' organization opposed any single item in the budget, the city council in question would have to then submit it to the state tax commission for arbitration. Moreover, the bill would have prevented the city council from putting a bond issue proposal to the people for a vote if the taxpayers' group objected. In fact, the proposed legislation empowered the group to sue any city official who the group believed had violated any of the bill's many provisions. "You only have to think contrary to the taxpayers to be sued for damages," observed the attorney for the city. If the bill became law, argued city officials, it would effectively "destroy local self-government and transfer governing powers from duly elected public officials to self-constituted taxpayers organizations."[58]

The B&L collapse represented an opportunity for those members of the El Paso County Taxpayers Association who were

politically ambitious. Judge Little had already run for public office
and would again. J. Herbert Pratt ran for county commissioner, and
Merrill Shoup had his eye on the governor's seat. They used the
fury of building and loan depositors to take down local politicians
and elevate themselves. They attacked the "city gang" and its "rotten" mayor, George Birdsall, whom they blamed for the scandal,
and used language that insinuated that the Springs was under the
thumb of corrupt machine pols—the rap against nearby Denver.[59]

Taxpayers' associations reveal a side of the 1930s that departs
from the feel-good, collectivist-oriented political activism we often
associate with that era. These activists were full of anger, but
not of the sort that compelled working people to come together
to resist evictions or farm auctions or to build or strengthen labor
unions. Instead, cross-class movements that deployed the trope of
the "little man" were predicated upon the idea that old-fashioned
self-reliance, not handouts to the "undeserving," was the cure for
what ailed America.[60] Journalist Lorena Hickok, who traveled
across the United States for the Roosevelt administration in order
to report back to the administration on its New Deal relief efforts,
wrote of many Americans' horror of dependence, and particularly
of white-collar people who, it seemed, would rather starve than
apply for relief. One Arizona man asked her what would happen to
men like himself, "men who have been the backbone of commerce,
who have had ambitions and hopes, who have always taken care of
our families."[61] It was a fear for both blue-collar and white-collar
Americans, and it helped to fuel these cross-class tax revolts across
America.

By the mid-thirties the anti-tax movement had lost steam nationally, but it had played an important role in state and local politics.[62]
Between 1932 and 1934, seven states enacted limitations on the
general property tax, and several dozen localities established similar limits.[63] Republicans (and some Democratic politicians, including Colorado's governor, Ed Johnson) took the anti-tax ball and ran

with it as they attacked the New Deal for expanding the power of the federal government. Often they opposed the New Deal on the grounds that it was "soaking the poor," whose taxes, they alleged, went to pay for all those proliferating alphabet agencies.[64] When it came to Colorado Springs, voters there did not overturn municipal ownership of public utilities or vote out Mayor Birdsall. Nor did the Colorado state legislature grant taxpayers' associations veto power over local budgets. However, Merrill Shoup did sit on Governor Johnson's tax advisory committee, and he claimed that the taxpayers' movement was instrumental in reducing taxes.[65]

The West's vexed, sometimes hostile relationship to the federal government is of long standing. The 2016 seizure by a right-wing militia group of the Malheur National Wildlife Refuge in Oregon is just the most recent example. And yet Westerners have depended upon the federal government in multiple ways—the conquering of native peoples, subsidizing (and then regulating) transcontinental railroads, and protecting the interests of cattle kings, to name a few. In the twentieth century, as public lands were set aside for national parks and forests, military bases and monuments, the government's involvement in the region intensified. The government subsidized the construction and maintenance of huge reclamation, irrigation, and hydroelectric projects. Despite (or perhaps because of) the New Deal's largesse toward the West, which received three times the national average of federal expenditures, Westerners all too often responded by "gnawing at the hand that fed them."[66] Historian Albert Hurtado has provocatively suggested that the West has so benefited from government largesse that the region might be better understood not so much as "the cradle of individualism" but rather as "the nursery of Big Brother." Doubtless the West's dependence on the federal government goes a long way toward explaining its twitchy, defensive relationship to it.[67]

It would take decades for the politics of these taxpayers' associations to achieve legitimacy on the national stage. It began to pay

off nationally in 1964 when the conservative Arizona businessman Barry Goldwater won the Republican Party's nomination for
the presidency. It was the New Deal, which Goldwater opposed,
that had gotten him started in politics. When he ran for the Senate in 1952 he sounded like Merrill Shoup: "Do you want federal
bureaus and federal agencies to take over an increasing portion of
your life?"[68] Indeed, Shoup was one of Goldwater's earliest supporters in Colorado.[69] In 1968, four years after Goldwater's failed
presidential bid, Richard Nixon would strike a familiar chord of
taxpayer rights in his appeal to the aggrieved "Silent Majority."
Even more aggressively than the taxpayers' leagues of the thirties, Nixon's pitch to the Silent Majority deployed what one historian calls a "populist discourse that obscured divisions between
working-class and middle-class white voters."[70] Less than a decade later anti-tax activist Howard Jarvis's Proposition 13 won
over voters in California and radically changed property tax assessment there.[71] In Colorado, where the seeds of tax rebellion
had been planted in the twenties and thirties, taxpayers would
once again organize in the 1980s. And then there was Ronald
Reagan, who famously argued that, far from being the solution to
our country's problems, government *was* the problem.[72]

The Depositors' Committee and the El Paso County Taxpayers Association show that anti-statist conservatism has a long
history. They also exemplify the phenomenon at the very heart of
this book—a kind of consciousness that was not peculiar to the
American West but which thrived in certain communities there.
Members of the Depositors' Committee and the El Paso County
Taxpayers Association opposed city-owned public utilities, and
they never endorsed stiffer government regulation of the B&L industry or of the companies looking to scam desperate depositors,
because all of these efforts involved imposing unfair limits on free
enterprise. Keeping government out of one's home and out of one's
bank account was a crucial component of their American dream.

It was precisely this vision of getting ahead that had allowed my grandfather to pull off his swindle in the first place.

Where the depositors and Walter Davis parted company was on the question of the money and to whom it rightly belonged. However, this remained a moot point that fall, as the police were no closer to nabbing him or the money than they had been in June. Chief Harper had played a role in taking down the notorious Fleagle gang only five years earlier.[73] Just as the scandal was unfolding he became president of the International Association of Chiefs of Police.[74] And yet when it came to knowing the whereabouts of Walter Davis, the legendary "manhunter" was clueless.

6

The Port of Missing Men

Three years into the Great Depression Americans learned that life could grow even bleaker. Economically, the winter of 1932–33 was the worst in all of U.S. history.[1] In 1930 1,345 banks failed, a number that hit 2,000 the following year. But in the winter of 1932–33, there were ten bank failures a day in America and countless bank runs.[2] By early 1933 between 25 and 30 percent of the country's workforce was unemployed. Relief funds were pathetically undersized. With tax revenues sharply down, cities slashed services. City government in Detroit went so far as to close its zoo and slaughter its animals, which were then fed to the city's hungry residents.[3] Beyond the city, farmers were so desperate that the president of the American Farm Bureau, a conservative, warned Congress that unless something was done to alleviate the suffering of America's farmers, the countryside would succumb to revolution.[4] Businessmen in Muncie, Indiana, were likely not the only people who, in anticipation of widespread revolt, stockpiled large quantities of canned food in their cellars.[5] And in rural Sikeston, Missouri, the local newspaper worried that Hoover's attentiveness to big business over suffering veterans would lead to "riots next winter in cities and Socialists at the next election."[6]

Shattered by bank runs, bankruptcies, and massive unemployment, Americans were no longer beguiled or amused by the excess
and extravagance now associated with the twenties. Something
else was driving this shift as well: revelations of widespread financial dubiousness and outright malfeasance in American banking
and finance. The headlines that year included the likes of Chicago's energy mogul Samuel Insull, who fled the country before
he could be arrested on charges of embezzlement. Insull couldn't
understand what all the fuss was about. "What have I done," he
asked, "that every banker and business magnate has not done in
the course of business?"[7] Financial wrongdoing was hardly limited to tycoons such as Insull and Wall Street financiers, even if it
proved especially lucrative for them. In New Mexico, seven bankers were sentenced to the state pen in October 1932 for a $73,000
shortage at the First National Bank of Santa Fe. Among those sentenced was the bank's assistant cashier, Otis Seligman; his father,
Arthur Seligman, was the bank's president and the state's governor.[8] Months earlier, investigators found that the operator of twelve
failed banks in Chicago, the Bain Banks, made $5 million in un-
secured "character loans" to relatives and politicians with whom he
was friendly.[9]

Prosecutors were aggressive in going after bankers. Sometimes
they were playing to angry depositors; it was a get-tough stance
that brought them favorable press and votes, even if the charges
didn't always stick. Even when bankers were vigorously prosecuted, vengeful depositors sometimes opted for vigilante justice.
In Illinois, two men kidnapped a banker who had been sentenced
to serve between one and three years in the state penitentiary.
The men, one of whom had lost $6,000 in the crash, attacked the
banker in his home, bound and gagged him, and took him for a
car ride lasting most of the night. The sixty-five-year-old man was
found the next day still alive but very badly beaten in a patch of
weeds where his attackers had left him to die.[10]

In Colorado Springs the prevailing opinion about Walter Davis was that he had not made the cultural turn away from extravagance, that he remained his same old conspicuously consuming self. By mid-October 1932 the dailies were certain that the "master criminal" had been plotting his escape for years and that he was now living the high life somewhere enviably exotic. Perhaps he was on some South Seas island, the press speculated, or maybe he was in Greece, where the indicted Insull had fled to escape extradition. Almost certainly his "paradise" included female companionship. One thing was for sure—he had vanished into "the port of missing men."

In fact, the only border that Walter crossed, and only very briefly at that, was the Canadian border when he visited Niagara Falls. The authorities were convinced he had fled the country, but the July 11 expiration date on his passport seems to have stumped him. He was also keenly aware that in much of Europe foreigners were expected to register with the police, who would have been alerted to be on the lookout for an American fitting his description. Life on the lam for my grandfather did not match the outsized fantasies that people back home harbored. His nearly two-hundred-page FBI file offers a fairly detailed account of his comings and goings, provided by the one man with whom he spent time while he was on the run.[11]

A day after Lula left New York for Colorado Springs, Walter went to Broadway Drive It Yourself, a car rental outfit close to Central Park. Introducing himself as William Arnold, he arranged to rent a car for four days and, through the shop's proprietor, hired a driver at $5 a day, all expenses paid. The man whose good fortune it was to be his driver was John Henry Bogans, a thirty-five-year-old African American. A World War I veteran, he lived at the coincidentally named Davis Apartments on 136th Street in Harlem. The two men traveled to Poughkeepsie, where they stayed for two nights, before heading off to Albany and coming back to the city via Yonkers.

Upon returning to Manhattan, Walter decided against going back to the Gramercy Park Hotel, even though he had paid for his room through the first week of July. Instead, he rented a room at the nearby Parkside Hotel, not the sort of luxury hotel where the police might have expected to find him.[12] As soon as they returned to the city, Walter presented his chauffeur with a proposition: if Bogans became his personal driver, he would pay him $40 a week and front him the money for a secondhand automobile. Bogans accepted the offer and Walter advanced him $250 with which to buy a used Ford. He also agreed to cover the expenses of the road—gas, oil, repairs, and the man's food and lodging. This was easily twice as much as many professional men were earning during the Depression.

From early July until sometime after Labor Day the two men were on the road together. They traveled to New London, then to Boston and Portland, usually stopping for one or two nights. Many of their visits included a five- to ten-minute trip to a bank, just long enough, presumably, for Walter to cash a Liberty Bond. After a quick stop in Northampton, Massachusetts, Bogans drove them to Albany, where they lingered for a full week. Once there, Walter took in the Seabury Commission hearings investigating corruption in New York mayor Jimmy Walker's administration. From Albany, they stopped in Schenectady, where they toured an electrical plant. On their way to Niagara Falls their route would have taken them close to Cooperstown, where just three years earlier Walter had attended his daughter's graduation. After stopping in Buffalo, they took in Akron, Pittsburgh, Cumberland, and Baltimore, Maryland. Finally, after five days in Asbury Park, where Walter declined to stay at a hotel that catered to Jewish visitors, they returned to New York City.

Hotels routinely practiced discrimination, usually against racial and ethnic minorities, and when they traveled Bogans had to locate lodging elsewhere for himself. Still, the two men spent a good deal of time in each other's company. And in Albany, where Walter rented a hotel apartment with a kitchen, the two men cooked breakfast together every morning for a week. Back in New York, Bogans picked up Walter each day from the hotel around midday and chauffeured him around the city. His favorite destination was South Shore Drive in Bay Ridge, Brooklyn. There he would take what must have been melancholy walks as he watched the ships passing through the Narrows on their way to sea or into the harbors of New York and New Jersey. Bogans noted that his employer seemed unusually well informed about the movements of cruise

Walter Davis, fall 1932. The September police circular advised that he might have lost weight during his time on the lam, and the suit's baggy fit suggests he had. (Author's archive)

ships. Of course, he probably would have been knowledgeable about departure times if just weeks earlier he had figured that Europe offered the best solution to his dilemma.

Bogans was the only person with whom my grandfather had any meaningful, face-to-face contact that summer and fall. Hotel staffers considered him the "perfect guest" because he paid his bills in cash and on time and never made a fuss. They often ran into him because he frequently went out on walks all over the city, and when they saw him they tried to cheer him up. Likewise, guests there knew him as a "man with a haunted look." Throughout his stay, he kept to himself and never spoke to anyone unless first addressed. But with his driver, Walter was uncharacteristically chatty. He gave Bogans financial advice, warning him against investing in first mortgages—the best mortgages in which to invest and the bread and butter of the soundest building and loan associations—steering him instead toward government bonds. It likely helped to forge something of a bond between them that Bogans was from a solid family. His uncle worked as a sales manager at an insurance firm in Chicago, so Walter could have talked with him about life insurance. The fact that Bogans also had spent time in Europe during the war meant that the two men could talk about their impressions of life abroad.[13]

My grandfather described himself, or the man he was impersonating, as a retired lawyer from Cincinnati, and on more than one occasion he boasted that he had enough money to last him the rest of his life. Bogans, who noticed that his boss's left-hand coat pocket always looked to be full of money, believed this to be true. Walter also made a point of emphasizing that a friend with whom he said he sometimes met was an old college chum of his, although Bogans never saw this alleged friend.

In many respects, Walter's narrative of this man's life as a successful, college-educated lawyer matched the life he had wanted for himself. Curiously, he never mentioned having a wife, a daughter, or, for that matter, a mistress. There was one woman in his story—his mother, whom he claimed lived in Bermuda with her second husband. He would be living with her, he explained, were it not for his stepfather, whom he apparently disliked. Impersonating a bachelor from Cincinnati lessened the possibility Bogans might ever link him to the missing Colorado banker. But one wonders if remaking himself into a single man may have also reflected his weariness with romantic entanglements. As for his stepfather, perhaps he was a stand-in for Walter's real-life brother Roy, who had taken on the role of the family patriarch after their dad's death.

My grandfather may have been a lone wolf, but life as a fugitive was largely solitary and offered little by way of pleasure. He was especially lonely for his wife and daughter, but communicating with them was dangerous. Nonetheless, he began to telephone Lula in early August, about a month after she returned home. The calls became more frequent when he was back in the city. Once or twice a week he ventured into a drugstore in the Murray Hill district and called her from a phone booth there. While he was traveling in July and August he had posted letters to her, but once he was back in New York he had to abandon conventional letter writing. Aware that the authorities were on the lookout for any communication that would reveal his whereabouts, he developed an alternative method of staying in touch.

On three occasions that fall he visited the nearby branch of Brentano's bookstore, at Fifth Avenue and 27th Street, and on each visit he purchased at least one book. (His choices were eclectic: *Nobody Starves*, Katherine Brody's proletarian novel about striking Detroit autoworkers; British novelist Warwick Deeping's *Smith*; a book of sophisticated cartoons entitled *Virgins in Cellophane*; *New York: The Wonder City*, an elegant book with photographs of many of the city's best-known buildings; and *Poems That Have Helped Me*.) Each time he asked the store to mail the book, first class and special delivery, to his wife in Colorado Springs. Walter then accompanied the clerk to the mail department and waited while the book was wrapped and prepared for shipping. He made one further request—that the sales clerk paste a small card, which Walter himself provided, on the inside cover of each book. At least one sales clerk found his attentiveness unusual, but he attributed it to the fact that the method of shipping was both involved and expensive. If Walter got letters to Lula this way, it was trickier for her to get letters to him. However, beginning sometime in November Lula reportedly mailed letters to him, using the address "William Arnold, General Delivery, Yonkers, New York." Bogans drove him to the Yonkers post office twice a week. Walter followed the same routine each time he was dropped off there. Although the weather had already turned cold, he removed his muffler and overcoat upon exiting the car, as if to signal his arrival to someone.

As winter began to set in, Walter weighed his options. He told Bogans he was thinking of spending the winter in Agua Caliente, a gaming resort that had opened in Tijuana, Mexico, in 1927. Agua Caliente attracted Americans looking to gamble and drink, and its visitors included mobsters as well as Hollywood stars. "Where the rainbow ends" (and, by inference, the proverbial pot of gold awaited) was how the resort billed itself. What drew my grandfather to it, besides the weather, was that, as its advertisements stressed, passports were not required. He planned to travel to Agua Caliente by train, but he promised Bogans he would advance him money so he could drive across the country to meet him there. Then, sometime in March, he would depart Mexico for Los Angeles, he told his chauffeur.

Leaving the city he loved doubtless had something to do with the cold weather, but Walter was also growing more anxious. Certainly by October he knew about the wanted poster that featured his picture. He knew it contained a veritable laundry list of his habits, traits, and idiosyncrasies. Practically everything about him—from his prodigious consumption of apples and his sartorial preferences to his health problems and peculiar posture—was noted. That degree of detail would have required the cooperation of colleagues, friends, and perhaps even family members, which would have added to his uneasiness. Most nerve-racking of all was the fact that the poster featured that enticing $1,000 reward.

Walter was right to worry about the wanted poster, which by late September was making the rounds of police departments, newspapers, and detective magazines.[14] Walter often walked in the park adjacent to his hotel. Manhattan's only privately owned park, Gramercy Park was—and is—off limits to the general public. As a resident of the Parkside, he would have had a key to the park's gates. It would seem that police detectives, or at least two such detectives, had ways of accessing the park, too. And so it happened that one day in October two detectives and my grandfather were walking at the same moment on the park's bluestone paths. The detectives appear to have been enjoying a stroll, but soon they found their attention drawn to the well-dressed middle-aged man walking ahead of them. He was not the type of man who would normally arouse suspicion, but why was it, they wondered, that he kept looking over his shoulder in their direction? Each time he turned his head, he gave them more time to scrutinize his face. "That bird thinks someone is looking for him, all right," muttered one to the other. Without anything more than his twitchy nervousness to go on, they shelved the idea of questioning him. In that neighborhood of well-heeled residents the presumption of innocence carried considerably more weight than in other parts of the city.[15]

If he was aware of the detectives that October, and it seems he may have been, the encounter doubtless further rattled him. Of course, being chauffeured around the city diminished the likelihood that he might be recognized. Maybe the dark glasses that he began wearing in mid-November helped in that regard. Staying in his room and rarely venturing outside would have maximized Walter's chances for freedom. But the only way he could relieve the feeling of claustrophobia that came with being cooped up in his hotel room was to take long walks, which he did each day. This was risky, as were his trips three or four times a week to the newsstand at 42nd Street and Sixth Avenue. There he purchased the *Denver Post*, as the police circular promised he would, and the *Kansas City Star*. Self-deluded though he could be, he would have understood the precariousness of his freedom.

However, there was no way that my grandfather could have known just how contingent his present circumstances were. It turns out that the detectives who had spotted him that October day in Gramercy Park read detective magazines. Not long after Walter crossed their radar one of the detectives recognized the "nervous man of Gramercy Park" in the pages of his favorite detective magazine. True, the man in the photograph looked unruffled and confident in contrast to the worried man they had spied, but the faces matched up. Now it all made sense: the man's backward glances, anxious face, and palpable unease, so out of place in that little island of tranquility. It was uncanny, the detective thought, how well the description of the fifty-one-year-old fugitive tallied with the man they had recently seen. He would be well dressed, the write-up promised, and living in a good hotel or apartment building, but he would also appear anxious, and he would likely look haggard, and noticeably slimmer than his given weight.

On Friday, December 9, Walter sat down at his desk in the Parkside and composed what was, for him, an unusually long letter. That night most New Yorkers were caught up in the drama of a projected snowstorm that made the front page of the *New York Times*. A lot was riding on this storm, the first of the season. While holiday shoppers and store operators hoped the storm would fizzle out, the fifteen thousand unemployed men who stood ready to clear the city's streets and roads prayed for a blizzard and the opportunity to finally earn a dollar or two. Snow was not on Walter's mind, however. He began this letter to Lula by offering her financial advice that managed to be both exceedingly precise and curiously opaque, rather like that telegram to Dorothy in June. He identified most of the people he mentioned by initials—initials that would have made sense to Lula but to few other people. He suggested she approach either Roy or some other man whom he identified only by initials, and to say that a friend had lent her $3,500 and had requested in return a trust deed for their Tejon Street house. After giving her exact instructions about trust deeds and insurance policies, he warned her to be careful about what she signed.

The letter then turned shambolic as he lurched from one topic to the next. Proclamations of love collided into possible business maneuverings and stark warnings about others, which then gave way to dark musings about his situation. He accused Roy of "always grinding some ax for himself" and of having "some crooked slant on things I have." She should not trust him "an inch." There was only one man he seemed at all inclined to trust, but he admitted he had no idea how he felt about what he called "the whole matter." Bottom line: "There isn't a man with sense back there." He returned to this theme in the next paragraph. She should expect that people back home "will misquote your every word and misinterpret every wink of your eye." But if others were untrustworthy, Walter was himself an unreliable narrator of his own recent past. Although he had been no further west than Akron, Ohio, he claimed that he had nearly suggested they meet up when a recent trip took him close to Colorado Springs.

Much of the letter concerned their future. Should Lula wait to join him until Dorothy (or "Charlie," as he called her) and her fiancé, Dewey, were settled together? He emphasized that the only reason he allowed Lula to stay in Colorado Springs was because of their daughter and the fact that she was not yet permanently settled. "A lot of angles," he mused. He wrote of how unbearable it was for him to have to wait for her, and then he turned self-pitying:

Am just marking time. Have never been to a stage show. Have never listened to a radio. Can't stand music. You know I am terribly in love with you, honey darling, and as sentimental as a kid where you are concerned, and music, cannot endure it.

Am living so simply. Spending so very little. Keeping it until you and I can enjoy it together. I can do little except work, read, walk. I do not drink and you can buy whiskey for $2 a gallon. Everybody drinks; not for me though. *Worry worry worry* about you and drinking wouldn't help.

The plan, to the extent that any emerged from the letter, was that whenever she was ready to join him, he would tell her where he was and they would reunite. All he wanted from the house, he said, were pictures, unmounted, of her and Dorothy. Finally, he encouraged her when she was feeling blue to remember "the millions who were out of work and destitute." After all, he reminded her, "we could have more to be unhappy about than we have." He added a postscript of sorts, apologizing for a letter that was "disjointed and badly written." However, he explained, "it is difficult to write and want to put down things which you can not." [16]

The following day he stopped by Brentano's again and purchased *Flowering Wilderness*, part of John Galsworthy's *Forsyte Saga*. For the fourth time he followed the clerk to the shipping department and arranged for his letter, neatly folded into an envelope, to be pasted inside the book's front cover. In a departure from his normal protocol, he requested that the package be addressed to Walter Clyde Davis at 1628 N. Tejon Street, Colorado Springs.

There was a snowstorm that weekend, but the much-anticipated blizzard never materialized, and on Sunday Walter headed out again with Bogans. Maybe the snow got in the way of a longer drive, because at about two o'clock Walter asked to be dropped off at the corner of 38th Street and Sixth Avenue. As much as he disliked the cold, he disliked being in his hotel room more. And the city, heavy with whiteness, was beautiful. After a lengthy walk, he entered the hotel lobby. As he waited for the elevator, two well-dressed men approached him from behind. "Are you Davis?" one of them asked. Slowly Walter turned around and faced them. Perhaps he remembered the detectives from that day in the park. "I'm your man," he said, nonchalantly. "He didn't turn a hair," one of the detectives observed. "I've handled a lot of cool fellows in my time," said Detective Dominick Pape, "but this Davis fellow is just as cool as any of them."

Questioned about where all the money was, he shrugged. The $200 he had on him was all he had left, "every cent in the world. I was going to surrender the next day or so," he said, "because I'm just about broke." He claimed he had been on the verge of turning himself in more than once. He quickly clarified that although he was without money on him, he did own $600,000 worth of real estate in Colorado, where his family was keeping several million in safekeeping for him. When the detectives asked him how much money he had stolen, he maintained his innocence. All of his troubles stemmed from a misunderstanding. When they pressed him, he clammed up and refused to talk anymore without legal representation. He then bragged about his lawyer daughter.

The detectives took him to the 22nd Street station, where he was booked. He was allowed a phone call, and he rang up Lula. Rather than tell her that he was in police custody, he said only that he was considering turning himself in. Before ringing off, he told her she was his one and only true love. When the police placed him in a cell they thought he seemed relieved to have been nabbed and almost eager to return home. Maybe the police were fooled by how upbeat my grandfather seemed or maybe he slipped the detectives some cash, but Walter was allowed to enter his jail cell without removing his silk tie. Later it was explained that the police extended him this courtesy because he was a banker. But according to established police policy, all prisoners were, without exception, meant to be relieved of belts and ties.

Once my grandfather was in his cell with the door locked, he turned gloomy. Whatever relief he had felt about no longer having to outsmart the police and about being able to focus on something other than all the angles of his predicament vanished once he was behind bars. Maybe the visceral reality of incarceration was too much for him. For most of that evening and night he sat on his cot. He appeared neither cool nor relieved. After all, there was a reason he had left Colorado, and six months later the situation had not improved. Would he be able to convince anyone besides his wife and his daughter that his problems were the result of a misunderstanding? More to the point, would a jury believe him? If Fred Bentall with his pint-sized association had had the book thrown at him, what might happen to him when he stood trial? He had read about the angry crowds at Sharer's trials and at the Depositors' Committee meetings. He also knew that many townspeople imagined that he was the master swindler behind the wrecking of all their associations. A successful appeal might take years.

I suspect that foremost in his consciousness that night was his family. In his letter to Lula he had said he was living simply so that they could enjoy the money together. But if he still had some part of the money cached away somewhere and it was discovered by the police, it would become part of the association's assets. Unless he had somehow managed to communicate to his family the whereabouts of the money, it was useless to them, no matter how big his stockpile. And then there is the possibility that he had told the police the truth and that he really was down to his last $200 of cash. All of these scenarios were equally dire for his family. How would his wife and daughter fend for themselves in the midst of this brutal and seemingly endless depression?

It seems unlikely that suicide had not already figured in Walter's deliberations long before he entered that jail cell. Two people who had contact with him that June before he left Colorado thought it quite likely he would end his life. "If they ever find him," Eva had told the press, "they'll find him dead." His lawyer, Bernard Seeman, told an employee of the City not to be surprised if his boss killed himself. And then there was the wanted poster, which said quite plainly, "Check bodies of all persons found dead."[17]

How likely is it that a man facing a $1.25 million shortfall, someone who had amassed over half a million dollars' worth of universal life insurance, had not considered suicide? And how could killing himself not have occurred to my grandfather when stories of suicide filled the newspapers? That year saw the high-profile suicides of millionaires George Eastman of Kodak and Ivar Kreuger, the match baron, not to mention those of many stockbrokers, businessmen, and professional men. That April, while Lula was staying at the Waldorf Astoria, the head of several large real estate corporations committed suicide while lodging there. The note he left behind read, "To whom it may concern, can't stand it any longer." And it wasn't just stockbrokers diving out of skyscrapers. The papers contained stories of unemployed and underemployed working people who found that they, too, could stand life no longer.[18] There is no evidence that shame figured in my grandfather's calculations. Maybe it was expedience, knowing that life would become a lot less bearable for him and everyone around him if he returned to Colorado.

That night Walter sat on his cot, stared at his cell door, and focused on another angle. Although money was doubtless part of his calculation, this time the angle involved inches and knots and bars. As it happened, there was a rowdy, noisy prisoner at the end of the corridor and the guard on duty that night walked down the corridor several times to shut him up. When he passed Walter's cell at 3:00 a.m. he saw him sitting on the edge of his cot staring ahead. But at 3:20 a.m. when he again walked past his cell the guard noticed that his prisoner seemed to be standing upright, pressed against the bars and steel shield on the lower half of the cell door. His fingers were gripping the upper part of the bars. The guard, believing that he was staring moodily at the wall, yelled, "Don't ride the door."

The policeman assumed his reprimand would have sent him back to his cot, but Walter was still leaning on the cell door when he passed him again. This time, the guard said, he realized that the prisoner's eyes were glazed and that his tie had been secured to an upper cross bar. The cells in the 22nd Street station did not offer an accommodating space for hanging oneself. When the guards opened his cell door they saw that only two inches stood between Walter's feet and the floor. My grandfather's heart was still beating faintly, and the police emergency crew thought there was a chance he might live. They brought in a doctor from St. Vincent's Hospital, and for nearly two hours they struggled to revive him. He never regained consciousness.

7

Orphans in the Storm

Hugh Harper was the first to receive the call about my grandfather's capture. The police chief could not take credit for his arrest, but at least he could be the one leading Colorado's most hated man, in handcuffs, off the train. Eager to bring him to justice, he was already on his way to New York when news of the arrest began to circulate in Colorado Springs. Lula learned of it from a local reporter and Eva from a New York City policeman. But most residents who got wind of his arrest that evening did so on Walter Winchell's nationally syndicated radio show. Immediately, skeptical callers, anxious for verification, flooded the switchboard at the *Gazette* and *Telegraph*. By the time the morning paper hit the newsstands and Harper got off the train in New York City Walter was already dead. For anyone who dreamed of a satisfying trial in which justice was served and the hidden money recovered, news of his suicide was disappointing. The boldface headline "Crime Doesn't Pay," accompanied by visual proof—photographs of him looking formidably composed before the scandal and emotionally shredded after his arrest—must have provided little solace.[1]

In the days following his suicide the authorities behaved as though they thought closure on the affair was just around the

Colorado Springs police chief Hugh Harper wielding an automatic as his colleague, inspector Irvin Bruce, looks on. "Manhunter" Harper counted among his close friends J. Edgar Hoover, the chief of the Bureau of Investigation (later renamed the Federal Bureau of Investigation). (Courtesy of the Irvin "Dad" Bruce Collection, the Pikes Peak Library District, MSS 0159)

corner. Reverting to their original hypothesis, they now said that Walter had absconded with anywhere from $250,000 to $500,000 in negotiable bonds and cash. They insisted he had stashed it somewhere. When reporters asked Harper if it wasn't true that upon his capture in New York Walter had claimed that the only cash he had left was $200, the chief smiled broadly. "We'll see about that," he said. Receiver Fertig was also optimistic, predicting that

DP Dec. 19, p.1 (72)

Pricemarks of Crime,

written by conscience, were stamped upon the face of Walter C. Davis as he faced the New York police camera after his arrest Sunday. Study these two portraits of this man who hanged himself rather than return to face depositors of the City Savings Building & Loan association. At the left is Davis, the successful man of finance, sleek, assured, well-groomed, self-confident. At the right is Davis, the trapped fugitive. Notice the sagging mouth, the flabbiness of cheek and chin, the dull, beaten eyes. Six haunted months worked this change. Crime never pays.

KEYS FOUND IN DAVIS' EFFECTS
MAY LEAD TO HIDDEN FORTUNE

Banker Who Hanged Self in Jail Believed to Have Taken $250,000 When He Fled From Colorado Springs—Keys May Be to Deposit Boxes.

The *Gazette* ran the same two photos with similar commentary two days later. (*Denver Post*) with nearly a quarter of a million dollars of life insurance coming their way, depositors would see a 13 percent dividend before much longer.[2]

No matter how sanguine the authorities were about the case, my grandfather's 3,600 depositors remained apprehensive. To begin with, more than a few of them doubted that the man who had committed suicide in the 22nd Street police station was actually Walter Clyde Davis. Six months earlier a C.W. Davis had killed himself in a Long Beach, California, hotel, and at the time the authorities suspected the dead man was Colorado's most wanted man. Some might have wondered whether he had tried to stage the suicide so that his family and depositors could collect the insurance money while he remained free. There were now so many rumors swirling about that when Harper visited the New York City morgue he arranged for Walter's corpse to be removed from its casket and photographed. Fingerprints were taken as well. Partly this was to ensure proper documentation for the insurance companies, but it was also to head off any rumors that he was still alive. Yet those rumors had staying power. Long after my grandfather died, Harper said that the police continued to receive "hot tips" about the whereabouts of the "loan baron swindler."[3]

People's suspicion that Walter Davis had put one over on everyone, that he had escaped to that port of missing men, was fueled by broader revelations about scandals in the banking industry. Nothing would do more to burnish bankers' reputation for greed and corruptibility than the spring 1933 hearings of the Senate Committee on Banking and Currency, better known as the Pecora Committee. Tasked with investigating the causes of the stock market crash, the committee uncovered a jaw-dropping amount of financial dubiousness and wrongdoing.[4] Hidden bonuses, exorbitant salaries, and unpaid personal income taxes—all of it turned out to be business as usual among America's highest-profile and most respected bankers, including Charles E. Mitchell of the National City Bank (today's Citibank) and J.P. Morgan Jr. of the House of Morgan. Mitchell and other top officers at National City took $2.4 million in interest-free personal loans from the bank in order to help them ride out the stock market crash.[5] Commenting on the country's bankers, the *Denver Post* suggested that "if the senate committee can find one who has been paying income taxes the last few years, that will be real news."[6] Another newspaper editor spoke for many when he claimed, "The only difference between a bank burglar and a bank president is that one works at night."[7] In his inaugural address, President Roosevelt made a point of condemning bankers, those "unscrupulous money changers."[8] This was the reputation of Walter Davis: just another "bankster."[9]

In the wake of Davis's death the press put out contradictory reports about his intentions and state of mind, but all were in agreement that the disgraced banker had chosen to kill himself because of his overpowering shame about having looted his business. The police offered corroborating evidence from his Gramercy Park apartment, where they found a gun and various powders, two of which were said to contain poison.[10] And yet it was equally likely that, for Walter, suicide meant avoiding jail and ensuring Lula and Dorothy an insurance payout that would make them financially secure. It also permitted dividend payments hefty enough to blunt the anger of his depositors, and hence further protect those close to him.[11]

Walter's funeral was a private affair, held at the family's home. Pallbearers included men with whom Walter had done business over the years: neighbor and lawyer Clyde Starrett, who had recently been elected district attorney; Mayor George Birdsall, the co-owner of the town's major car dealership; the Northwestern Mutual Life district manager; the owner of a title and abstract company; the president of a local paint supply company; and the family physician, Dr. Peter Hanford. Conspicuous by their absence as pallbearers were Walter's three brothers. He was buried at Evergreen Cemetery and, although the press did not report it, without a gravestone. The next day the *Denver Post* observed that at the same time that Walter's body was being lowered into the grave, authorities in New York were opening a safety deposit box that he had rented there. Instead of the hundreds of thousands of dollars and bonds they had hoped to find inside it, they found his out-of-date passport and two silver mementos of little value. Even in death, the *Post* writer remarked, Walter Davis seemed to "get a laugh on the authorities."[12]

The search for the money continued to unfold on a national stage. Intensifying the urgency of the search was the news that after the authorities sold his two Packard automobiles to satisfy his debts, Walter's estate amounted to $485, the value of his Cadillac.[13] Every time the authorities thought they had found a promising safety deposit box they came up empty-handed. As for all the keys the authorities confiscated from his New York hotel room and his Springs office, they matched no bank boxes. With headlines in the local dailies such as "Search for Davis's Box Nears Crisis," Harper suddenly decided that Fertig, an insurance broker with no law enforcement experience, should really be in charge of searching for the hidden treasure. The conflict was resolved when the Justice Department, agreeing with local authorities that federal laws had been broken, came onboard. The very next day it was announced that J. Edgar Hoover's Bureau of Investigation (later renamed the Federal Bureau of Investigation or FBI) would be taking over the investigation. Careful to emphasize Harper's important spadework, the article in the *Gazette* declared the "worldwide secret organization of the federal government has started the machinery in motion which eventually is certain to uncover for the defrauded depositors the stolen fortune which Davis is known to have concealed." It also warned readers that there would likely be little news in the weeks ahead because the bureau did not publicize its efforts.[14]

In the immediate aftermath of Walter's suicide the authorities kept very little from the press. However, there was one item they did keep from reporters. What went unreported is that local authorities and Colorado's attorney general believed they had enough evidence to move forward with charges of mail fraud against Lula. Much of the correspondence between the authorities that is included in my grandfather's FBI file concerns Lula's culpability. The Brentano's package containing the December "code letter" and the discovery that Walter had communicated with Lula several times using this method rekindled their suspicions. The telephone company records indicating that the couple had also spoken on the phone a number of times from August onward did not help her cause.[15]

In their view the most persuasive evidence against Lula was her November 1931 withdrawal of $10,000 from an account she and Walter shared at New York's Bowery Savings Bank. She put $500 of the money in their safety deposit box and took the remainder of it—in the form of a check—with her to Colorado Springs. Harper and Fertig were convinced that for anywhere from two to six years Walter had used Lula as a courier for transferring money and securities belonging to the association to New York City. By late November 1931, with depositors pressing him hard for money, they reasoned, he sent Lula to New York to retrieve some of that money. Perhaps Lula was his courier, but he had been with her in New York just weeks earlier. Why hadn't he withdrawn it himself?

In the wake of his suicide and with Lula in the authorities' crosshairs, Eva Terry, the woman whom the authorities and the public once regarded as Walter's key accomplice, began to recede from the narrative. At first the press hounded her. Once reporters learned of Walter's suicide they descended upon her uncle's home. Her aunt Hattie met them on the porch, and after enduring a fusillade of questions she said, "The lies they have told about her. It would be different if the girl had been implicated. We can say nothing." Eva's faint voice was then heard from inside the house. "Shut the doors," she told her aunt. By the afternoon Eva modulated her response, calling the offices of the local paper to say that she would cooperate in any way to help the authorities solve the mystery of the missing money. But the police finally began to believe what Eva had been saying all along, and moved on. The embezzlement charges that the DA had filed against her were quietly dropped. It would take another four years, but the authorities ended up even returning to Eva the ring and $3,000 that they had once claimed were property of the depositors.[16]

I am not sure that either my mother or my grandmother understood that the authorities considered Lula their prime suspect, but surely they could feel the press turning against her. Walter had not helped matters for his family by boasting to the New York police that his relatives were keeping "three or four million dollars" for him so that he would be "well taken care of" upon his return to Colorado.[17] Lula's unwillingness to talk to the press worked against her, too. Asked to comment on her husband's arrest, she demurred. "I've got nothing to say. What is there for me to say?" she asked. The following day the paper published its usual headshot of Lula with the censorious caption, in bold print, "Refuses to Talk."[18]

Lula would learn that plenty of people expected that at last she would have something to say. But she stayed silent, and worse, I suppose, she conducted herself with the sort of brisk efficiency not normally associated with a grieving widow. Less than two weeks after Walter's funeral, readers of the local dailies learned that she had retained a lawyer to help sort out her finances. This move worried depositors who feared it indicated that she might challenge her husband's redistribution of insurance monies, which would slow down and might even jeopardize the disbursement of that promised first dividend payment.[19]

Lula did retain a lawyer, but not one in Colorado Springs, where, my mother maintained, no one was willing to represent the family. They turned to the brilliant and controversial Denver lawyer Horace N. Hawkins. Known as "Colorado's Clarence Darrow," Hawkins had been active in the fight against Colorado's Ku Klux Klan, and he had represented the United Mine Workers during the deadly strike in Ludlow, the site of the 1914 massacre of striking workers and their families. Hawkins had not made his name as a criminal lawyer, but perhaps the Depression, which was hard on even very talented lawyers such as Hawkins, led him to take their case. A year later he represented the trio of accused embezzlers in the Railway Savings Building and Loan case.[20]

On January 5, 1933, just three weeks after Walter's death, Hawkins met for the first time with the authorities. He must have realized that they were contemplating filing charges against Lula. Afterward he wrote to my mother, whom he called his "junior counsel," and asked her to provide him with a complete list of the family's travel from as far back as she could recall. Fertig and Harper were none too happy to be going up against Hawkins. In a letter to J. Edgar Hoover, Harper described Hawkins as a "high class trial lawyer with a high standing at this bar." He had "the reputation of being very smooth," he added.

As the search for the missing money floundered, the police started playing hardball with Lula and Dorothy. That May they questioned the family's former laundress, Lillian Ferguson. Had she been at Walter's funeral? Had she noticed the delivery of a package from Chicago? Had she or the woman who was then working as the family housekeeper, Ruie Stewart, lost money in the City's crash? And did Dewey Sample, my mother's fiancé, sleep over when he was in town? Apparently they were considering charging Lula with running a lewd and disorderly house. Then, that spring, El Paso County convened a grand jury to investigate, among other issues, the B&L scandal. Lula was not brought before the grand jury, but Jim Fleming, the City's handyman, was hauled

Goes to Aid of Fiancee

DEWEY R. SAMPLE,
Student at the University of Colorado, who has dropped his studies to aid and comfort his bride-to-be, Dorothy Davis, daughter of Walter C. Davis, alleged embezzler and suicide victim.

Dorothy's fiancé, Dewey Sample, stood by her and Lula. However, my mother eventually called off their engagement. After working as a lecturer in the geology department at the University of Colorado in Boulder, Dewey found a permanent position in the office of the U.S. Geological Survey. He never married, and when Dorothy wrote him in 1945 to tell him of her imminent wedding, he wrote back to say she was the only woman he had ever loved. (*Denver Post*) before it and threatened with formal charges. Lula asked Hawkins to counsel Fleming's lawyer, which he did, and in the end the indictment was quashed.[21]

Receiver Charles Fertig also made it abundantly clear that he was not going to make Lula's life easy moving forward. He contacted those insurance companies holding policies—totaling $100,000—in which Walter had designated Lula the beneficiary, and told them they must hold off issuing her a payment. Immediately Fertig and Hawkins were at loggerheads, and so they would remain until that spring, when Fertig collapsed from nervous exhaustion, brought on, the dailies claimed, by the stress of untangling Walter's financial mess and grappling with angry depositors. Five weeks later he was dead. T.C. Turner, the receiver's lawyer, was appointed the City's co-receiver.[22]

Meanwhile, the depositors were convinced that Lula was holding up the insurance settlement that would allow the dividend disbursement to go forward. One depositor, an accountant with connections to *Common Sense Weekly*, phoned Lula that May to say that if an insurance agreement was not soon forthcoming he would go after her brother-in-law Roy with a gun. He promised to harm Lula and Dorothy as well, although he didn't spell out precisely how. It turned out that employees of the City (who were now working for the receivership) had been spreading the word that Lula was the one to blame for the delay in the payment of dividends to depositors.[23]

At the end of June the new receiver went on the offensive in an effort, it would seem, to force Lula to relinquish all claims for any bit of the insurance money. Turner filed three lawsuits against Walter's estate. One lawsuit claimed that between January 1926 and June 1932 Walter had drawn a salary of $27,582 from the El Paso Industrial Bank without it being approved by the company's board of directors. The second suit alleged he had done the same with Fleming and Company in the amount of $80,000 during the period between July 1927 and June 1, 1932. The final suit claimed that on June 1, 1932, Walter had helped himself to $30,000 belonging to the City and had deposited it in a safety deposit box in Denver for his own use. That same day he took another $30,000 from the City and with it purchased all of the capital stock of the El Paso Industrial Bank—another one of his financial entities—taking the stock in his own name. Turner was suing the estate for a total of $167,582.[24] In the end, he chose against moving forward with these lawsuits, and they went unmentioned in the press. Did Turner decide that he lacked sufficient evidence to prevail, or had he only ever filed suit to force Lula's hand?

On August 9, 1933, six weeks after Turner had filed those lawsuits and eight months after Walter's death, the two parties finally reached a compromise about the insurance. Accordingly, the City would receive almost $200,000, with the possibility of collecting $140,000 more on contested policies. In exchange for giving up all claims to shares of stock in all her husband's businesses, Lula was to receive $82,000 of the disputed life insurance money. She was also permitted to keep the house, which had always been in her name, and all its furnishings. Several items that had belonged to Walter but had been in the receiver's possession—an umbrella walking cane, a small revolver, a gold pin, sixty miscellaneous books, and a lady's wedding ring—were to be handed over to Dorothy. The agreement represented a compromise, with neither side getting all that each had wanted. Lula and Dorothy had hoped that some of the foreclosed property belonging to Fleming and Company might land in their hands, but the agreement mandated that they give up all such claims. With the equivalent of $1.5 million in today's terms going to Lula, it was an agreement that seemed to prove Horace Hawkins's talents as a negotiator. After all, Walter may have purchased and paid for those insurance policies, but he reportedly did so with money from the association.

The settlement offers us the best evidence of what Turner

believed he had on Walter and possibly Lula. It details Walter's "unauthorized" annual salaries—one at $5,000 and another at $16,000. Then there was the $30,000 withdrawal from the City that Walter made on June 1 before fleeing the Springs for New York.[25] Finally, the settlement also alleged that in October 1931, before leaving for New York, Walter arranged for Fleming and Company to execute a promissory note to him for $60,000 and another to Lula for $35,000. The loans were paid from proceeds of the sale of real estate belonging to Fleming and Company.

Without a doubt Walter's business maneuvers crossed the line ethically. Given Coloradans' antipathy toward B&L men, my grandfather surely would have been convicted had his case gone to trial. But the authorities had a mixed record when prosecuting cases of financial wrongdoing. Take New York's powerhouse banker Charles E. Mitchell. Senator Carter Glass damned "Sunshine Charley" as the banker most responsible for the stock market crash. Mitchell resigned his position, yet efforts to charge him with anything, including tax evasion, failed. He died some twenty years later an eminent Wall Street banker.[26] Mitchell's lawyer argued that the charges against his client were about "appeasing mob psychology," as though they stemmed entirely from prosecutorial overreach.[27]

Throughout the country the public did push prosecutors to go after bankers whose banks had failed. The problem for prosecutors was the inadequacy of the laws, which did not address a whole host of practices that should have been unlawful. For example, bankers routinely made loans to themselves and to friends and family. Prosecutors often charged bankers who made such loans with embezzlement only to have their cases crumble on appeal because such loans were not illegal.[28] When it came to B&Ls, the inadequacy and ambiguity of the laws governing the thrift industry further complicated prosecutors' efforts. One can see how this played out with the litigation involving Pueblo's Railway Savings B&L. At the midway point in this drawn-out case, it had already generated twenty-seven volumes and a one-thousand-page abstract. Over the years convictions against the Pueblans would be secured and then reversed (for failing to prove intent) before finally being reinstated. Such vacillations happened in Los Angeles, too. Early in the scandal, the *Rocky Mountain News* departed from many papers in editorializing that the B&L heads who were under fire acted within the law, but only because the "law is worse than useless."[29]

According to standard accounts, the Depression was the period when the thrift industry sloughed off the last vestiges of its past as an amateur, semi-philanthropic movement and professionalized itself.[30] In this it was aided by the federal government, which mandated a strict regulatory regime and established safeguards—a mortgage reserve bank, federal charters for associations, and a system of deposit insurance. Under the new regime, the central task of the thrift business would be residential mortgage lending, while banks would handle commercial lending, including commercial real estate lending. Thrift institutions would offer fixed-rate, long-term residential mortgages, financed through short-term passbook savings deposits, which were federally insured.[31] It is true that by 1934 businesses calling themselves "savings and loans," regulated and insured by the federal government, were starting up across the country—the result of a big push by the thrift industry's trade group. "Savings and loan" would become the standard locution throughout the country, as the industry moved with speed to rebrand itself.[32]

What these accounts typically fail to reckon with are all those building and loan associations that by decade's end were still in receivership and winding down their affairs, and all those that had avoided receivership but were barely hanging on. One lawyer claimed, with some justification, that in contrast to factories and banks, which "owed their salvation" to the federal government, pre-Depression B&Ls had been abandoned by the government like so many "orphans in the storm."[33]

B&L depositors rather than operators were the true orphans of this storm, and depositors of the City found themselves in a terrible predicament. At the time of the insurance settlement in August 1933, co-receiver Turner predicted that depositors would receive their first dividend payment within two to three months. However, for reasons unrelated to the insurance imbroglio, this was not to be. First of all, there was considerable legal wrangling in the state over whether the claims of those who maintained that they had loaned money to now-insolvent building and loan associations should take precedence over the claims of association shareholders. Ultimately, the courts ruled that everyone would have to suffer equally, but this took two years to resolve, during which time no dividends could be paid.

The more persistent obstacle in moving forward with dividend payments had to do with efforts to end the City's receivership. Not long after the courts had named Fertig the receiver of the City, a group of association members and unnamed outside "investors" whom they brought onboard tried to engineer the dissolution of the court-ordered receivership. The people behind this effort were more financially comfortable than many depositors, and they hired Judge John Little of the Depositors' Committee and the Taxpayers Association as their lawyer. They needed two-thirds of the City's membership to support their effort before the district court judge would approve the creation of a liquidation corporation, as had happened much earlier with Sims's association.

Advocates of liquidation maintained it would be a more "eco-nomical" and speedier way of terminating the business. There were some costs—property taxes, insurance, and upkeep—that a liquidation corporation could no more avoid than a receivership could. But the corporation planned to prioritize selling off all the City's property as quickly as possible. While this would necessitate selling the association's assets at a terrible loss, members would no longer be responsible for the taxes, insurance, and maintenance on these properties. On the other hand, if association-owned properties were rented, they were bringing in some revenue, and would do so until the receiver determined that the market had rebounded and the properties could be profitably sold.

Opponents of receivership argued that liquidation enabled members themselves to bear the brunt of the work, so association members would be spared the expense of paying receivers and their staff. It is true that these costs were considerable. During 1936 the cost of paying the City's co-receivers and the office staff came to $5,400, and that was nearly four years into the receivership.[34] Throughout the country people worried that those on the receivership's payroll would use it for their own personal profit, and some did. The lawyer for California's building and loan commissioner actually denounced "receivership racketeers."[35] The scandal in the Springs spawned no such "racketeers," but the handling of Pueblo's Railway crash was another story. There the judge actually appointed the association's lawyer, a longtime Democratic politician and one of the embezzling trio, to act as the association's receiver. After public outrage forced the judge to change course he appointed a wealthy businessman as its receiver, with a salary of $1,000 a month.[36]

Nonetheless, in contrast to a liquidating corporation, a receivership offered real transparency. Its records were a matter of public record, and there was court oversight. Moreover, if the receiver, lawyer, and staff were paid, it was because closing down these businesses required considerable work. By August 1934, the co-receivers of the City were working with twenty large boxes of depositors' claims. Tellingly, as late as November 1937 members of the Assurance, who had opted for liquidation on the grounds that it would be speedier and less costly, had yet to see a penny.

As it happened, this group of wealthier depositors of the City failed three times to reorganize as a liquidating corporation. Despite their failed efforts, a new organization calling itself the Colorado Springs Liquidation Corporation (CSLC) stepped forward and announced its intention to liquidate the association. The men behind the CSLC repeated the usual arguments about the costliness of the receivership model. They promised more generous and quicker dividend payments than was possible with the receivers, whose process, they argued, was slow and cumbersome and made more so by the courts. They also bragged that they had the financial backing of a number of unidentified "rich men." [37]

Many depositors and shareholders of the City were desperate. Those who were part of the Taxpayers Association were, as we have seen, suspicious of the state and its proxies—the court-appointed lawyers and real estate men who were serving as receivers and lawyers and allegedly draining the assets of their B&L. Originally there were reportedly 3,609 claimants of the City, with claims totaling $1,876,000.[38] However, the CSLC peeled away so many of them that before long it controlled $1,263,000—or two-thirds—of the claims. Individual claims that were assigned ranged from $1.94 to $6,000, but the greatest number by far were between $200 and $2,500. In October 1934, knowing that the receivers were contemplating making their first dividend payment, officials of the CSLC filed in district court a notice that any dividend money to claimants should be paid instead to the corporation on the grounds that it held 70 percent of the claims against the City.

Having seen the success of the CSLC, other companies and individuals now got into the act. It became something of a cottage industry in the Springs, as businessmen who had obtained these consents and agreements sold them to others. And so it was throughout America as businessmen bought up passbooks on troubled banks and B&Ls. This was, of course, the tactic that Henry Potter had tried against George Bailey. In some places newspapers even printed the weekly rates for buying and selling these passbooks. However, it would seem that elsewhere in America actual money was sometimes exchanged for passbooks, although the sum could be as low as 25 cents on the dollar.[39] Springs businessmen such as C.M. Marshall seem to have not even offered that much.

Among those who assigned their claims to Marshall was an elderly widow, Mrs. Newton Dotson, who lived in a North End bungalow. She was among the City's middle-class depositors. We know what happened in this case because Mrs. Dotson's daughter, who lived across the street from her mother, witnessed the sales pitch of one of Marshall's smooth-talking salesmen. In exchange for Mrs. Dotson's assignment the salesman promised to give her stock for the Colorado National Gold Company. He brushed off questions about the soundness of the company, assuring them that the company "shipped carloads of gold every day." She could count on obtaining 50 percent of her claim, he said. Mrs. Dotson's daughter believed he was running a scam, and she was sure that she had convinced her mother of this, too. She was so confident that her mother shared her view that she left her mother's home before the salesman had. When she returned she discovered that her mother had turned over her claim in exchange for Marshall's worthless stock. After Marshall had accumulated fifty-five of these assignments he sold them at between 10 and 15 percent of their face value of $39,565 to a man named I.J. Marker.

What brought Dotson's case to court was that she, like other victims of this scam, had received zero compensation for her claim. Now word was spreading that the improbable was happening: the receivers were finally in a position to deliver on Fertig's promise, and at a full sixteen percent. More and more people wanted out of these assignment agreements so they could take part in the dividend payment. And they were discovering that the CSLC had lied to them about being able to break off their agreements. Not only that, but all the talk about rich men being a part of the CSLC was a bunch of hooey. The corporation turned out to have no cash capital. Complicating matters further, many people were confused about what they had signed because they had never been given a copy of the agreement with the CSLC. Journalists who got hold of a copy of one of these agreements found that it promised the claimants nothing by way of remuneration. It wasn't just vulnerable elderly people or those with little schooling who were taken advantage of. A clerk working for District Judge Cornforth on these cases had himself signed over his claim.

When these cases first began working their way through the court system in spring 1935, three years after Ed Sharer was first on trial, it must have felt like déjà vu. Once again the courtroom was packed, full of desperate people. These consents and assignments created problems for everyone, and not just the depositors who had assigned their claims and now found themselves stuck in a legal limbo. The delays and confusion they caused—with the lawyer for the CSLC asking for delay after delay and then appearing in court without the requested documents—meant that even those who had held on to their claims had to wait longer than they should have for those dividend payments. In the end, Judge Cornforth was scathing in his criticism of those such as Marshall and Marker who had tried to circumvent the court-ordered receivership. Null and void was his judgment of the CSLC assignments, and many others, including I.J. Marker's.[40] He later said that in his sixteen years on the bench these assignment cases had proven the most troublesome cases of all.

Despite all the suffering they caused, for three long years the CSLC and its ilk were able to operate with virtually no interference. The one article in the local press warning depositors against assignment scams appeared in August 1932. In a front-page article, District Attorney John Meikle, at the urging of receiver Fertig, cautioned "B&L victims" that they should beware of "fly-by-night stocks and bonds salesmen," eager to lure them into assigning their claims. However, no one else seems to have spoken up, or if they did, the press ignored them. As best as I can tell, the city manager, city council, mayor, newly elected district attorney Starrett, and, for that matter, the Depositors' Committee were all silent.[41]

In California one finds much the same deplorable situation, as a very brisk trade in passbooks emerged there. However, in the Golden State the villains seem to have been associations in liquidation that still had considerable assets and had "pegged" the price of depositors' passbooks at half or less of their actual value. Distraught depositors found themselves forced by their circumstances to trade in their passbooks for a fraction of their original worth. However, they also pushed politicians to do something about this, and progressive Democrats took the lead. In January 1935 the state legislature held hearings to investigate ongoing fraud in the building and loan business. Before a crowd of five hundred, one association member spoke of "aged and destitute people selling their passbooks at 48 cents on the dollar when the association had 100 cents on the dollar in property and other assets."[42] This speaker may have been exaggerating the health of his association, but the investigating committee of the state assembly called the traffic in passbooks one of the "worst scandals" in the state's history. In May 1935 the Republican governor signed a bill designed to eliminate the trade in passbooks.[43]

What happened in California shows what could be done in a different political climate. Colorado boasted liberal Democrat Edward Costigan, who captured a Senate seat in 1930. Costigan promised voters a "new deal" in his Senate run, a full two years before FDR used the term.[44] But while Colorado's Republicans were in the doldrums between 1930 and 1938, the Democrats were deeply divided, with conservatives such as William (Billy) Adams and Edwin Johnson standing in the way of committed New Dealers like Costigan.[45] Democrats were likely too divided to stop the fraud in consents and assignments. After all, politicians of both parties had a long history of looking the other way when it came to regulating this industry. Their history of inaction meant that the laws and regulations governing B&Ls were a muddle—badly written and therefore poorly understood. Complicating matters further was that certain details, such as whether particular claims took precedence over others, had not been legally established, at least not beyond contestation. Shortly after Walter's suicide Colorado's attorney general announced that he had appointed a committee mandated to develop a system of penalties for lax B&L commissioners. Whom did he choose to chair the committee? Bernard Seeman, the lawyer who had represented both Walter Davis and the unscrupulous Pueblo B&L operators. No effective regulation was pursued by the state legislature.[46]

Colorado's failure to regulate the B&L industry in the first instance, along with its unwillingness to stop this business of consents and assignments, demonstrates something more fundamental than politicians' refusal to strengthen the state's regulatory machinery. In Colorado there was a determined opposition to regulation itself. How else can one explain the relative absence of public criticism of these consent and assignment schemes and the failure of successive district attorneys or anyone else to investigate them? Colorado Springs, like much of the West, was loath to erect or enact anything that might act as a roadblock to ingenuity and enterprise. For example, in May 1931, when the state legislature was debating changes in the laws governing B&Ls and the enactment of blue-sky laws to protect consumers against securities fraud, opponents characterized these bills as "destroyers and not builders."[47] It was a culture that encouraged ambitious men with entrepreneurial drive, and with predictable results when enterprise edged over into fraud, whether with the hustlers of the CSLC or with my grandfather and the rest of the local building and loan crew. Even the horror of dust storms was not at first enough to convince the farmers and ranchers of nearby Baca County, a hard-hit dust bowl county, to agree to a federal plan to control soil erosion. Farmers and ranchers there "preferred dealing with the problem individually."[48]

As an open-shop town, the Springs had become a place that fostered individualistic solutions rather than one where the working classes pulled together as a group. There was a broad consensus, stretching from the Chamber of Commerce to its opponent *Common Sense Weekly*, that unions were "rackets." When people did come together they usually did so in cross-class organizations such as the town's voluntary associations, lodges and clubs, and groups such as the Depositors' Committee and the EPCTA. In the end it was a culture invested in the idea of its own rugged individualism. Even the Depositors' Committee fizzled out when the Pratts left town. They did so shortly after J. Herbert Pratt, running as a Republican, lost the election as county commissioner and a scheme to keep *Common Sense Weekly* afloat unraveled. The Pratts had devised a subscription drive to keep the paper alive: contestants with the most renewals or new subscriptions were promised a "magnificent array of prizes and commissions" totaling $3,000. Their "rustling ability," readers were told, would determine their success. However, the drive came to an abrupt and mysterious end, reportedly because of a con man with extraordinary rustling ability.[49]

The El Paso County Taxpayers Association persisted, but not without internecine squabbling. By April 1934, a splinter group calling itself the Real Estate Owners Protective Association announced its intention to organize a special election, primarily to have the city entirely put on a "cash basis."[50] The Republican elite, too, was divided, but in the years ahead its members would pull together in an audacious effort to woo the U.S. military to the area. Among many other residents, however, the tradition of looking out for one's own interest was firmly established, which is why two-thirds of the City's members broke away from the receivership in order to cut their own deals. Over the decades it had become an individualistic culture whose valorization of free enterprise and rugged individualism inclined people to understand those in need as entirely responsibility for their own sad fate.

As the cases involving those consent agreements worked their way through the courts, the search for the missing money continued. In March 1935, after J. Edgar Hoover's men proved unable to uncover Walter Davis's hidden fortune, Scotland Yard was asked to scour the banks of London for it.[51] Nearly three years later the authorities remained convinced that Walter had absconded with a vast fortune, possibly as much as a half million. Was it the report of him with scads of securities practically falling out of his pockets at a doctor's office in Denver that persuaded them?[52] Could it have been the chauffeur's description of his boss cashing Liberty Bonds in banks as they traveled? Or was it his last letter to Lula, where he claimed he was saving all the money for when they could be together?

The mystery for me isn't what happened to the half million dollars. For twelve years he had offered inflated rates of interest, which meant that he had paid out $450,000 more in interest to depositors than their money had actually earned. Moreover, for some time at the City withdrawals had outpaced deposits. Then there was the fact that his investments were in the failing real estate market.[53] Seven years of extravagant living also made a dent, as did the insurance.[54] That said, Walter made substantial withdrawals—$90,000 for himself and $35,000 for Lula—in the eight months leading up to the collapse of his business. The mystery is what happened to *that* money.

The authorities continued their search for the missing money, but they abandoned their plan to file charges against Lula for mail fraud or for anything else. She escaped prosecution, but had Lula knowingly aided and abetted her husband's embezzlement? The woman who emerges in those telegrams and letters was certainly nobody's fool. She had worked by Walter's side when he was a loan shark, and her head was hardly buried in the sand when it came to his relationship with Eva. At the very least she knew her husband was capable of emotional dishonesty. And yet Lula seems to have never entertained the possibility that Walter was guilty. How else can one make sense of the fact that she pressed forward with the insurance claims and contested the ownership of properties belonging to Fleming and Company, all the while with the conviction that she was in the right?

Walter Davis believed in his own innocence and doubtless gave Lula persuasive explanations for his shortfall. Maybe he claimed that the inflated interest rates he paid depositors meant he now owed them nothing.[55] Or maybe he stuck to legalistic defenses of his business practices. In the end, he was ambitious and hard-driving, and there was no law against that. No matter how sharply the money had been earned, Lula and Dorothy believed it was his and theirs. My mother only ever said of his failure, "I felt so damn sorry for him."

Lula may not have been knowingly complicit, but her well-developed instinct for self-preservation sometimes did trump her truthfulness. There was the time in the summer of 1932 when she presented herself to the authorities as virtually penniless. Lula later revealed to her lawyer that she could have easily paid substantial insurance premiums to keep Walter's policies in force.[56] Thirteen years later, at the end of her life, Lula wrote daily letters from her hospital bed to Dorothy, who was then living in the East. In one such letter she voiced her apprehensions about having asked Jim Fleming, Walter's former handyman, to find a crucial bit of paperwork in her desk at home: "Of course, everybody is going to know all our business and all our house if I keep on out here." Yes, Lula had secrets.

Few residents of the Springs would have been surprised to learn that Lula had been less than totally honest with the authorities.

After the newspaper announced the terms of the insurance settlement, Lula found this letter in the mailbox:

> We will call at your???? home
> for the missing money and bonds
> also a part of the insurance money.
> will also visit your ????? attorney in Denver. *BE READY.*

It was signed, "The crowd of poor you owe."[57]

Among the depositors, the presumption that Lula, Roy, and Eva were all guilty died hard. For nearly a decade Roy struggled to keep his typewriter shop open. As for my mother, her most vivid memories of those times were of being "cut dead" on the streets and in the stores by people she had once counted as friends. After three years of feeling like a pariah she left town, not to marry her fiancé, Dewey, but to work as a journalist for the oil press bureau, first in Tulsa and then in Dallas. Likely Eva, who spent the rest of her life working as a stenographer and secretary in the Springs, was also threatened by depositors, especially after the press revealed the return of Walter's gifts to her. Remarkably, despite the snubs, the whispers, and the threats, all of the principals stayed put in Colorado Springs, the town where the daily paper predicted that in ten years' time the name of Walter Clyde Davis "would still arouse hatred and reviling."[58]

During the building and loan crisis the authorities, anxious to underscore the venality of the accused B&L operators, emphasized that it was indeed poor people who had been disproportionately victimized. Whether their concern was genuine or gestural, actual poor people would not find much sympathy or understanding during these years from officials at the city, county, or state level. Humiliation came with poverty and even (or perhaps especially)

```
                                    Colo, Spgs, Colo.

Mrs. Lula M. Davis.
City;
         We willcall  at your???? home for the missing money and bonds
also a part of the insurance money.

will also visit your????? attorney in denver. BE READY.
                                                        ----------

                        The crowd of poor you owe.
```

The letter was meant to be from the poor, but whoever sent this letter used good stationery that included an envelope with a gilt-edged flap. (Author's archive) with the programs meant to ameliorate it. This was certainly the case with old-age pensions, which my great-uncle Roy Davis helped to enact and the Pratts supported.[59] Historians estimate that in 1934, 50 percent of all elderly Americans lacked sufficient income to be self-supporting. In Colorado, the measure mandated that only citizens sixty-five and older who had resided in the state for at least fifteen years and whose homes were worth less than $1,000 were eligible. Yet in Colorado resistance to the law was substantial, with the *Gazette* opposing it and the statewide Federation of Taxpayers' Associations, of which the EPCTA was a member, fighting it all the way to the state supreme court.[60] In El Paso County payments came to less than $28 a month, an amount sufficient to arouse suspicions that some pensioners had misrepresented their circumstances. In March 1936, county officials dumped four hundred people from the rolls. Officials assured the press that this culling would be followed by a reinvestigation of blind pensioners and of those women receiving mothers' compensation. Their aim was to keep "an almost continuous check" on pensioners.[61]

As for those on relief—an even less "deserving" group—the scrutiny was perhaps even more intense. By Thanksgiving 1934, one-quarter of Coloradans fit this definition. The situation had not improved seventeen months later when L.G. Niles, El Paso County commissioner in charge of administering to the poor, declared that World War I veterans on the county welfare rolls who were due to receive bonus certificates would find themselves automatically dropped from the rolls.[62] Six months later, in January 1937, the *Gazette* acknowledged that relief did have its virtues—"homes kept intact, hungry children fed and clothed, jobless persons kept at work, and in the more material sense, of lasting civic improvements." However, the newspaper bemoaned what it called the "relief snowball," which it said had grown at an "appalling" rate. In less than four years the city went from having no relief program to being in the relief business to the tune of nearly $3.5 million.[63]

R—Denver: Partly cloudy and unsettled.

Seventy-Fifth Year; Founded

E 74; NO. 221   DENVER, COLO., WEDNESDAY, AUGUST 9. 1933   IN TWO SECTIONS—SECTION

DLE MEN TO GET FLOOD A

County Expects Them to Live on a Dollar a Week

Old age came to these people and the legislature of Colorado remembered them. The old-age pension law was passed. The state prepared to settle its obligation to its indi- and infirm old men and women. Life has been a series of sad episodes for them. Another cruel blow was dealt yesterday when county court granted them 34 a month on ch to live. Left to right: Andrew P. Anderson, Mrs. I. Zora Baldwin, John Naava and W. A. Shreve. Their faces show the typical lines of care and worry seen on the faces old men and women who jammed county court yesterday.

LORADO RAPS LCOVA PLANS

aska and Wyoming Join ainst Plea of Prosser and Hinderlider

ORGE SANFORD HOLMES
Washington Correspondent
INGTON, Aug. 8.—Colorado
thru Attorney General Paul
er and State Engineer M. C.
ider, presented a powerful
against unconditional ap-
of the Casper-Alcova project
ederal public works board.
rrow they will take up with
blic works administration what
lieves offers a practical and
ery solution of the whole in-
controversy, namely, federal
on of a storage dam at Tor-
Wyo., close to the Nebraska

proposal will be discussed with
. ld. Waite, deputy administra-
public works, with a view to
g the government that build-
reservoir would insure water
three states involved in the
Alcova row, guarantee the
ation sought by Colorado, pro-
e necessary amount for the

Court Exceeds Authority In Issuing Miserly Sums To Old Age Pensioners

Luxford Grants Only $4 Per Month to 55 Denver Residents, Claiming There Isn't Enough Money to Go Around

BY GENE CERVI

For more than eight years The Rocky Mountain News carried on a fight to bring about passage of an old-age pension law.

This campaign bore fruit in the last general assembly when a measure designed to care for the indigent aged became a law.

Yesterday an example of how Denver County administers this law—or rather—fails to administer the law—was given in county court by Judge George A. Luxford.

Fifty-five aged residents of Denver appeared before the court to be heard on their applications for the old-age pension.

Notwithstanding the fact it is mandatory upon the city to provide a living for persons who have reached the age of

Tent-Dweller Commits Suicide, Sums of Pension Low, A · 1 Wife

U. S. BOYCOTT IS CONSIDERED

Government May Withhold Contracts From Firms Not in NRA List

BY THOMAS L. STOKES
(United Press Staff Correspondent)
WASHINGTON, Aug. 8.—With-
holding of government contracts from
industries which refuse to adopt
President Roosevelt's voluntary blan-
ket code is being considered by Gen.
Hugh S. Johnson, national recovery
administrator.

Johnson said today he had discussed such a measure—which would

Labor has faced faster than
employers at the hands of NRA
to date, says an editorial on
Page 20.

be a "government boycott"—with several administration officials.
He has not made any final decision, but indicated this weapon would
be employed if necessary.
The government is now distribut-
ing valuable business in its public
building projects under the $3,300,-
000,000 appropriation by congress.
At the same time Johnson said

Denver Woman Faints, Forgets Husband, Child

Strange Case of Amnesia Caused by Worry Over Children, Say Doctors

BY JOHN C. POLLY

ONE of Denver's strangest
cases of amnesia, in which a
young mother fails to recognize
her husband or one-year-old
daughter, was revealed last night
at Denver General Hospital
where she was taken after faint-
ing on the street.

The victim of the attack of
amnesia is Mrs. Vivian Gdovian,
25, of 2550 16th st.

Physicians said the attack apparently was brought on by Mrs.
Gdovian's worry for more than
two years over the health of her
children. Usually amnesia is
caused by a blow on the head or
sudden shock.

Faints and Falls
To Pavement

Mrs. Gdovian left home last
night for a short walk on the
16th st. viaduct. Her husband,
Albert, remained at home with
the children, Betty, three, and
Elma, one. He expected his wife
to be absent only a short time.
After walking a few feet, Mrs.

The *Rocky Mountain News*, August 9, 1933.

The era's massive relief efforts troubled many people who worried that the "dole" would sap the self-sufficiency of recipients, who would grow lazy and dependent. "Chiselers," "shovel-leaners," and "bums"—these were just a few of the terms commonly used to disparage people on relief.[64] In the West, conservative Democrats attacked the New Deal. William B. King, Democratic senator from Utah, railed against such spending on the grounds that the rich didn't have enough money to support the poor. Moreover, he argued, relief was eroding the very individualism that had made the United States the "greatest republic in the world." In truth, even President Roosevelt was ambivalent about the welfare state being created on his watch. However, Republicans as a group hated relief, not only because they believed it was destroying individualism and industriousness but also because they believed its beneficiaries would vote Democratic.[65]

Colorado initially supported the Democrats, giving landslide victories to progressive Edward Costigan in 1930 and Roosevelt in 1932. Roosevelt even won traditionally Republican El Paso County in 1932 and 1936.[66] Over time ordinary Coloradans' opposition to the New Deal grew. In 1936, when failing health caused the state's liberal senator, Edward Costigan, to exit politics, Coloradans voted for conservative Democrat Edwin C. "Big Ed" Johnson, who had held the governorship since 1933. And in 1940 and 1944 Coloradans, in contrast to most of the nation, voted for Roosevelt's Republican rivals.[67] Throughout his presidency, the Colorado Springs newspapers, the *Daily Twins*, attacked Roosevelt as well as those benefiting from New Deal relief programs. In 1944 Big Ed Johnson went so far as call the New Deal "the worst fraud ever perpetrated on the American people."[68] For many Westerners, taking government aid was nothing less than "a confession of failure."[69]

Few people of means in Colorado Springs spoke out for the "economically damned" during the Depression. In January 1931, when a politically nonaligned group of unemployed men asked the local taxpayers' organization to go on record supporting a public works project for the unemployed, the taxpayers declined. At the meeting with the Organization of the Unemployed, some taxpayers attacked members of the group whom they claimed had turned down offers of employment in order to stay on relief—a sensible move, actually, given the difficulties in getting approved again for relief.[70] The taxpayers were not about to make common cause with people they regarded as rabble. They certainly were not going to meet with the local chapter of the Communist-led National Council of the Unemployed. The Colorado Springs chapter attracted 175 unemployed men and women to a planning meeting for a hunger march in Denver. Members of the chapter also went before the city council and demanded that it provide its unemployed with free water and electricity and enact nondiscrimination policies toward Spanish-speaking workers and "colored" workers.[71] There is no evidence those demands were taken seriously. When the group's leader appeared before the city council in 1933 to request a permit for a May Day parade, police chief Harper made it clear he would not tolerate an "organized communist demonstration" in the streets of Colorado Springs, certainly not one "planned by New York communists."[72]

There were other pockets of dissent, too. For a brief while the *Colorado Springs Independent*, the westside weekly and onetime KKK mouthpiece, became a surprisingly spiky left-wing alternative to the local dailies. The *Independent* had been an anodyne paper for some time. Its coverage of the B&L scandal had been subdued. But in the middle of the Depression, its editor took to denouncing not just Colorado Springs but capitalism as well. Week after week, the paper excoriated officials at the local Works Progress Administration (WPA) for the humiliating way in which they treated female relief workers. He attributed administrators' punitive policies to the town's history as a resort area, which meant that the city was skewed toward those who were somewhere on the spectrum between rich and comfortable. These people, argued the paper, were uniformly and tenaciously anti-union.[73] These were the people who controlled the Chamber of Commerce, which openly opposed relief, and its members were determined to keep the city's relief numbers down. The paper also blamed negative attitudes toward relief on the fact that the Springs was a city that lacked large industries and therefore lacked a substantial working class. In the beginning of 1937 the *Independent* was sold to a man who returned it to its bland ways.

By now, onetime members of the City with uncontested claims had received two dividend checks—one in August 1935 and the other in October 1936—amounting to 22 percent of their claims. A third payment of 9 percent went out the following November, so by the end of 1937 depositors had recovered 31 percent of their money. The assignment mess held up the checks, and so did the receivers' decision to hold off on selling the association's real estate assets until the market rebounded. As late as fall 1942, depositors were still waiting for the fourth and final dividend check of 10 percent. With that final payment they would have recovered 41 percent of their money.[74] The receivers for Railway Savings B&L had taken a different route, dumping hundreds of properties on the market at once, with disastrous consequences for Pueblo's real estate market. Going slowly rather than quickly unloading the association's holdings—136 of which were in Pueblo's already saturated market—meant that the City's depositors were forced to wait for that final dividend payment a full decade after the City had put a stop on withdrawals in the spring of 1932.

In the end, what helped some residents of the Springs hold on to their property was the Home Owners' Loan Corporation.[75] A New Deal agency, HOLC was meant to refinance home mortgages that were in default so that those holding such mortgages could escape the maw of foreclosure. Beginning in the summer of 1933, the

HOLC office in the Springs began converting first mortgages held by receivers of building and loan associations into HOLC bonds, with terms more favorable to consumers. As early as March 1934, the HOLC had authorized $260,000 in loans at 6 percent interest to 160 homeowners in the region. Two years later that number had grown to 684 homeowners, whose combined loans came to $1,202,739. By 1936, when the agency's active lending program ended, more than a million homeowners, accounting for roughly one-tenth of all mortgages across the nation, had been assisted by a loan from the HOLC.[76]

Even with the HOLC rescue effort, the fallout from the thrift industry's collapse was long-lasting and substantial. In Chicago, one HOLC study found that as late as 1940 only a sliver of the city's pre-Depression building and loan associations had survived, and most of those that had pulled through were in poor shape. Complicating any industry-wide recovery were lingering allegations of fraud, and not just in the scams involving assignments and passbooks. In the spring of 1937 the *Gazette*'s lead story concerned irregularities in the B&L business that had been uncovered by a special committee of Colorado's house of representatives. Once again there were calls for a grand jury investigation. And then there was the Railway B&L case, which kept turning up in the news like a bad penny. The lawsuit against the three Railway B&Lers was not resolved until 1942, a decade after it was initiated. The Supreme Court of Colorado upheld the Pueblans' convictions on charges of embezzlement. All of these stories kept alive the connection between building and loan associations and financial wrongdoing.[77]

In Colorado Springs, updates on pending dividend payments and on Ed Sharer's endless appeals kept the B&L scandal in the news most of the decade. The drama around Sharer was not resolved until April 1935, when the Supreme Court of Colorado reversed his convictions on forgery on a technicality. He had already been freed on $10,000 bond in November 1934, after having spent two and a half years in the county jail. No other charges against him were pursued, and he lived the rest of his life in Los Angeles.[78]

Another reminder of the industry's crookedness came on May 9, 1938, when the local press announced that Fred Bentall had been freed on parole. His release came nearly six years after his arrest and eighteen months after depositors received their final dividend check. A model prisoner, Bentall had been transferred early in his sentence to a low-security state reformatory, where he worked as a bookkeeper and later as a teacher. The B&L man's losses had been so large the authorities suspected him of having salted away association funds. The total disbursement to depositors amounted to 13 percent. Bentall's talk about devoting himself to paying back defrauded depositors proved to be just that.[79]

Understandably, people in Colorado Springs remained extremely wary of the industry, even the new federally chartered and insured savings and loans. The first such outfit to open up in the Springs called itself the Federal Savings and Loan Association. "It will be as different from those defunct associations," promised a spokesman for the Federal, "as a national bank is from a pawn broker's office."[80] It would be an old-fashioned mutual organization, he said, and he emphasized that it would not offer bloated interest rates and that all deposits, up to $5,000, would be insured by the federal government, just as with banks. Federal Savings and Loan, which opened its doors in 1934, grew slowly. As records of the HOLC reveal, people mistrusted these associations, even if the word "building" appeared nowhere in their name.[81]

In 1938 one HOLC official in Denver conducted an informal study in which he tried to gauge the "typical" attitude toward building and loan associations. Many thousands of people in the Denver area had been members either of Railway or of the Silver State Building and Loan Association, both of which had failed. The sixty-three people whom the official questioned held a variety of jobs, from office workers and salespeople to barbers. He also polled virtually everyone in HOLC's Denver office. What he discovered was that absolutely no one he surveyed saved in a building and loan. Nearly 70 percent emphasized that they stayed away from them because of negative experiences that they, their family, or friends had had during the meltdown. Many termed the whole business "crooked" and said that even with the guarantee of federal deposit insurance they would avoid thrifts at all costs.[82] A 1936 report, this one from the HOLC field office in Pueblo, reported "intense bitterness towards anything that smacked of 'building and loan'" and predicted that it would be a long time before that bitterness dissipated.[83]

That bitterness may not have entirely receded ten years later when *It's a Wonderful Life* was released. Hopes ran high for the movie—the first postwar Hollywood movie for both Jimmy Stewart and Frank Capra. For director Capra the movie was a chance to explore something more daring than the "Hollywood version of how life should be lived." Yet as production wound down, there were worries that Capra had produced too un-Hollywood a movie, and its release was scheduled for just before Christmas 1946. Releasing it during a time of holiday cheer failed to save the film. *It's a Wonderful Life* lost over a half million dollars at the box office and won no Oscars. The movie also attracted the attention of the FBI's Red-hunting Los Angeles field office, which believed its treatment of Henry Potter was meant to discredit bankers. It was, the FBI claimed, "a common trick used by Communists."[84] Discerning critics disliked the film, too, but on different grounds. "A figment of simple Pollyanna platitudes" was the *New York Times*' judgment.[85] The *New Yorker* found it "so mincing as to border on baby talk." As for audiences, it's hard to know whether they felt patronized by the ending, depressed by everything but the film's final eight minutes, or annoyed by the whole package. Perhaps the traumas of bankruptcy, bank runs, suicide, and war were too much a part of America's recent past for audiences to stomach the movie.[86]

It would take more than a decade before Americans once again began to trust the thrift industry. That they did owes a lot to thrift leaders who oversaw the creation of new federally chartered and insured savings and loans. Crucial to the eventual success of the thrift industry was the insurance offered by the Federal Housing Administration (FHA). With their own risks diminished, savings and loans attracted customers with mortgage loans that featured low interest rates of 4 percent to 5 percent and required as little as 10 percent down. These shifts ushered in an era of easy and inexpensive credit for many, one that made homeownership in many cases a better bargain than renting, particularly for whites. African Americans continued to face racial discrimination in the housing market, and savings and loans were sometimes part of the system of exploitation that entrapped black homebuyers.[87]

By 1950 savings and loan associations were the dominant provider of residential mortgage finance.[88] For nearly thirty years S&Ls performed well. Doubtless there were savings and loan men who, working with developers and lenders, used their positions to line their own pockets. That was the view of Richard Netzer, a professor of economics and prominent municipal finance expert. According to Netzer, even during the industry's so-called halcyon years S&L operators treated their businesses like veritable "honey pots." The thrift business, he argued, was full of "self-dealing, kickbacks, and other ways in which money collected from homeowners taking out mortgages was intercepted on its way to depositors."[89] However self-serving some of their operators' wheeling and dealing may have been, the industry was no longer beset by outright embezzlement and malfeasance. Indeed, savings and loan businessmen such as Los Angeles's own Mark Taper and Walter Ahmanson developed such solid reputations as civic leaders and philanthropists that their names today grace university buildings, theaters, and museums throughout L.A.[90]

———

As for Colorado Springs, conditions there during the Depression bordered on the dire. Cripple Creek gold mining briefly rebounded, but it would never again be the city's engine of growth.[91] By the end of the thirties my mother's hometown was little more than a "Depression-ridden resort town."[92] One resident recalled that by decade's end, with people leaving and nearly 20 percent of the city's housing stock vacant, it began to feel like a ghost town. Even the town's heartiest supporters knew that it could not depend solely on tourism for its survival. As war in Europe once again loomed, some of them set about reinventing the place. Aware of how lucrative military installations could be, they "decided to try to get something out of" that war.[93]

In courting the military, Colorado Springs boosters touted the area's ample sunshine and all its available land, some of it farmland that had gone dry and been abandoned as a result of the drought. They practically turned the city's two leading hotels—the Broadmoor and the Antlers—into "war facilities." Charles Tutt Jr., the son of Spencer Penrose's onetime business partner, helped to spearhead a group of boosters committed to luring the military there. The president of the Broadmoor Hotel, Tutt and his friends wined and dined the Army's top brass, who came to view the Springs as offering them an essential "time-out," where they could "get tight and tell their woes." Between 1941 and early 1942 the Army announced that Colorado Springs would be the location for Camp Carson and the Peterson Army Air Base. During the war more than a hundred thousand men trained at Camp Carson.

The town's courting of the military continued, and in 1950 the Air Force (now an autonomous branch of the armed forces) chose the city as the site for its Air Defense Command, now known as NORAD. The city's Chamber of Commerce helped to seal the deal by offering a shuttered airfield on attractive terms and by promising to build a thousand housing units for the needed workforce. Four years later the Springs was named the site of the future Air Force

Academy, in no small part because the state legislature appropriated $1 million to buy a huge parcel of land north of the city for its site. The military sector of the local economy was further solidified when, in the early 1960s, the Air Force opted to keep Fort Carson open. Twenty years later the Air Force "permanized" its presence in Colorado Springs when it chose it as the site for its Consolidated Space Operations Center, the unified United States Space Command, and the new SDI National Test Bed Facility.[94] By the 1980s, 60 percent of the Colorado Springs economy was tied to the military.[95]

Bolstering the city's economy further during the Cold War years were high-tech companies, many from California, that began relocating or opening facilities there. A big draw was the city's relative cheapness, the absence of unions, and its "tractable blue-collar work force."[96] Colorado Springs had been an open-shop town for decades, and in 1949 the city charter was even amended to bar the city from negotiating with labor unions.[97] The Springs became, as one study puts it, "an archetype of the new military-industrial city," or what the Chamber of Commerce preferred to call the "Space Capital of the Free World."[98] The city's dependence on the government did nothing to diminish its ideological commitment to free enterprise.

That free enterprise and anti-statism remained articles of faith in the city owed a lot to the grip the hard right had on the local media. In 1946 R.C. Hoiles, then the owner and publisher of California's right-wing *Orange County Register*, acquired the local daily, and it stayed under that family's control for sixty-five years.[99] When, in the mid-fifties, Merrill Shoup led a new group to protest "reckless" spending, he would find an important ally in Hoiles.[100]

The military remade Colorado Springs. Life changed for some members of the Davis family as well. Roy Davis became the main supplier of office machines for the town's military. Perhaps being the town's biggest seller of Liberty Bonds during World War II helped him snag that contract.[101] And in the final months of the war, my thirty-five-year-old mother met an army lieutenant (a former HOLC employee from Washington, D.C.) whom she would marry. She had spent the past seven years living with her mother and working at a downtown bookstore owned and operated by Edith Farnsworth, a member of the town's social set. Hers was a nine-to-five existence with few diversions. Sometimes she characterized this period as hell, and it certainly wasn't the way she had imagined her life unfolding. On the other hand, talking about and selling books brought her pleasure. So did knowing that customers were curious about her. Farnsworth may have taken a gamble on my mother, but she may have also figured that Dorothy Davis might be something of a draw for her shop. At least my mother, who seems to have used her notoriety to feel like somebody, thought so.

As long as interest rates did not rise America's savings and loans did well, as they earned an income spread on the difference between the higher long-term interest rates they received from their mortgage loans and the lower short-term interest they paid out to depositors.[102] However, in the latter part of the seventies, growing numbers of consumers started to invest their money in a new product—lucrative money market mutual funds. S&Ls were stuck with hundreds of billions of dollars on their books that were tied up in thirty-year fixed-rate loans (usually at 6 percent), and with their interest rates on new deposits limited to 5.5 percent. The once-thriving thrift industry began to sink. It declined further in 1979 when interest rates climbed higher in the wake of efforts by the Federal Reserve to bring down inflation. The Fed's move triggered a recession that resulted in S&L defaults and foreclosures. Under President Reagan the push to deregulate accelerated, particularly when it came to the thrift industry, which many believed

The first time I came across this picture I didn't recognize the woman on horseback as my mother. By the time she was raising me, my mother no longer had the bearing, daring, or flirtatiousness of the woman pictured here. At first I imagined that this photograph pre-dated the scandal, and that it was her father's ruin that had changed her, but this photo was taken in 1937. My mother recalled these years as having been extraordinarily trying, but this photograph suggests she was still a spirited woman. (Author's archive)

had been unfairly hampered by nearly fifty-year-old restrictions, born of a different era.

Faced with a thrift industry teetering on insolvency, the Reagan administration, with crucial support in Congress, decided that the "self-regulating mechanisms of the free market" should determine the industry's fate. S&Ls would no longer be restricted in what they could offer depositors by way of interest. At the same time, in a distinctly non-free-market move, FSLIC insurance for S&Ls was increased from $40,000 to $100,000 per deposit. Even at the time, some worried that this would enable risk-free fraud. When the industry failed to recover, further deregulation was pursued. With the Garn–St. Germain Depository Institutions Act of 1982, S&Ls were allowed to increase their consumer loans, make commercial corporate and business loans, and invest in nonresidential property, up to 40 percent of their total assets. Thrifts were also permitted to provide 100 percent financing, without any down payment from the borrower. "I think we've hit a home run," Reagan said upon signing the bill.

De-regulation was "like a freight train . . . and everybody just got on board," recalled one thrift regulator. The fact that the history of the building and loan industry was largely unknown meant that there was no effective way of countering those who dismissed Depression-era regulations as "anachronistic and debilitating." Savings and loans, now promoted as "moneymaking machines," did indeed emerge from their doldrums. The only problem was that these new free-market thrifts proved to be the "perfect vehicle for self-enrichment." What happened in the eighties was nothing short of "collective embezzlement," as operators, enabled by politically connected co-conspirators, plundered their businesses as they went on ludicrously outsized spending sprees. "The best way to rob a bank is to own one" was the judgment of the commissioner of the California Department of Savings and Loans. It's been estimated that the cost of the S&L crisis to taxpayers was somewhere between $150 billion and $175 billion.[103]

Texas was the hardest-hit state, but Colorado did not escape unscathed. Denver-based Silverado Savings & Loan, whose board of directors included Neil Bush, son of President George H.W. Bush, suffered one of the worst crashes of all, which was said to cost American taxpayers $1.3 billion. Some analysts now believe that the government's bailout of the S&L industry set a dangerous precedent in which the government subsidized risky behavior, a move that may have encouraged the recklessness that led to the subprime mortgage crisis of 2007.[104]

Colorado Springs' right-wing media and its militarized economy consolidated the town's reputation for conservatism. It became a magnet for conservatives such as the libertarian Robert LeFevre, who in 1954 moved there and began writing editorials for the *Gazette-Telegraph*. Within two years LeFevre established the Freedom School, which he operated there for twenty years. In the early twentieth century Colorado Springs had boasted that it was "the City of Churches," and as its economy struggled through a downturn in the 1980s city leaders decided to pursue economic development through Christian evangelism. Of the groups that settled there, none was more powerful than Dr. James Dobson's California-based Focus on the Family, whose recruitment the city sealed with a $4 million grant from a local foundation. By the mid-1990s there were nearly a hundred conservative Christian groups in Colorado Springs as well as Ted Haggard's New Life mega-church, which had set up shop there in 1984. In 1992 evangelical conservatives made Colorado the first state to pass an amendment preventing localities from outlawing discrimination on the basis of sexual orientation. With a lopsided two-to-one vote in favor of the bill, its supporters proclaimed Colorado Springs the "Vatican of evangelical Christians." Although the courts eventually overturned the amendment, it gave rise to similar efforts in four other states.[105]

During this period, taxes continued to galvanize Springs residents. It was California's Howard Jarvis who in the 1970s captured headlines with the property-tax-slashing Proposition 13. However, by the late 1980s anti-tax activists in Colorado Springs once again took the lead nationally when former El Paso County commissioner and state representative Douglas Bruce devised what he called the "Taxpayers' Bill of Rights."[106] Some sixty years after the taxpayers' league in El Paso County first mobilized, at least some of that group's dreams came to fruition. TABOR, as it is known, called for amending Colorado's constitution to prohibit state government from raising taxes or tax rates without a referendum. It also proposed that state government be barred from spending the money it collects under existing taxes if tax collections rise faster than the rate of inflation or population growth. Surplus revenue, under the law's terms, must be given back to taxpayers, no matter the needs of the state. 1992's TABOR law became a model for the anti-tax movement nationally, but it has proven hugely complicating for the state of Colorado, whose system of public education has suffered under it.[107] The libertarian law raises a fundamental question: is a government that cannot tax really a government?[108]

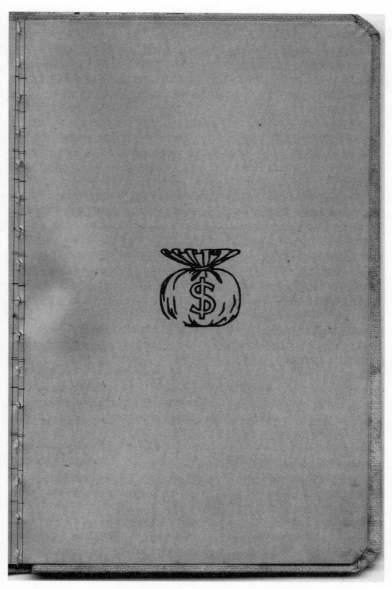

The back cover of a passbook for the City Savings Building and Loan. (Author's archive)

Epilogue

In the spring of 1956, when I was five years old, a moving van pulled up to our house. Out came furniture, steamer trunks, and well over a hundred boxes. It had all been in storage in Colorado Springs ever since Lula's death in the spring of 1945, just weeks after Dorothy's wedding to a lieutenant stationed in Colorado Springs at Peterson Army Air Force Base. The van was timed to arrive as we were making the two-mile move from Bethesda to Chevy Chase Village, where my parents had purchased a house big enough to hold Lula and Walter's belongings. Days later, my father was taking stock of it all when he came upon a box filled entirely with gloves. As he lifted a pair he noticed that its fingers were stiff. By the time he had removed all the hundred-dollar bills that Lula had rolled up and deposited into the fingers of all those gloves, he was staring at something like $2,500.

I have no idea if my mother knew about the money-stuffed gloves. The fur coats were another matter. She had expected that her mother's furs would be heavy with cash when they arrived in Maryland. And they would have been if the furriers had not ignored her instructions to store the furs whole rather than taking them apart—apparently the preferred method for long-term fur storage. Had the furriers felt curious bulges in the lining of the coats and, knowing the Davis name and reputation, decided to open them up? Probably. But the $2,500 was hardly all that remained of my grandfather's onetime fortune. Take, for example, my grandfather's black diamond ring, which my parents sold to a District of Columbia jeweler in 1958. That alone netted them $16,000. And this was in addition to Lula's estate. After that was settled in 1945 my mother inherited $85,000.

Lula died with an estate that in today's dollars was worth roughly $1 million. That figure does not include the cash and jewelry that went uncounted in the final estate tally. In planning for their future in the wake of Walter's suicide, Lula might well have figured that she would live beyond age sixty-two—the age at which she died. Still, what those numbers suggest is that my mother and grandmother could have parted with thousands of dollars without themselves suffering during the Depression.[1] Would it have mattered to those depositors? I would wager that for many of them just about any size check would have made a difference. And here's the thing: although my parents were not frivolous, it wasn't as if that money went for essentials. Mostly it paid for a house in the tony suburb of Chevy Chase Village and private schools and colleges. Rejected by the charmed circle back in the Springs, my mother tried her best to launch her rebellious daughters into it in Washington, D.C. No luck there.

Like many girls of the sixties, I systematically thwarted my mother's social ambitions for me. Still, her father's money shaped me, even the terms of my rebellion. It gave me opportunities I understood at the time to be primarily the consequence of my father's hard work. Growing up, the value of hard work (and implicitly the payoff that follows from it) was drummed into me. To be clear, it's not as though I came to this project with any naiveté about the American dream. Coming of age in the sixties, I developed a healthy skepticism toward national narratives that claim America to be a meritocracy, that imagine free enterprise and individualism as guarantors of our freedom. But somehow that political analysis didn't quite extend to me. *Shortfall* has made me rethink just about everything. What if I hadn't attended Sidwell Friends, among D.C.'s preppiest prep schools? What if Walter hadn't been both ambitious and ethically challenged? Perhaps nothing other than my grandfather's ingenuity at stealing other people's money separated us from my great-uncle Willard and his wife, stuck in a ramshackle house on west Colorado Avenue.

My grandfather had a cruel disregard for his customers, whether they were looking for security, a lifeline, or fast money. I wish he had been an outlier, a lone maverick, but he wasn't. Whether in Colorado Springs, Los Angeles, Philadelphia, or many other places, the building and loan business bore little resemblance to Bailey Brothers. However, this book is not just the story of one small group of people in a Western town; it's also a history of America's uneven playing field, or one significant corner of it. It takes aim as well at a larger cultural narrative, the fairy tale at the heart of *It's a Wonderful Life*—that capitalism is redeemable, and not because of bank examiners and government regulators, but because of wonderful people like George Bailey. I'm not sure how much traction this fantasy has any longer, but it's worth asking why it has had such a hold on Americans. Have we needed George Bailey to keep at bay all the real-life Walter Davises of the world, to keep us from losing faith in the fairness of our system?[2] And might it be that we ourselves are more deeply implicated than we know in this cultural fantasy of capitalism's goodness? What if our own investments in this system, and our own hopes of making it, also have figured in this fairy tale?

Acknowledgments

Shortfall took me somewhat beyond my comfort zone as a historian. Researching this book meant leaving behind the long sixties, immersing myself in multiple histories—of the American West, banking, and conservatism—and plunging deeper into early twentieth-century U.S. history. Not all of my colleagues and friends were persuaded that this should be my next book project. Years ago, historian Moshe Sluhovsky was the first friend to ask the question I imagined I had already answered: "But why should we care about this?" Figuring that out took a while.

Ultimately, getting to that larger story required a deeper immersion both in the archives and in the relevant secondary sources. In the early stages of writing, my literary agent, Geri Thoma, wisely advised "pulling back the camera" and giving readers a wide-angle view of the story, a judgment seconded by my friend Wini Breines. My college roommate and friend Torrey Reade, who worked for years as a Wall Street investment banker, read a later draft of the book in the summer of 2015. She shared with me what she believed needed fleshing out and clarifying, and at that moment when my spirits were flagging she restored my faith in the project. Barry Qualls, Anne Hyde (a professor for two decades at Colorado College in Colorado Springs), and Charlotte Nekola read and commented on the manuscript in ways that improved it immeasurably. Many thanks to all those who usefully read and commented on drafts of the prologue: Steve Aron, William Deverell, Karen Halttunen, Susan Johnson, Seth Koven, Constance Samaras, Jacob Soll, and Marla Stone.

Over the years my thinking was sharpened by conversations with the following colleagues, friends, and acquaintances: Elinor Accampo, Joe Boone, Anthony Tirado Chase, Ellen DuBois, Ann Fabian, Ray and Joy Flint, Daniel Goode, Sofia Gruskin, Bill Handley, Sharon Hays, Janis Holm, Maria Lepowsky, Tania Modleski, Donna Murch, Becky Nicolaides, Molly Pulda, Steve Ross, Brett Sheehan, Bette Skandalis, Ann Snitow, Jeff Solomon, Carole Vance, Devra Weber, Ginny Yans, Pat Yeghessian, and Gilda Zwerman. The friend who crucially got me working on this book with her discovery of those *New York Times* articles is Alice Wexler, with whom I have had many a conversation about the challenges of writing one's own family history.

This book forced me to retool, and the University of Southern California gave me the time and support to do so. An early sabbatical through USC's Advancing Scholarship in the Humanities and Social Sciences, an initiative of then Vice Provost Beth Meyerowitz, proved helpful at a critical juncture in the research of this book. Thanks are also due to Vice Dean Peter Mancall and then Dean Steve Kay.

Every lecture I gave on this project generated valuable feedback. In April 2013 I presented my research to members of the Western History Workshop at the Autry National Center. One participant suggested I examine the court cases that he was sure followed from the building and loan meltdown. He was right, as subsequent trips to the Colorado State Archives proved. UCLA historian Steve Aron, that workshop's organizer, asked crucial questions about the centrality of the West to my book. Faculty in the History Department at USC raised questions about the scope and ambitions of this project. Louis Hyman's response to my paper at 2016's Histories of Capitalism Conference at Cornell enabled me to see that I needed to clarify one piece of my argument. Many thanks to my interlocutors at the fall 2016 Colloquium on Political Economy, sponsored by the Center for the Study of Work, Labor and Democracy at the University of California, Santa Barbara, particularly the center's director, Nelson Lichtenstein, as well as Eileen Boris, Miroslava Chavez-Garcia, Mickey and Richard Flacks, Mary Furner, Lisa Jacobson, Laura Kalman, Alice O'Connor, Constance Penley, Howard Winant, and everyone who took part in that wide-ranging and energetic discussion.

Over the past fifteen years I have conducted research in many libraries and archives, and the people who have assisted me deserve special thanks. Tim Blevins, the division head of Special Collections in the Pikes Peak Library District, is a scholar in his own right, which is doubtless why he proved to be so tenacious at finding hard-to-get sources. It was Tim who uncovered a partial run of an obscure but essential local newspaper, *Common Sense Weekly*. I also want to thank the other wonderful librarians, archivists, and staff at the PPLD, particularly Erinn Barnes, Dennis Dailey, Jody Jones, Chris Nicholl, and William Thomas. The able, overworked archivists at the Colorado State Archives in Denver found the right boxes—no small feat. Paul Levit did whatever it took to retrieve pesky, seemingly lost files. Also able were James Chipman, Lance Christensen, and Tracie Seurer. Librarians at the Texas State Archives in Austin were likewise terrific. Thanks are due to Leah Witherow at the Pioneers Museum, the librarians in Special Collections at Colorado College, Bill Stookey, the title examiner in the El Paso County Assessor's Office, the staff in Special Collections and Archives at the University of Colorado in Boulder, and Kathy Reynolds, the director of the Cripple Creek District Museum. Many years ago I examined HOLC records at the National Archives at College Park, Maryland, where the staff guided me expertly to the right materials. Finally, thanks to the staff at the Greensburg Carnegie Public Library in Greensburg, Indiana.

In Colorado Springs, I was lucky enough to meet with veteran local journalist John Hazlehurst, whose mother, Edith Farnsworth, turns up briefly in these pages. Deeply knowledgeable about the region, John shared with me his thoughts about his hometown. Thanks also to Dwight Haverkorn, a local historian often to be found at a microfilm reader at CC.

Anyone who has stared at a microfilm reader for long hours knows that it is hard work. The staff at the Mining Exchange Hotel, located just blocks from the downtown branch of the Colorado Springs Public Library, always made my stays there comfortable. And here at home, Moth, LucyFur, and Walter Gomez provided much-needed distraction, often when trying to pry me away from this book.

The New Press has provided a wonderful home for *Shortfall*. Working with Carl Bromley and Marc Favreau, my extraordinarily talented editor, has been a dream. Marc has a laser-like vision for what needs further explanation or outright overhauling. Maredith Sheridan, the marketing manager and associate publicist at the press, and Emily Albarillo, the production editor, were terrific. Susan Warga's copyediting was superb.

Without my father's revelation to me some twenty years ago, there would be no *Shortfall*. I'm grateful that he finally spilled the beans. Over the years my sister, Martha Jane Echols, has been generous in sharing with me her thoughts about our family. She is several years older than me, which doubtless goes some way toward explaining why our memories do not always converge. My sister also gave me several boxes of photographs and family papers, for which I am grateful. Many thanks are also due to Lucy O'Brien, who generously went through the many boxes that had been left behind in what was now her attic.

One regret I have is that my mother's graciousness and kindness do not come across in this book. A lifelong Episcopalian, in the last years of her life she pushed herself to be more empathic to people different from herself. For her, it was about becoming a true Christian. I loved her deeply. I still miss her and our talks about her parents and her life with them in Colorado Springs.

Finally, Kate Flint came into my life a little more than twelve years ago. A polymath *and* an indefatigable sleuth, Kate is brilliant. A generous and demanding critic, she managed throughout to be utterly supportive while at the same time conveying that whatever draft she had just read was not quite there. Always this news was conveyed in an upbeat fashion, usually by the phrase "Almost there!" There were times when she also tracked down something—about, say, tourism or banking—before I had gotten there. Kate often accompanied me on trips to Colorado Springs, where she would photograph the houses, buildings, stores, and hotels that figure in this book. She did this even though she was working on her own book, a cultural history of flash photography. Having Kate in my life (and, indeed, being married to her) is a blessing. I cherish her every day.

Notes

Prologue: Captain Nothing

1. Calculating worth over time is a vexed task. One can employ different measures of worth. I have chosen to use the Consumer Price Index (CPI) throughout. See the very useful essay by Lawrence H. Officer and Samuel H. Williamson, "Measures of Worth," Measuring Worth website, www.measuringworth.com/worthmeasures.php, accessed January 25, 2017.

2. "Why Banker Davis Was Glad," *San Antonio Light*, January 22, 1933. This feature article, which included an artist's renderings of the principals in the scandal, seems to have been nationally syndicated. It also appeared in the *Milwaukee Sentinel*.

3. Davis is mentioned in Stephen J. Leonard's invaluable history, *Trials and Triumphs: A Colorado Portrait of the Great Depression with FSA Photographs* (Niwot, CO: University Press of Colorado, 1993).

4. For example, in the standard history of the thrift industry, its author, David L. Mason, argues that B&Ls had an impressively low failure rate nationwide in 1931 and 1932. He puts the figure at just over 2 percent, by comparison to the failure rate of banks, which he puts at 20 percent. However,

the problems with B&Ls—with associations becoming frozen, going into receivership, being liquidated or consolidated—lasted into the early forties. To get an accurate reading on the condition of the B&L industry, one would have to consult state archives in every state rather than rely on the numbers put out by the thrift industry itself. See Mason, *From Buildings and Loans to Bail-Outs: A History of the American Savings and Loan Industry, 1831–1995* (New York: Cambridge University Press, 2004), 78. Mason often relies upon thrift industry insider Josephine Hedges Ewalt's *A Business Reborn: The Savings and Loan Story, 1930–1960* (Chicago: American Savings and Loan Institute Press, 1962). He also cites the history written by the general counsel of the U.S. Savings and Loan League, an industry trade group. See Horace Russell, *Savings and Loan Associations* (Albany, NY: Matthew Bender, 1956). In discussing the Great Depression, Mason downplays financial wrongdoing and fraud, but he mentions one 1920s case involving seventeen Philadelphia thrifts with interlocking directorates.

5. See Mehrsa Baradaran, *How the Other Half Banks: Exclusion, Exploitation, and the Threat to Democracy* (Cambridge, MA: Harvard University Press, 2015), 86. Baradaran's book is on target in its critique of the banking industry today, but she treats Bailey Brothers Building and Loan Association as though it typified the building and loan business. And in the opening paragraphs of *From Buildings and Loans to Bail-Outs*, Mason claims that *It's a Wonderful Life* "provided an accurate sketch of America's thrift industry during its heyday of the late 1940s and early 1950s."

Here and there one comes across references to building and loan failures in a particular city during the 1930s. See, for example, Lizabeth Cohen, *Making a New Deal: Industrial Workers in Chicago, 1919–1939* (New York: Cambridge University Press, 1991), 227–38, and Gerald Jaynes, "The Economy and the Black Citizen, 1900 to World War II," in *The Oxford Handbook of African American Citizenship, 1865–Present*, ed. Henry Louis Gates Jr. et al. (New York: Oxford University Press, 2012), 308. Jaynes notes that in 1930 there were seventy black-owned B&Ls with assets of more than $6.5 million. By 1938 that number had fallen to fifty B&Ls with assets of $3.6 million. One scholar who does acknowledge the extent of failure in the thrift industry, but refers to "amateur management" and "conflicts of interest" rather than flat-out financial wrongdoing, is Kenneth A. Snowden in his essential article, "The Transition from Building and Loan to Savings and Loan, 1890–1940," in *Finance, Intermediaries, and Economic Development*, ed. Stanley L. Engerman, Philip T. Hoffman, Jean-Laurent Rosenthal, and Kenneth L. Sokoloff (New York: Cambridge University Press, 2003), 167–69. Barry Eichengreen describes B&Ls as among the worst offenders when it comes to real estate speculation in the 1920s. See Eichengreen, *Hall of Mirrors: The Great*

Depression, the Great Recession, and the Uses—and Misuses—of History (New York: Oxford University Press, 2015), 29.

6. Molly Pulda, "Unknown Knowns: State Secrets and Family Secrets," *Biography* 35, no. 3 (2012).

7. Beryl Satter, "Reflections: On Family Properties: Race, Real Estate, and the Exploitation of Black Urban America," *Reviews in American History* 41, no. 1 (March 2013): 179.

8. The Davis family archive included material that my sister subsequently contributed.

9. "Federal Savings Reelects Officers," *CSG*, January 20, 1938, 1.

10. Letter to the Editor, *CSW*, May 13, 1932, 1.

11. U.S. Department of Commerce, *Fifteenth Census of the United States: Population*, vol. 6, *Families* (Washington, DC: Government Printing Office, 1933), 213. Accounts of the number of depositors in the four Colorado Springs building and loan associations varies from a high of 10,000 to a low of 5,000. See "Depositors Demand Arrest of Gross," *DP*, July 2, 1932; Republican Central Committee of El Paso County Announcement to B&L Stockholders, *CSG*, November 5, 1932; Editorial, *CSW*, July 18, 1932, 4.

12. For a number of important essays emphasizing instead the "anonymous, often invisible, workings" of capitalism, see Michael Zakim and Gary J. Kornblith, eds., *Capitalism Takes Command: The Social Transformation of Nineteenth-Century America* (Chicago: University of Chicago Press, 2012), 12.

13. For dubious mortgage lending schemes, including interest-only balloon mortgages and the "mortgage racket" more generally, see Louis Hyman's *Borrow: The American Way of Debt* (New York: Vintage, 2012), 65–78. For low-down-payment loans, see Eichengreen, *Hall of Mirrors*, 29. Historian Jacob Soll persuasively argues that poor accounting exacerbated the Great Depression. See Soll, *The Reckoning: Financial Accountability and the Rise and Fall of Nations* (New York: Basic Books, 2014), 192.

14. For the failure rates of Colorado B&Ls, see the Index to Liquidations Archives Number 69-261, CSA. For the effects of the crash on Pueblo, see "District Attorney Traces Saunders' $100,000 Check," *DP*, July 22, 1932, 3.

15. See *Annual Report of Building and Loan Associations* (1929–1944) of the Texas Department of Banking at the Texas State Library and Archives, Austin, Texas.

16. Eichengreen, *Hall of Mirrors*, 29. Snowden notes that the sunny predictions for industry growth and integrity made in 1930 by Morton Bodfish, the powerful leader of the B&L trade group, were colossally wrong. The thirties, says Snowden, represented nothing less than a "decade of demise" for the B&L industry. Snowden, "Transition," 157.

17. My estimate of the failure rate in Colorado is derived from the State of Colorado's Biennial Reports of the Bureau of Building and Loan Associations, which are available at the Colorado State Archives, Denver, Colorado. When it comes to the figures nationally, there is a gulf separating the figures put forward by David Mason in *From Buildings and Loans* and those put forward by Kenneth Snowden in "Transition." That discrepancy is largely attributable to the fact that Mason stops counting after 1932, and Snowden wisely continues counting until 1941. It turns out that one must examine figures until at least 1941 because associations typically "froze," often for years, until they were liquidated or consolidated into another B&L. Complicating any effort to calculate the closure rate is that while many B&Ls were effectively frozen, new "savings and loans" associations were being established while the older B&Ls languished. The new S&Ls were federally chartered and offered depositors federally insured insurance. See Snowden, "Transition," on this development.

18. For quotes stressing the semi-philanthropic nature of B&Ls, see Elaine Lewinnek, *The Working Man's Reward* (New York: Oxford University Press, 2014), 95, 99; Snowden, "Transition," 170; Mason, *From Buildings and Loans*, 24–27. It was New York University professor of economics Richard Netzer who characterized the post–World War II S&L industry as dominated by men who treated their associations like nothing so much as "honey pots." In the aftermath of the S&L crisis, prevailing wisdom held that deregulation had destroyed the S&L industry. Netzer believed otherwise: that the industry had always tolerated unethical practices. See his letter to the editor, "Savings and Loans Were Always a Scandal," *NYT*, August 24, 1990.

19. There is a vast and contentious literature on social mobility in the United States. Historian Stephan Thernstrom penned two of the most influential books about it. Thernstrom's 1964 classic, *Poverty and Progress: Social Mobility in a Nineteenth Century City* (reprint, Cambridge, MA: Harvard University Press, 2009) argued for limited mobility. His prize-winning 1976 book, *The Other Bostonians: Poverty and Progress in the American Metropolis, 1880–1970* (Cambridge, MA: Harvard University Press, 1976) found evidence of significantly greater mobility. My discussion draws on these books, and his preface to the 1987 edition of *Poverty and Progress*. I have also been influenced by other studies, including the critique of Thernstrom's work in Kenneth Kusmer's *Down and Out, on the Road: The Homeless in American History* (New York: Oxford University Press, 2003). See also Howard Chudacoff's excellent essay "Success and Security: The Meaning of Social Mobility in America," *Reviews in American History* 10, no. 4 (December 1982); Michael B. Katz, Michael B. Doucet, and Mark J. Stern, *The Social Organization of Early Industrial Capitalism* (Cambridge, MA: Harvard University Press, 1982). Economist Thomas Piketty's *Capital in the 21st Century*

(Cambridge, MA: Belknap, 2014) has generated substantial debate about income inequality and social mobility. Piketty argues that American rates of social mobility actually lag behind those of Europe and have for some time. It's worth noting that claims about social mobility have not always been attentive to place, time, race, and gender. For income inequality, see also Emanuel Saez, "Striking It Richer: The Evolution of Top Incomes in the Unites States," September 3, 2013, 3, http://eml.berkeley.edu/~saez/saez-UStopincomes -2012.pdf.

20. The idea that what's truly problematic about American capitalism is Wall Street (and titans of capital) was demonstrated in an exchange between 2016 Democratic Party presidential candidates Hillary Clinton and Bernie Sanders. Asked if it was actually true that he was not a capitalist, Sanders deflected the question and instead attacked the "casino-capitalist process" whereby "Wall Street greed and recklessness wrecked this economy." Clinton said, "When I think about capitalism, I think about all the small businesses that were started." She then moved on to discuss the need to address the excesses of capitalism. See Amy Davidson, "Comment: Radical Measures," *The New Yorker*, January 25, 2016, 19.

21. The description here is that of Wall Street reformer Ferdinand Pecora in his 1939 book, *Wall Street Under Oath: The Story of Our Modern Money Changers* (ebook, Los Angeles: Graymalkin Media, 2014). John Kenneth Galbraith emphasized Wall Street in his classic study of the Depression, *The Great Crash 1929* (New York: Penguin Books, 1975), and others have as well. See, for example, David M. Kennedy's *The American People in the Great Depression, Freedom from Fear, Part One* (New York: Oxford University Press, 2001), and Ira Katznelson's *Fear Itself: The New Deal and the Origins of Our Time* (New York: Norton, 2014).

22. Peter Conn is critical of this tendency in *The American 1930s: A Literary History* (New York: Cambridge University Press, 2009), 6.

23. The language here is that of Wilfred M. McClay, invoked by labor historians Jefferson Cowie and Nick Salvatore, in their provocative article "The Long Exception: Rethinking the Place of the New Deal in American History," *International Labor and Working-Class History* 74 (Fall 2008). See McClay, "Individualism and Its Discontents," *Virginia Quarterly Review* 77, no. 3 (Summer 2001): 395.

24. Jefferson Cowie and Nick Salvatore advance the idea that the New Deal was "the long exception" in U.S. history. See Cowie and Salvatore, "The Long Exception." The same issue includes pithy responses from Jennifer Klein, Michael Kazin, Kevin Boyle, and Nancy MacLean. There is a growing literature about the New Deal that reveals the extent to which gender and racial inequality were built into the welfare state that New Dealers forged. Devra Weber, *Dark Sweat, White Gold: California Farm Workers, Cotton,*

and the New Deal (Berkeley: University of California Press, 1994); Katznelson, *Fear Itself*; Suzanne Mettler, *Dividing Citizens: Gender and Federalism in New Deal Public Policy* (Ithaca, NY: Cornell University Press, 1998).

25. It was Joshua B. Freeman who in a pioneering 1989 essay, "Putting Conservatism Back into the 1960s," argued that it was time for historians of the sixties to address conservatism. Conservatism was not, he argued, simply a reaction to the rebellious decade, and seeing it as such "presents too great a discontinuity between the conservative triumph late in the decade and earlier conservative developments." See "Teaching the Sixties: A Symposium," in *Radical History Review* 44 (Spring 1989): 95. Freeman's piece was followed by Alan Brinkley's influential essay "The Problem of American Conservatism," *American Historical Review* 99 (April 1994).

Historians' interest in mapping modern American conservatism accelerated as the New Deal coalition began to further unravel. There are now many excellent books about American conservatism. David Kennedy argues that it was during the thirties, the years when New Deal liberalism was ascendant, that the hostility to federal power that we associate with much modern conservatism consolidated. See *American People*, 341. An important account that locates anti-statism firmly in the 1920s is Lyn Dumenil's *The Modern Temper: American Culture and Society in the 1920s* (New York: Hill & Wang, 1995), 26. Three essential books that focus on businessmen's pushback against the New Deal are Kim Phillips-Fein, *Invisible Hands: The Businessmen's Crusade Against the New Deal* (New York: Norton, 2009); Kathryn S. Olmsted, *Right out of California: The 1930s and the Big Business Roots of Modern Conservatism* (New York: The New Press, 2015); and Elizabeth Tandy Shermer, *Sunbelt Capitalism: Phoenix and the Transformation of American Politics* (Philadelphia: University of Pennsylvania Press, 2013). Shandy, in particular, makes the point that the business conservatives she studied were not across the board anti-statist. They often turned to the federal government for "help constructing the infrastructure upon which commerce depended." See Shermer, *Sunbelt Capitalism*, 35–36.

Other significant studies on the subject include Lisa McGirr, *Suburban Warriors: The Origins of the New American Right* (Princeton, NJ: Princeton University Press, 2001); Becky M. Nicolaides, *My Blue Heaven: Life and Politics in the Working-Class Suburbs of Los Angeles* (Chicago: University of Chicago Press, 2002); Nelson Lichtenstein and Elizabeth Tandy Shermer, eds., *The Right and Labor in America: Politics, Ideology, and Imagination* (Philadelphia, PA: University of Pennsylvania Press, 2012); Elizabeth A. Fones-Wolf, *Selling Free Enterprise: The Business Assault on Labor and Liberalism, 1945–60* (Urbana: University of Illinois Press, 1994); Robert O. Self, *American Babylon: Race and the Struggle for Postwar Oakland* (Princeton, NJ: Princeton University Press, 2003); Matthew Lassiter, *The Silent Majority:*

Suburban Politics in the Sunbelt South (Princeton, NJ: Princeton University Press, 2006); Kevin Kruse, *One Nation Under God: How America Invented Christian America* (New York: Basic Books, 2015); Robert Kuttner, *Revolt of the Haves: Tax Rebellions and Hard Times* (New York: Simon & Schuster, 1980); and David Bieto, *Taxpayers in Revolt: Tax Resistance During the Great Depression* (Chapel Hill: University of North Carolina Press, 1989).

26. Indispensable to understanding the region are two magisterial books—Elizabeth Jameson's *All That Glitters: Class, Conflict, and Community in Cripple Creek* (Urbana, IL: University of Illinois Press, 1998) and Thomas A. Andrews's *Killing for Coal: America's Deadliest Labor War* (Cambridge, MA: Harvard University Press, 2008).

27. The city's streets-paved-with-gold scheme was hatched *after* gold mining was already in decline. The local taxpayers' association, whose activities I chronicle later in this book, unsuccessfully challenged the bond issue. "'Taxpayers' Launch Campaign on Paving," *CSG*, March 5, 1920. See also the oral history by J. Juan Reid, "Growing Up in the Twenties: One Man's View of Colorado Springs," 1980, in the holdings of the Colorado Springs Pioneers Museum. "Springs Streets Really Paved with Gold," *CSG*, May 23, 1965.

28. Adam M. Sowards, *United States West Coast: An Environmental History* (Santa Barbara, CA: ABC-CLIO, 2007), 81; Patricia N. Limerick, *The Legacy of Conquest: The Unbroken Past of the American West* (New York: Norton, 1987), 100. Limerick observes that today in the American West what we have is not just a persistence of attitude but also the revival of mining activity. See Limerick, *Something in the Soul: Legacies and Reckonings in the New West* (New York: Norton, 2000), 225; William Deverell, ed., *A Companion to the American West* (Oxford: Blackwell Publishing, 2004).

29. Historian Catherine McNicol Stock has argued persuasively that in order to understand how America's heartland, once the home of Populism, became more conservative, one needs to factor in changing attitudes toward the military: "The creation of a military economy in the heartland not only made obvious the association between local politicians and the military, but it took away their most potent anti-militarist view: that rich easterners and financiers on Wall Street were profiting from war while poor farm boys did the fighting and dying." See Stock, "Making War Their Business: The Short History of Populist Anti-Militarism," *Journal of the Gilded Age and Progressive Era* 13, no. 3 (July 2014): 396.

30. In arguing for the prototypical quality of Colorado Springs I am aware that Mike Davis already made the case for California, which he says "acts as a kind of prefigurative microcosm of national politics; its intentional antinomies tend to anticipate the form and content of social conflict in the rest of the country." See Davis, *Prisoners of the American Dream: Politics and Economy in the History of the U.S. Working Class* (London: Verso, 1986), 158. Lisa

McGirr has made the case that Orange County, California, was a prototype, arguing that it was "the first functional form of a new conservative milieu that appeared less distinctly elsewhere." She likens several other cities, including Colorado Springs, to Orange County in the conservative cultures they have fostered. However, her focus is on a later period than mine—the 1960s. See her groundbreaking book, *Suburban Warriors*, 13. Focusing on the Republican establishment in 1940s California, Kristoffer Smemo argues that it pioneered a "new conservative statism" foreshadowing the moderate-liberal Republicanism of Dwight D. Eisenhower. See Smemo, "The Little People's Century: Industrial Pluralism, Economic Development, and the Emergence of Liberal Republicanism in California, 1942–1946," *Journal of American History* 101, no. 4 (March 2015): 1168.

31. Robert O. Self, "California and the New Suburban History," *Reviews in American History* 31, no. 1 (March 2003).

32. Michael Kazin, "A Liberal Nation in Spite of Itself," *International Labor and Working-Class History* 74 (Fall 2008). Here Kazin is rephrasing the paradox noted by Lloyd Free and Hadley Cantril, scholars of American public opinion. They maintained that most Americans are conservative ideologically but in practice liberal. Free and Cantril, *The Political Beliefs of Americans: A Study of Public Opinion* (New Brunswick, NJ: Rutgers University Press, 1967).

33. It was Robert G. Athearn who characterized Westerners' response to the federal government as "politically schizophrenic." He was referring specifically to the New Deal years, but he believed this attitude predated the Depression. See his book *The Mythic West in Twentieth-Century America* (Lawrence: University of Kansas Press, 1986), 103. DeVoto's pithy assessment is quoted in Albert L. Hurtado's "Whose Misfortune? Richard White's Ambivalent Region," in *Reviews in American History* 22, no. 2 (June 1994): 288.

34. For more about Phoenix, see Shermer, *Sunbelt Capitalism*. Later in the 1960s, after Goldwater's defeat in 1964, Richard Nixon was able to successfully exploit the surge of suburban populist conservatism. Matthew Lassiter has demonstrated that "consumer status, taxpayer rights and meritocratic individualism" were the key building blocks in the mobilization of white suburban voters, Nixon's "Silent Majority." Taxpayer rights and a meritocratic individualism existed decades earlier in Colorado Springs but, as best as I can tell, largely disconnected in any overt way from race and suburbanization. See Lassiter, *The Silent Majority*, 198.

35. "Palmer Removes Residence from El Paso County," *CSG*, March 14, 1884, 4. His move was projected to reduce the county assessment by $60,000. It doesn't appear that Palmer actually did move out of the county. From the 1920s onward Colorado Springs prioritized low taxes. See "Springs' Taxes Lower than Most Cities, Survey Shows," *CSG*, February 26, 1950, B1. And

"Springs One of Colorado Cities with Lowest Taxes," *CSG*, September 19, 1949, B1.

36. Thomas Frank, *What's the Matter with Kansas? How Conservatives Won the Heart of America* (New York: Metropolitan Books, 2004).

37. See Richard Harris, "Working-Class Home Ownership in the American Metropolis," *Journal of Urban History* 17 (November 1990): 63. One essential, in-depth study of a hardscrabble, white working-class suburb of south Los Angeles suggests that the antitax activism that erupted there during the Depression presaged the conservative tax revolts that would break out in California several decades later. See Nicolaides, *My Blue Heaven*. Many people of color yearned to own their homes as well, but racially discriminatory lending practices very often effectively put successful homeownership off-limits. See Beryl Satter, *Family Properties: How the Struggle over Race and Real Estate Transformed Chicago and Urban America* (New York: Metropolitan Books, 2009); Margaret Garb, *City of American Dream: A History of Home Ownership and Housing Reform in Chicago, 1871–1919* (Chicago: University of Chicago Press, 2005), 188; Margaret Garb, "Drawing the Color Line: Race and Real Estate in Early Twentieth-Century Chicago," *Journal of Urban History* 32, no. 5 (July 2006).

38. Upton Sinclair, *The Jungle* (New York: Grosset & Dunlap, 1906), 212.

39. According to Margaret Garb, studies of neighborhood housing suggest that Sinclair's rendering of the Rudkuses' sad experience with homeownership was a fair depiction. See Garb, *City of American Dream*, 154–55. She argues that a neighborhood B&L was more apt to let a few missed payments be forgiven. However, that would not have been the case with a building and loan of the "nationals" variety.

40. Lewinnek, *The Working Man's Reward*, 100.

41. *Shortfall* builds upon the work of left-leaning scholars who have explored a fuller range of working-class experiences and consciousness than the celebratory accounts of working-class resistance that has characterized much labor history. I have in mind three extraordinary books: Seth Koven's *The Match Girl and the Heiress* (Princeton, NJ: Princeton University Press, 2014); Alison Light's *Common People: The History of an English Family* (London: Penguin, 2014); and Carolyn Steedman's *Landscape for a Good Woman* (New Brunswick, NJ: Rutgers University Press, 1987). All three books focus on British class feelings.

42. Both "working people" and "working class" are less than totally satisfactory terms. "Working people" is too baggy a term, and it reinforces the notion of the so-called classlessness of American society. Yet "working class" can obscure more than it clarifies, especially in a tourist town like the Springs with so few industrial workers. Certainly occupational categories tell us only so much. How do we categorize a barber or a contractor? Did the barber

own his own shop or work in another man's, and might that contractor have been better described as a carpenter? And what do we make of the Colorado City factory hand who reportedly attended college—usually a marker of middle-class status? Complicating matters further, the move from blue-collar to white-collar work did not always represent upward mobility. Then there is the question of self-identification. Many Americans prefer to see themselves as a "people not a class"—a preference not entirely reducible to disidentification with one's class of origin. On the trickiness of "upward mobility," see Chudacoff, "Success and Security," 105. The succinct formulation about Americans and class is Michael Kazin's in his essay "A People Not a Class: Rethinking the Political Language of the Modern US Labor Movement," in *Reshaping the U.S. Left: Popular Struggles in the 1980s*, ed. Mike Davis and Michael Sprinker (London: Verso, 1988), 257–86. This is also the view of David E. Kyvig in his book *Daily Life in the United States, 1920–1940* (Chicago: Ivan R. Dee, 2002), 165. It was British historian E.P. Thompson who defined a class as "a very loosely defined body of people who share the same congeries of interests, social experiences, traditions, and value-system, who have a disposition to behave as a class, to define themselves in their actions and in their consciousness in relation to other groups of people in class ways." Quoted in Ira Katznelson and Aristide R. Zolberg, *Class Formation: Nineteenth-Century Patterns in Western Europe and the United States* (Princeton, NJ: Princeton University Press), 18.

43. Light, *Common People*, xxviii.

1: Advertisements for Himself

1. This account of Palmer's remaking of the Pikes Peak region is drawn from Andrews, *Killing for Coal*, 27–50.

2. PikeView Coal Company operated north of town, but in the years ahead most industry would be located to the west in Colorado City.

3. Marshall Sprague, *Newport of the Rockies: The Life and Good Times of Colorado Springs* (Athens, OH: Swallow Press, 1988), 18.

4. Isabella Lucy Bird, *A Lady's Life in the Rocky Mountains* (New York: G.P. Putnam, 1882), 177–78.

5. Many who came were said to be the second sons of British aristocracy.

6. See Christine Bold, *The Frontier Club: Popular Westerns and Cultural Power, 1880–1924* (New York: Oxford University Press, 2013), 58–61.

7. *The WPA Guide to 1930s Colorado* (Lawrence: University of Kansas Press, 1987), 56–57.

8. Jameson, *All That Glitters*, 24.

9. Melvyn Dubofsky, *Hard Work: The Making of Labor History* (Urbana: University of Illinois Press, 2000), 43.

10. One of the best sources about Colorado is *The WPA Guide to 1930s Colorado*. See its section on Colorado Springs, 111–23.

11. By 1917 when residents of Colorado City voted to be part of Colorado Springs, some of this would change. By that point the Golden Cycle Mill was still operating, but with a much diminished labor force. The far northern side of town also featured coal works. The city's business leaders, eager to keep its tourist trade, aggressively attacked anything that might undermine its pristine reputation, such as the knock-on effects of Manitou's lack of a sewer system. "Manitou and Fountain Creek," *CSG*, December 10, 1904.

12. See "City of Sunshine: Colorado Springs: Health, Education, Recreation, Residence, All Year Round," 1917, Special Collections, Penrose Library, Pikes Peak Library District: "Into whatever part of the city he may go, his first impressions of beauty, taste and cleanliness deepen. . . . Many of the residences are mansions with spacious grounds. . . . Colorado Springs is cosmopolitan and metropolitan" (79).

13. *WPA Guide*, 112.

14. It was the view of Charles Mulford Robinson, "noted good roads expert," who outlined a system of parking in his report to city officials, "Would Transform Streets into Lanes of Greensward," *CSG*, August 2, 1905 (included in "Evolution of Historic Medians," https://coloradosprings.gov/sites/default/files/planning/historicmedians.pdf).

15. H.W. Brands, *The Age of Gold: The California Gold Rush and the New American Dream* (New York: Anchor, 2003), 442. Recent work on the great California gold rush has complicated Brands's view. It turns out that some of those who came looking for gold wanted to launch a successful small business or farm with their profits, not to become instantly rich. See, for example, Malcolm Rohrbough, *Rush to Gold: The French and the California Gold Rush, 1848–1854* (New Haven, CT: Yale University Press, 2013). I would argue that for the men who became mine owners during the Cripple Creek gold rush, the dream of striking it rich (or richer in the case of those who arrived on the scene already moneyed) was often a powerful lure.

16. J.R. Robinson, "The Ideal City," in Colorado Springs City Council, Town Incorporation, City Organization and Reorganization (Colorado Springs: City Council, 1901–2). Robinson, the mayor, cited the state's "unlimited mineral wealth."

17. Limerick, *Legacy of Conquest*, 100; Limerick, *Something in the Soul*, 225.

18. Frank Norris, *The Octopus: A Story of California* (New York: Doubleday, Page, 1901).

19. Sprague, *Newport in the Rockies*, 163.

20. "To Establish Resort in Bear Creek Canyon," *CSG*, February 27, 1902. The plan was to build a summer resort for tourists in the area known as Jones Park.

21. "'Coney Island' Resort in Ivywild to Cost $75,000," *CSG*, January 5, 1906, 1; "New Bath House at Zoo, Open to Public, Finest in the State," *CSG*, August 6, 1911; "Landell Bartlett Recalls Zoo and 'Bathhouse John,'" *CSGT*, June 1, 1958, 2.

22. Jameson, *All That Glitters*, 22–23.

23. *WPA Guide*, 117.

24. Jameson, *All That Glitters*, 48.

25. Unfortunately, many of those in the region who were most in need of the Myron Stratton Home became ineligible when the community of miners in Cripple Creek broke away from Republican-dominated El Paso County to form Teller County in 1899. See Jameson, *All That Glitters*, 47.

26. Also useful is "The Standard and Colorado-Philadelphia Mills," adapted with minor revisions from *Red Rock Rag* 4, no. 7 (July 2003), Friends of Red Rock Canyon website, http://redrockcanyonopenspace.org/education /history/the-standard-and-colorado-philadelphia-mills.

27. Jan MacKell, *Brothels, Bordellos, and Bad Girls: Prostitution in Colorado, 1860–1930* (Albuquerque: University of New Mexico Press, 2007), 131. The six-hundred-man figure is my best guess based upon the two hundred men who were employed at the Standard in 1905.

28. *WPA Guide*, 116.

29. The Golden Cycle adopted this new technology after a fire destroyed the mill. See Jameson, *All That Glitters*, 246. For the Haywood quote, see *WPA Guide*, 116.

30. "High Winds Bring Clouds of Dust and Protests to City and County Officials," *CSG*, March 25, 1914.

31. *WPA Guide*, 116.

32. Jameson, *All That Glitters*, 25.

33. Andrews, *Killing for Coal*, 240.

34. Jameson, *All That Glitters*, ch. 7; George G. Suggs Jr., *Colorado's War on Militant Unionism: James H. Peabody and the Western Federation of Miners* (Norman: University of Oklahoma Press, 1991), 20; Richard White, *It's Your Misfortune and None of My Own: A New History of the American West* (Norman: University of Oklahoma Press, 1991), 374–75.

35. Jameson, *All That Glitters*, 199–205.

36. Dubofsky, *Hard Work*, 51.

37. Jameson, *All That Glitters*, 199–202; Melvyn Dubofsky, *We Shall Be All: A History of the Industrial Workers of the World* (Urbana: University of Illinois Press, 2000), 23; Suggs, *Colorado's War*, 82–83.

38. Suggs, *Colorado's War*, 4, 111–12.

39. Jameson, *All That Glitters*, 245–52.

40. Ibid., 244.

41. Reid, "Growing Up in the Twenties," 55.

42. The question of which side was most responsible for the violence is still debated. Certainly pro-union miners were no angels. Take the brutal murder of mine foreman Martin Gleason, which happened well before the strike, and was likely at their hands. Gleason's body was completely mangled, with virtually every bone in it broken. After shooting him in the head, his murderers threw his body into an abandoned shaft that dropped some five hundred feet. Whoever killed him took neither his watch nor his money. "Mart Gleason Murdered and His Body Found in An Abandoned Shaft," *Cripple Creek Evening Star*, December 27, 1901, 1. His murder occurred just two months after his employer, the Woods Investment Company, announced that those working at their Victor mine would have to live there rather than in Cripple Creek, a shift in policy that one of the local papers attacked. See "You Can Work for Stratton," *Cripple Creek Star*, October 15, 1901, 5. A year and a half earlier Gleason had hired an African American miner to work in the Wild Horse Mine, whose workers Gleason supervised—a move that his crew successfully opposed. Still, a number of recent studies argue that some of the worst violence during the strike was the work of agents provocateurs, not WFM members. See Jameson, *All That Glitters*, 152.

43. Bold, *Frontier Club*, 1.

44. Limerick, *Legacy of Conquest*, 48. The chapter in which she discusses this is called "Empire of Innocence." Christine Bold has dubbed this process the "perpetrator-victim reversal" in *Frontier Club*, 15. Historian Richard White wrote about this dynamic as well in *It's Your Misfortune*, 603: "For people who were the beneficiaries of conquest, white westerners have had a persistent knack for portraying themselves as victims—of Indians, of the federal government, of eastern corporations."

45. Scott Martelle, *Blood Passion: The Massacre and Class War in the American West* (New Brunswick, NJ: Rutgers University Press, 2008), 19–20.

46. Quoted in James Green, "Re-interpreting Ludlow," *Dissent*, Spring 2009, 135.

47. The phrase "corporation-ridden" turns up in a number of places, including "Ex-Governor Adams Dies in Battle Creek After Long Illness," *DP*, November 2, 1922, 1.

48. "Simon, His Convention," *CSG*, September 13, 1908, 10.

49. Martelle, *Blood Passion*, 7.

50. John Green, "A Colorado Miners' Store," *Consumers' Cooperation: Organ of the Consumers' Cooperative Movement in the U.S.A.* 3, no. 5 (May 1917).

51. "Tutt Chosen Head of Open Shop Society," *CSG,* December 22, 1922. For more on the politics of the NAM, see Phillips-Fein, *Invisible Hands.* Elizabeth Shermer has argued that the post–World War II discourse of the right-to-work movement helped to unravel the New Deal's support of labor unions and the idea that they were a "legitimate part of the tripartite body politic." In the West, she says, leaders of the open shop exploited fears about unions' coerciveness and racketeering. Again, there is evidence that these fears were mobilized earlier in Colorado. See Shermer, "Is Freedom of the Individual Un-American? Right-to-Work Campaigns and Anti-Union Conservatism, 1943–1958," in *The Right and Labor in America: Politics, Ideology, and Imagination,* ed. Nelson Lichtenstein and Elizabeth Tandy Shermer (Philadelphia: University of Pennsylvania Press, 2012), 135–36.

52. Sinclair Lewis, *Babbitt* (1922; reprint, New York: Oxford University Press, 2010), 306–7.

53. In an August 25, 2014, email, Jameson said she imagines that the defeat of the union was a devastating defeat for striking workers and their supporters in Colorado City.

54. MacNeill quoted in *Mining and Engineering World* 23 (July–December 1905): 105; "Standard Mill to Close About Jan. 1," *CSG,* December 2, 1911; "Mill Being Torn Down," *Colorado City Iris,* January 19, 1917, 1.

55. The *Colorado Springs Independent,* a westside paper with a more working-class readership, regularly referred to the *Gazette* and the *Evening Telegraph* as the "Daily Twins." See, for example, a page-one article in the July 6, 1933 issue.

56. Reid, "Growing Up." I have reached this conclusion based upon the meeting places of the KKK, which were on the west side, the residence of KKK candidates for public office, and the precinct voting records from 1924 through 1930. The KKK was listed in the town's city directory.

57. See "Klan Puts Coolidge Ahead in Colorado," *NYT,* October 2, 1924, 4. Both the *Times* and the local dailies were critical of the KKK. "Form Anti-Klan Body in Colorado," *NYT,* May 13, 1925, 2; Robert Alan Goldberg, *Hooded Empire: The Ku Klux Klan in Colorado* (Urbana: University of Illinois Press, 1981) is the standard treatment. See also David M. Chalmers, *Hooded Americanism: The History of the Ku Klux Klan,* 3rd ed. (Raleigh, NC: Duke University Press, 1987); Ed Quillen, "Welcome to Kolorado, Klan Country," *Colorado Springs Independent,* May 22, 2003 (the name is the same as that of the newspaper that promoted the KKK, but the *Independent* did not have an uninterrupted publishing history; this is a different paper).

58. According to Goldberg, the local Masonic lodge was a KKK bastion. Goldberg, *Hooded Empire,* 53.

59. The *Independent* published an article that put the number of Klansmen in the Springs at one thousand. See "K.K.K. Meeting Pulls Full House,"

CSI, October 10, 1924, 1. Later the paper claimed that there were many more Klansmen in the larger Pikes Peak region, but I suspect that the paper's number exaggerates the membership numbers. See "Say 6,000 Klansmen in This Region—Number Increasing," *CSI*, November 14, 1925.

60. "Strong Opposition to R.O.T.C. in High Schools of This City," *CSI*, October 10, 1924, 1.

61. One gets a good sense of the important role played by the figure of the "pioneer" in the newspaper obituaries.

62. James J. Lorence, *The Unemployed People's Movement: Leftists, Liberals, and Labor in Georgia, 1929–1941* (Athens: University of Georgia Press, 2009), 126. Writing about the effects of the failed 1934 strike in the South, historian Jefferson Cowie notes, "Widespread industrial revolt would never again happen in the region." See Cowie, *The Great Exception: The New Deal and the Limits of American Politics* (Princeton, NJ: Princeton University Press, 2016), 107.

63. What little we know of Walter Davis's father indicates that he, too, was not a union man. When the barbers' union in nearby Columbus announced that its members would be levying an additional charge for neck shaving, Allen Davis came out loudly against it in the pages of the Greensburg newspaper.

64. Sheila Rothman, *Living in the Shadow of Death: Tuberculosis and the Social Experience of Illness in American History* (Baltimore: Johns Hopkins University Press, 1995), 187.

65. Bird, *A Lady's Life*, 154.

66. There are many articles about the TB industry in the *Gazette*, including the recent article by Scott Rappold, "America's Greatest Sanitarium," *Gazette*, June 17, 2007. For the connection between TB and street cleaning, see William French, "Drug Store Cowboy," his recollections of downtown Colorado Springs circa 1936, Special Collections, Pioneers Museum, Colorado Springs. Contemporary articles include "Where Colorado Springs Proves Its Brotherhood," *CSG*, October 5, 1913. Also very helpful is Chris Nichol et al., eds., *Doctors, Disease, and Dying in the Pikes Peak Region* (Colorado Springs: PPLD, 2012).

67. Henry Sewall quoted in Roy Porter, *The Greatest Benefit to Mankind: A Medical History of Humanity* (New York: Norton, 1999), 422.

68. Allen Davis Probate, File D113, box 43672, February 4, 1908, CSA.

69. "Human Vultures Thrive in Colorado Springs," *CSW*, May 27, 1932, 1.

70. The Moffat Tunnel project, which proposed to unite the eastern and western slopes of the Rockies, was controversial in large part because the tunnel would eliminate Pueblo's lock on westbound traffic. Legislation for it became bogged down in the general assembly more than once. It took a devastating flood in Pueblo, killing one hundred people, before the circumstances

were such that Governor Oliver Shoup could see his way to pushing the legislation through. Linking the passage of the tunnel bill to one for emergency funds for the disaster and for flood relief in and around Pueblo proved crucial to getting it passed. The final roadblock was caused by Shoup's insistence that the commission overseeing the tunnel's construction be composed entirely of his own choices. Roy's maneuverings got the legislation through the lower house, but with the proviso that the Moffat Tunnel commission be drawn from county commissioners of the four principal districts that were most affected. Roy's compromise was bitterly opposed by the Denver delegation, and it made him enemies, including quite possibly Shoup himself. See "Davis Wins Victory," *CSG*, April 27, 1922, 1; Kathleen Wallace, "Historical Perspectives: Who Was That Man Shoup?" *New Falcon Herald* 8, no. 6 (June 2011).

71. See Lynn Dumenil, *Modern Temper*, 197.

72. The Rotary Club magazine took note of Sinclair Lewis's *Babbitt* in Arthur E. Hobbs, "Is There Anything Wrong with Rotary?" *The Rotarian*, November 1925.

73. Walter Davis, Bureau of Investigation File, Davis family archive.

74. H. Dewey Anderson and Percy Erwin Davidson, *Occupational Trends in the United States* (Stanford: Stanford University Press, 1940), 599. Historian Sharon H. Strom argues that while jobs that were classified as "stenographer" and "typist" were becoming feminized as early as 1910, the absolute numbers of male stenographers and typists did not decline until 1930. She further argues that the impact of mechanization on the gendering of office work was somewhat more ambiguous than usually assumed. See Strom's authoritative study, *Beyond the Typewriter: Gender, Class, and the Origins of Modern American Office Work, 1900–1930* (Urbana: University of Illinois Press, 1994), 48.

75. Arthur Brooks Baker, "The Velvet Hammer," undated newspaper column, possibly written for the *Denver Post*. In this piece Baker touted Roy Davis's skills as a state legislator, but he made mention of his office machines.

76. Andrews, *Killing for Coal*, 59–61.

77. "Economical Conditions in Europe Are Poor, Says Davis on Return from Rotary Trip," *CSG*, July 19, 1927; John J. Lipsey, "Legionnaires to Paris," letter to the editor, *CSG*, July 22, 1927.

78. Devon E. Francis, "Statehouse Gossip," *CSG*, April 14, 1929.

79. See Susan Tucker, Katherine Ott, and Patricia Buckler, eds., *The Scrapbook in American Life* (Philadelphia: Temple University Press, 2006).

80. See Daniel J. Kevles, *In the Name of Eugenics: Genetics and the Uses of Human Heredity* (New York: Knopf, 1985); Paul A. Lombardo, *Three Generations, No Imbeciles: Eugenics, the Supreme Court, and Buck v. Bell* (Baltimore: Johns Hopkins University Press, 2010); Martin S. Pernick, *The Black*

Stork: Eugenics and the Death of "Defective" Babies in American Medicine and Motion Pictures Since 1915 (New York: Oxford University Press, 1996).

81. "Whitmore in Danger," *LAT,* December 17, 1930; "Beesemyer in Deeper," *LAT,* December 19, 1930.

2: The Loan Man

1. Peter R. Shergold, "The Loan Shark: The Small Loan Business in Early Twentieth-Century Pittsburgh," *Pennsylvania History* 45, no. 3 (July 1978): 196.

2. Lendol Calder, *Financing the American Dream: A Cultural History of Consumer Credit* (Princeton, NJ: Princeton University Press, 1999), 52. The case of the eighteen-year installment plan is drawn from Elizabeth Ewen's *Immigrant Women in the Land of Dollars: Life and Culture on the Lower East Side, 1890–1925* (New York: New Feminist Library, 1985), 170.

3. Calder, *Financing*, 50, 56.

4. Ibid., 58–60.

5. For a fascinating study of how personal debt moved from the shadows and into the mainstream of American capitalism, see Louis Hyman, *Debtor Nation: The History of America in Red Ink* (Princeton, NJ: Princeton University Press, 2011).

6. J.M. Oskison, "Exploiters of the Needy," *Collier's*, October 2, 1909, 17.

7. "Everybody's Business," *Jewish Social Service* 5 (1914): 122.

8. For example, what "lunchpail lending" giant Household Finance Corporation made in profits a hundred years ago would be dwarfed by what it would make in the 1990s and beyond. In 2001 HFC reported profits of $1.8 billion. Within a year the financial titan HSBC acquired HFC for $16.4 billion. Or take payday lending. In 2008, approximately 14 million households made use of a payday lender, and collectively they borrowed a staggering $40 billion in installments of $200 or $500 or $800. Respectable banks such as Wachovia, Bank of America, JPMorgan Chase, and Wells Fargo helped to finance the growth and expansion of the industry. Now the business of personal indebtedness is an engine of American capitalism. See Gary Rivlin, *Broke USA: From Pawnshops to Poverty, Inc.—How the Poor Became Big Business* (New York: Harper, 2010), 18, 27.

9. Calder, *Financing*, 26.

10. Thanks to Anne Hyde for this observation.

11. Shergold, "Loan Shark," 198–99. Small loans for short periods and with little by way of security could sometimes be obtained at immigrant banks, but usually even this opportunity was extended only to bankers' friends. See also Rivlin, *Broke USA*, 4.

12. A 1911 *New York Times* article quoted a well-known advocate of anti-loan-shark legislation, who cited as typical the figure given him by a business

insider—a $10,000 investment that had yielded $10,000 in profits in a little more than three months. See "Says Loan Sharks Bought Legislation," *NYT*, June 27, 1911.

13. Wells Fargo Messenger, "Borrowing Money: How Salaried Men Should NOT Do It," *B and O Magazine* 2, no. 1 (October 14, 1914): 47. The article borrows liberally from an older article by Chas. F. Bigelow, "The Borrower and His Pitfalls," which was published in the *Proceedings of the National Federation of Remedial Loan Associations* (Buffalo, NY: 1909).

14. J.A. Reichart, "Loan Shark Still Flourishes," *Forbes*, May 13, 1922, 31.

15. One defender of payday lending argues in an op-ed piece that "hardworking Americans" of modest means use payday lenders and check-cashing businesses because they are often a better option than checking accounts at banks whose fees put them out of the range of these consumers. Lisa Servon, "Are Banks Too Expensive to Use?" *NYT*, October 30, 2014. Another journalist offers a more measured account, but argues that even some consumer advocates who favor stronger regulation of payday lending acknowledge that the very people whom tighter regulations are meant to protect will likely be the ones most hurt by it. See Stacy Cowley, "To Curb Abuse, Loan Rules May Cut a Lifeline," *NYT*, July 23, 2016. And someone associated with EZ Pawn depicts the business as though it was a benevolent society: "We're there to help the community and to help people who need short-term 'bridge' loans." See Corey Kilgannon, "Chronicle of a Changing City," *NYT*, January 16, 2011.

16. Benjamin Blumberg, *Industrial Lenders News* 5, no. 12 (June 1921). Blumberg presented this paper in Indianapolis at the meeting of the Indiana Licensed Lenders Association in 1921. The article also claimed that the "borrower actually prefers to do business with money lenders so that he can preserve his pride, guard his dignity and avoid charity and alms."

17. Rivlin, *Broke USA*, 35.

18. Shergold, "Loan Shark," 210.

19. Charles Rogers, "American Unthrift," *Atlantic Monthly*, May 1911.

20. Some loan sharks would move their operations from "dank backrooms" into the personal loan businesses, now legal in states with the new small loan law. See Hyman, *Debtor Nation*, 12. Shergold argues that at first the result of the uniform small loan laws was to severely reduce the number of lenders, which caused a slight reduction in the capital available for loans. In the 1920s the number of authorized loan companies apparently declined. However, the continued inability of small loan companies to cope with the needs of low-income, high risk borrowers created an opening for the mob, which moved in and provided loans at much higher interest rates than were legally approved. See Shergold, "Loan Shark," 222–3.

21. Calder, *Financing*, 134. It is worth noting as regards today's payday lending that a Federal Deposit Insurance Corporation study focusing on

the profitability of payday lending found that the industry's interest rates were necessary because of the overhead associated with operating a retail outlet and borrowers' high rates of delinquency. See Cowley, "To Curb Abuse."

22. Some of today's loan sharks have developed an endless appetite for poor people with bad credit or no credit, and for people who repeatedly default on their loans. In fact, as one local branch manager for Household Finance Corporation admitted, the company actually targets consumers with terrible credit, people with scads of maxed-out credit cards. These are precisely the people that HFC and other such companies cultivate for new loans—at higher rates, and with a whole new slew of up-front fees appended. Rivlin, *Broke USA*, 6.

23. See Calder, *Financing*, 53–54.

24. Herbert Corey, "Silence Is Trait of Money Kings," 1927, newspaper clipping, Davis family archive.

25. In his guide to moneylending, Denver's leading loan shark, Charles E. Stratton, emphasized the necessity for secrecy in his line of work. See Oskison, "Exploiters of the Needy," 18.

26. Hugh Harper in June 24, 1932, letter to J. Edgar Hoover, director, Bureau of Investigation, from Walter Clyde Davis FBI file, 62-27247.

27. Glass quoted in Kennedy, *American People*, 66.

28. Garb, *City of American Dream*, 48; Cohen, *Making a New Deal*, 82; Snowden, "Transition," 170–72.

29. One 1893 national survey showed that B&L membership was drawn disproportionately from the working classes. Mason, *From Buildings and Loans*, 28–29.

30. Morton H. Bodfish, influential thrift industry leader, quoted in Calder, *Financing*, 67. Bodfish's 1931 *History of Building and Loan in the United States* was published by the industry trade group, the United States Building and Loan League.

31. For example, in the suburbs of Boston, Massachusetts, a house and lot that cost $3,000 would often be financed in the following fashion: A prospective homebuilder would accumulate savings of $1,500. He would then pay $500 cash for the property and $1,000 for the material and labor to build the house. The remaining $1,500 he owed would be raised through not one but two mortgages. The first would be obtained from a savings bank or from one of many private small investors working through mortgage dealers. The first mortgage would be for $1,200 at 5–6 percent interest, and it would enjoy legal priority over all other debts. When the building was almost finished a second mortgage for $300 at 6–8 percent interest was obtained from a real estate professional. By the time the house was finished, he still owed $1,500 and was required to pay interest payments semiannually for the next three to

eight years, and the payment of the principal in a lump sum at the end of the term. Calder, *Financing*, 65–66.

32. Ibid., 65–67.

33. Snowden, "Transition," 166–67; Calder, *Financing*, 67.

34. Mason, *From Buildings and Loans*, 28–29.

35. Mason emphasizes that many leaders of the "thrift business" identified with the movement toward economic, political, and social cooperation; ibid., 22–23. See also Alex Gourevitch, *From Slavery to the Cooperative Commonwealth: Labor and Republican Liberty* (New York: Cambridge University Press, 2014), 123. Robert Nelson, who is at work on a dissertation about the Knights of Labor, estimates that there were between fifteen and twenty Knights-affiliated building and loans, as well as proposals, which were never realized, for setting up another fifty. For the most part, the Knights of Labor focused on productive property rather than residential property. Email communication with Nelson, January 7, 2017.

36. Mason, *From Buildings and Loans*, 32–35.

37. Snowden, "Transition," 172.

38. The plaintiff in the case was Isadore Neuman and the defendant was the New York Mutual Savings and Loan Association. On April 18, 1891, Neuman subscribed for twenty-six shares in the New York association at $100 a share. He then borrowed $2,600 from the association. He was meant to pay interest at 6 percent a year, payable monthly. An agent of New York Mutual assured Neuman that his debt would be much smaller because the association enjoyed robust profits—on average between 15 and 20 percent—and that percentage would be deducted annually from Neuman's debt. In fact, the agent explained, because his interest would be between 3½ and 4 percent, Neuman's debt would be canceled within seven years. Neuman secured his loan with a first lien on real estate, which he owned, and by assignment of his twenty-six shares. However, he discovered that his obligations to the association included payments of $5.20 a month on the principal and another $13 a month in interest, as well as additional monthly fees of $10.40. These additional charges of $18.20 for principal and interest and $10.40 for handling costs came to $28.60 monthly and were said to cover the association's expenses, such as its salaries and commissions. All in all, the expenses involved in procuring the loan came to $79.40 and were deducted from the amount given Neuman, who received $2,520.60. From May 1, 1891, until March 1, 1894 Neuman paid the $26 entrance fee, $176.80 on the principal in dues at 20 cents a month, $448.00 interest at 6 percent, and $858.00 in additional dues for expenses—a total of $998.40. Deducting the interest at 6 percent, which he had paid for thirty-four months, it seemed that Neuman had paid $554.40 on the principal, but the association credited him with only $190.86 paid on the principal. See "Two Ways to Lend Money," *NYT*, July 13, 1897.

39. "Biennial Report of C.H. Leckenby, Auditor of the State of Colorado, from December 1, 1916 to November 30, 1918," CSA.

40. Mason, *From Buildings and Loans*, 37–38.

41. Ibid., 38.

42. Ibid., 71.

43. See Snowden, "Transition," 171.

44. The United States League of Local Building and Loan Associations, its institute, and allied associations also published histories of the industry. These self-serving industry accounts, which historians have often relied upon, are one reason that histories of America's thrifts in the decades before the S&L debacle tend toward the triumphalist. For example, Henry Morton Bodfish was both the executive director of the League and a historian of the building and loan industry whose work is much cited in accounts of the industry. See Bodfish, *History of Building and Loan*. Another prominent example of a history sponsored and published by the industry is Josephine Hedges Ewalt's *A Business Reborn*.

45. Mason, *From Buildings and Loans*, 74.

46. Once the state regulators of the B&L industry formed their own national organization in 1920 they held their annual meetings in conjunction with those of the League in order to share information. In 1922, thirty years after the founding of the League, representatives of the thrift, lumber, and real estate trade associations would come together to form another powerful trade association, the American Savings, Building and Loan Institute. See Mason, *From Buildings and Loans*, 72.

47. Ibid., 49.

48. Calder, *Financing*, 64.

49. No better evidence of the rising tide of radicalism was the success of the Socialist Party in 1912: its presidential candidate, Eugene Debs, snagged 6 percent of the vote, and twelve hundred of its candidates were elected to a variety of state and local offices.

50. Nicolaides, *My Blue Heaven*, 17.

51. Hoover quoted in "No Rent-Receipt Song," *NYT*, December 6, 1931.

52. Lewinnek, *The Working Man's Reward*, 86.

53. See W. E. B. Du Bois, *Black Reconstruction in America, 1860–1880* (New York: Free Press, 1998); David Roediger, *The Wages of Whiteness* (New York: Verso, 1991); Cheryl I. Harris, "Whiteness as Property," *Harvard Law Review* 106, no. 8 (June 1993).

54. For a useful discussion of black homeownership in the Chicago area, see Lewinnek, *The Working Man's Reward*, 92–93.

55. *Biennial Report of Roady Kenehan, Auditor of State of Colorado, from December 1, 1912, to November 30, 1914, Inclusive* (Denver: Smith-Brooks, 1914), 52, Box 13827, CSA.

56. 63rd Congress, *Rural Credits: Joint Hearings Before the Subcommittees of the Committees on Banking and Currency* (Washington, DC: Government Printing Office, 1914), 312.

57. Eli Gross, Commissioner of Building and Loan Associations, letter to Governor William H. Adams, January 5, 1933, Box 13829, CSA.

58. *Biennial Report of Roady Kenehan*, 40–41; *Biennial Report of M.A. Leddy, Auditor of State of Colorado, from December 1, 1910, to November 30, 1912, Inclusive* (Denver: Smith-Brooks, 1912), 237. Despite the concerns raised in these reports, it was the growth of out-of-state corporations masquerading as local building and loan associations that state officials found most troubling, and worked to eliminate. These were companies doing business as contract investment companies or contract loan companies, and their sharp business practices drew many complaints from consumers.

59. *Biennial Report of H.E. Mulnix, Auditor of State of Colorado, from December 1, 1915, to November 30, 1916, Inclusive* (Denver: Smith-Brooks, 1916), 128, Box 13827, CSA.

60. These figures are from the biennial report of 1920.

61. "Miller Hid Money Under Dining Table," *DP*, July 19, 1932; "Building-Loan in New Hands," *LAT*, July 16, 1927.

62. By June 1931 when Eli Gross was appointed commissioner of building and loan associations, a position that represented an improvement upon the position of deputy inspector, the assets of Colorado's B&Ls were reported to be $64 million, outstripping the reported assets of Colorado's state banks by $14 million, and yet the powers and funding conferred upon the commissioner were considerably less than those of the state banking commissioner. "Report: Governor's Special Committee on Building and Loan Associations," State of Colorado, Denver, 1932, Box 13829, CSA.

63. *People of the State of Colorado vs. The City Savings, Building and Loan Association, in the Claim of the Exchange National Bank of Colorado Springs, Colorado, Administrator de Bonis of the Estate of Thomas F. Woody, Deceased*, case no. 18902, February 27, 1934, Box 38445, CSA.

64. *The City Savings Building and Loan Association vs. P.J. Hecox*, case no. 16827, Box 37675, CSA.

65. A typical ad: "To Have Money When You Need It" was in large, bold type. The ad claimed that the City had long allowed depositors to withdraw "part or all of their money as needed without sacrificing accrued interest." *CSG*, January 1, 1923, 3.

66. *People vs. City Savings . . . Estate of Thomas F. Woody*.

67. Franklin W. Ryan, "Why Usury Laws Have Failed," *NYT*, April 9, 1922.

68. Edward Ewing Pratt, "Cooperative Savings and Loan Associations," *Proceedings of the Academy of Political Science in the City of New York* 2, no. 2 (January 1912).

69. The movie script was based upon a twenty-four-page story, "The Greatest Gift," that the writer and book editor, Philip Van Doren Stern, distributed as a Christmas card in 1943. Stern had been unable to sell his story to the glossies, but his Hollywood agent succeeded in selling it to Capra for $10,000. His holiday story of uplift was about a small-town bank clerk who, feeling trapped by the narrowness and the uneventfulness of his life and wishing he'd never been born, contemplates suicide. The protagonist is not a B&L owner whose business has enabled working people to become homeowners, but a bank clerk. The story was subsequently reworked by Marc Connelly, Dalton Trumbo, and Clifford Odets, who produced early scripts. Connelly created two Georges, a strategy then followed by Odets. Originally Cary Grant was set to play Bailey. See Jeanine Basinger, *The* It's a Wonderful Life *Book* (New York: Knopf, 1986), 103–7; Doug Molitor, "A Different Life: Cary Grant as George Bailey," letter to the editor, *LAT*, January 1, 2005. Molitor reveals that Michael Wilson, a victim of the Hollywood blacklist, performed an uncredited polish of the script.

3: Racketeers and Suckers

1. It was Nancy Cott, writing about gender-based solidarity among women, who used the term "we-ness." See Cott, *The Grounding of Modern Feminism* (New Haven, CT: Yale University Press, 1987), 5. For a very useful exploration of how historical scholarship on consumption has shifted, see Meg Jacobs, "State of the Field: The Politics of Consumption," *Reviews in American History* 39, no. 3 (2011). For examples of more upbeat appraisals of consumption: Roy Rosenzweig, *Eight Hours for What We Will: Workers and Leisure in an Industrial City 1870–1920* (New York: Cambridge University Press, 1985); Kathy Peiss, *Cheap Amusements: Working Women and Leisure in Turn of the Century New York* (Philadelphia: Temple University Press, 1986); Cohen, *Making a New Deal*; James Livingston, *Against Thrift: Why Consumer Culture Is Good for the Economy, the Environment, and Your Soul* (New York: Basic Books, 2011).

2. Hyman, *Debtor Nation*, 10.

3. Ibid., 31–33. It wasn't until the mid-1930s that the government went after auto finance companies such as General Motors Acceptance Corporation (GMAC) for deceptive advertising that claimed interest charges of 6 percent that turned out to be 12 percent. "Auto and Finance Firms Attacked," *CSG*, December 4, 1936, 1.

4. See Calder, *Financing*, 283–86, 260–61. Andrew L. Yarrow writes of the way that installment buying encouraged a "psychology of affluence." See Yarrow, *Thrift: The History of an American Cultural Movement* (Amherst: University of Massachusetts Press, 2014), 30–32. Some scholars have exaggerated the divide between the "producerist" nineteenth century and the

consumerism of the twentieth century. Veblen was an influential early critic and was followed by Galbraith, Vance Packard, Warren Sussman, and Christopher Lasch. Their influence has been enormous.

5. Mason, *From Buildings and Loans*, 61.

6. Ibid., 60.

7. "Building and Loan Associations Show Growth Since War," *New York Herald Tribune*, September 1, 1929, D1.

8. "Building and Loan Associations Gain Millions in Assets," *New York Herald Tribune*, May 31, 1925, B2.

9. Snowden, "Transition," 167–69.

10. Mason, *From Buildings and Loans*, 57.

11. See the Historical Society of Pennsylvania's digital history website, "Closed for Business: The Story of Bankers Trust Company During the Great Depression," by R. Daniel Wadhwani, http://digitalhistory.hsp.org/bnktr /essay/soothing-peoples-panic-banking-crisis-1930s-philadelphia.

12. "Report Governor's Special Committee on Building and Loan Associations," State of Colorado, September 1932, Biennial Reports, Box 13829, CSA, 9.

13. It was the 1932 Special Committee to the Governor on the B&L crisis that attributed the industry's collapse to the growth of this new-style B&L. It is, however, worth noting that there certainly were building and loan associations operating on this supposedly new-style basis well before 1920. The City was one, and so was Pueblo's mega-association, Railway Savings, which also predated my grandfather's business. See "Report Governor's Special Committee."

14. Mason puts the figure at 22 million; *From Buildings and Loans*, 44. Also see Cedric Cowing, *Populists, Plungers, and Progressives: A Social History of Stock and Commodity Speculation* (Princeton, NJ: Princeton University Press, 2015), 95–96; Cohen, *Making a New Deal*, 74.

15. Well-placed articles in the press promoted the "investment merit" of building and loans as well as the personal attention given to customers accustomed to being treated elsewhere like a "mere cog in the financial wheel." See, for example, "Building and Loan Associations Are Helping America," *Atlanta Constitution*, May 16, 1927, 10.

16. See Julia Ott, *When Wall Street Met Main Street* (Cambridge, MA: Harvard University Press, 2011), 65; Cowing, *Populists*, 95–96.

17. See *WPA Guide*, 116.

18. My discussion is informed by David Hochfelder, "'Where the Common People Could Speculate': The Ticker, Bucket Shops, and the Origins of Popular Participation in Financial Markets, 1880–1920," *Journal of American History* 93, no. 2 (September 2006).

19. Benjamin Roth, *The Great Depression: A Diary*, ed. James Ledbetter and Daniel B. Roth (New York: Public Affairs, 2009), 6.

20. *Merton E. Stubbs vs. Colorado Investment & Realty Co.*, District Court, County of El Paso, case no. 16738, October 6, 1928, Box 37675, CSA.

21. In her study of New York City in the twenties, Ann Douglas argued that with the arrival of mass culture Americans increasingly came to see that "everyone, wittingly or unwittingly, gets to play the 'sucker' one minute and the 'racketeer' the next." See Douglas, *Terrible Honesty: Mongrel Manhattan in the 1920s* (New York: Farrar, Straus and Giroux, 1996), 20.

22. J.R. Robinson, "The Ideal City," in Colorado Springs City Council, Town Incorporation, City Organization and Reorganization (Colorado Springs: City Council, 1901–2). Robinson, the mayor, cited the state's "unlimited mineral wealth."

23. Governor Shoup quoted in *House Journal of the Twenty-third General Assembly of the State of Colorado* (Denver: Smith-Brooks, 1921), 19.

24. Edgar T. Hunter, "A Thumbnail Sketch of the Cripple Creek/Victor Mining District's History," www.ccvgoldmining.com/downloads/History.pdf (accessed November 16, 2014). Hunter explains that gold production in the mining district began to slide after the turn of the century "because as the mines went deeper, ore grades decreased with depth, and water increased with depth." Production continued to decline even with the expensive construction of drain tunnels to facilitate mining. With the exception of one discovery of a lucrative cavity in 1914, gold production grew less and less profitable. Things improved somewhat in 1934 when the price of gold was raised from $20.67 to $35 per ounce. However, with U.S. entry into World War II, the gold mines were shut down as the government restricted the mining of nonessential metals.

25. According to the local press, gold production in the state was in decline in the 1910s, but really fell off during and after World War I. By 1926 profits from gold mining stood at just under $7 million; compare this to 1905, when profits were $25 million. See "History of Gold Output in State," *SGT*, March 6, 1927.

26. The Pikes Peak Highway, originally a toll road, was made free in 1936. "Pike, Palmer & Penrose Lauded," *CSG*, June 29, 1936; "Thrilling Two-Day Program to Mark Opening of Free Peak Auto Highway," *CSG*, June 14, 1936; "M.V. Park Spring Should Make City Famous Spa, Belief of Enthusiasts," *CSG*, Dec 17, 1922, 1. Earlier, in 1909, businessmen hit on the idea of constructing a tourist attraction in addition to the area's Short Line, the Midland railroad, and the Pikes Peak cog road. This new venture, what came to be called the Crystal Park Road, was meant to include a hotel and numerous cottages in the park, but these plans never materialized. The road itself went into the hands of a receiver in 1919, at which point it was consolidated with the Pikes Peak cog road. In 1925, Penrose acquired the cog railroad, Crystal Park highway, and Manitou Street Car Company. "Cog Railroad and Crystal Park Change Hands," *CSG*, June 25, 1925.

27. "Yount's Deep Drilling for Hot Water Recalls Other Manitou Well Projects," *SGT,* August 3, 1930, 8.

28. "Taxpayers' Association Opposed to Gas Franchise," *CSG,* June 25, 1931, 1.

29. "A Residential City of Rare Charm at the Gateway to the Roofgarden of America," *The "Greater Colorado" Edition of the Sunday Gazette and Telegraph,* April 6, 1930.

30. For the aerospace industry see William Deverell, Daniel Lewis, and Peter Westwick, "The End of the Aerospace Century," *LA Observed,* January 7, 2010, www.laobserved.com/visiting/2010/01/the_end_of_the_aerospace_centu.php.

31. *The WPA Guide,* 113.

32. Four million out of a total population of 120 million may sound small, but it was an unprecedented number. See Jules Tygiel, *The Great Los Angeles Swindle: Oil, Stocks, and Scandal During the Roaring Twenties* (New York: Oxford University Press, 1994), 10; Roth, *The Great Depression,* xv.

33. In 1921, Congress repealed the wartime excess profits tax, eliminated many luxury taxes, lowered corporate taxes, and slashed the maximum personal income tax from 65 percent to 32 percent. Mellon successfully advocated further reductions which created "windfalls for the wealthy." See Tygiel, *Great Los Angeles Swindle,*10.

34. Mayo quoted in Christopher Hawthorne, "Reading L.A.: Louis Adamic and Morrow Mayo" Culture Monster blog, *LAT,* January 31, 2011, http://latimesblogs.latimes.com/culturemonster/2011/01/reading-la-louis-adamic-and-morrow-mayo-1.html.

35. Associated Cultural Resource Experts, *Highway to the Sky: A Context and History of Colorado's Highway System* (Denver: Colorado Department of Transportation, 2002), ch. 5, "The Automobile Age Begins," https://www.codot.gov/programs/environmental/archaeology-and-history/highways-to-the-sky/ch5.pdf.

36. Much of what I know about Sims is gathered from newspaper articles about him that appeared in the local press and from Wilbur Fiske Stone, ed., *History of Colorado* (Chicago: S.J. Clarke, 1918), 2: 676–78.

37. My discussion of credit rating agencies draws on Scott A. Sandage's *Born Losers: A History of Failure in America* (Cambridge, MA: Harvard University Press, 2005), 148, and more generally chs. 5 and 6.

38. Yarrow, *Thrift,* 43. See David Kennedy, *Over Here: The First World War and American Society* (New York: Oxford University Press, 2004) 105.

39. Typical of the men involved with Assurance was Edgar Ensign, who was president of the association and Colorado's first commissioner of forestry. It was likely his death that precipitated the firm's sale to Sims.

40. "Springs Building Records Go Up by Leaps and Bounds," *CSG*, March 27, 1922.

41. "Lennon Park Name of New Townsite," *CSG*, April 15, 1921, 2. The *Gazette* published real estate advertisements for Lennon Park in April and May 1921. Adams Crossing is roughly at the intersection of Columbia Road and West Colorado Avenue, the main road that runs between Manitou Springs and Colorado Springs. It was named after the Civil War general Charles Adams, who came to Colorado after being wounded in the war to work as an agent for the White River Ute tribe in northwestern Colorado. Some believe that Adams's two-story Victorian was located right by the crossing and inside the current boundary of the RV campground. The crossing is roughly where Fountain Creek crosses West Colorado Avenue.

42. Often embezzlers are lower-level employees, although that description does not describe those who embezzled in the B&L scandal or in the S&L crisis fifty years later. See Kitty Calavita, Henry N. Pontell, and Robert H. Tillman, *Big Money Crime: Fraud and Politics in the Savings and Loan Crisis* (Berkeley: University of California Press, 1997), 63. For a useful treatment of today's most notorious embezzler, Bernard Madoff, see Diana B. Henriques, *The Wizard of Lies: Bernie Madoff and the Death of Trust* (New York: St. Martin's Griffin, 2012), 93.

43. Bentall differed from your average KKKer in that he belonged to downtown's First Baptist Church and not to the Pikes Peak Baptist Church in west Colorado Springs, whose membership was heavily Klan. Bentall was a deacon at the First Baptist and may have played a role in the sudden departure of its anti-Klan minister, Reverend Fulton, who resigned, without public explanation, in 1927. Years later, one resident recalled that the local KKK included no one "with any promise." There was at least one exception to that rule, however: lawyer and judge John E. Little. Goldberg, *Hooded Empire*, 55.

44. Less than four months after his association opened, Bentall arranged through the Home to loan $700 to a local laborer, Mike Daniels. As was customary, Daniels's loan was secured with a trust deed, in his case on a westside property. Six weeks later, Daniels showed up at the Home's office and paid $20 on the loan. Three weeks later he appeared at the association, this time with a check to pay off his loan in its entirety. People didn't usually pay off such a substantial loan that quickly. Most peculiar of all, Daniels paid it off with a check in the amount of $1,350. The check was from his friend Elmer Gunckle, a railroad repairman. Daniels directed whoever was working that day to have the association take the $680 (plus interest) that he still owed on the $700 loan and return the rest to him. Instead, the association cashed the check, released the trust deed on Daniels's property, and kept

the remaining $670. Daniels was an immigrant who had come to the United States in 1907. He had few skills or resources, as evidenced by the fact that he was still working as an unskilled laborer—a ditchdigger—in 1930. See *Mike Daniel vs. The Home Savings*, case no. 16449, Box 37618, CSA. For the state of Bentall's bookkeeping, see "$100,000 Shortage Denied by Bentall," *CSG*, July 8, 1932.

45. This is what happened to them in Sheridan, Wyoming, where they ended up selling many acres of rich land to their better-capitalized sometime partners Oliver Shoup and Verner Reed. Reed and Shoup paid them a half million dollars, so McKinnie and Davie made some money on the venture.

46. The newspaper article emphasized that in their Arizona ventures the two men relied upon the purchase of "script" rather than their own money. "Cropping of Desert Acres," *Arizona Republican*, May 27, 1912.

47. He was the president of the Manitou Mineral Water Company until sometime in 1920 or 1921, when the governor's son, Oliver Shoup Jr., assumed that position. Spencer Penrose, who was famously "wet," purchased the company from Shoup after the enactment of Prohibition, some say as a front to import alcohol; the company closed down after Prohibition was repealed. Dave Philipps, "Changing Hands Left Springs in the Shadows," *CSG*, July 17, 2011.

48. "Auditor, Former Employees Tell About E.C. Sharer's Acts When Dollar Co. Audit Was Demanded," *CSG*, September 28, 1932.

49. "Report Governor's Special Committee."

50. Kathleen Day, *S&L Hell: The People and the Politics Behind the $1 Trillion Savings and Loan Scandal* (New York: Norton, 1993), 191.

51. This is Louis Hyman's characterization. See *Borrow*, 74.

52. Roth, *The Great Depression*, 26; Galbraith, *The Great Crash*, 152–55.

53. For example, building and loans, which were by law made to keep their deposits in banks, sometimes were forced to close when the banks holding their money failed.

54. Sandage, *Born Losers*, 254–55.

55. Having brokered the legislation for the Moffat Tunnel in 1922, Roy was a rising star in Republican politics in Colorado.

56. Julie Berebitsky, *Sex and the Office: A History of Gender, Power, and Desire* (New Haven, CT: Yale University Press, 2012), 61.

57. In piecing together her past I have relied upon census records and city directories.

58. It was the brother of C.C. Hamlin, the *Gazette's* publisher and a leading member of the Mine Owners' Association, who brought Luke Terry's body back to the Springs for burial. News accounts claimed that he was a student at Colorado College, but he is not listed in the records, and in one

account of Ludlow he is identified as a mine guard. See Martelle, *Blood Passion*, 131. Martelle puts the number of dead during the fifteen-month strike at more than seventy-five. Historian Thomas Andrews, whose book *Killing for Coal* is beautifully written and extremely useful, cautions against what he calls "the perpetuation of the Ludlow-as-massacre story" on the grounds that it distorts our understanding of the relationships between the workers, the owners, and the state. I understand the desire to avoid the trope of victimization—after all, the striking workers were violent—but, as with the 1903–4 smelters strike discussed earlier, there is no getting around the imbalance of power between the strike owners and the striking workers. See Green, "Re-interpreting Ludlow."

59. By the 1920s courts were actually granting alimony more frequently, but the percentage of divorced women awarded alimony stood at only about 15 percent, according to U.S. Census Bureau statistics. See Amanda Barusch, *Brooks/Cole Empowerment Series: Foundations of Social Policy* (Belmont, CA: Centage, 2014), 384.

60. This was reported in Walter's FBI file.

61. For example, even the sons of Governor Oliver Shoup faced unwanted publicity when their marriages "went on the reef." In 1932, the *Rocky Mountain News* gloated, "Surprise piled upon surprise in the matrimonial affairs" of Oliver Shoup Jr. when his wife, claiming mental cruelty, filed for divorce, and his own dalliance with a divorcée became known. "Mrs. Oliver Shoup Jr. Files Suit for Divorce," *RMN*, April 28, 1932, 1. Three years into their marriage, Merrill Shoup's first wife sued for divorce because, she claimed, he had treated her cruelly and had refused to support her. See "Merrill Shoup Is Sued for Divorce," *CSG*, July 8, 1925, 10.

62. Lula shared with her daughter updates about Walter and Eva. Dorothy noted in her diary during the summer of 1927: "Mother saw E driving up and down Cascade to pick him up after he telephoned from drugstore—didn't tell him."

63. Knox was not cheap. Tuition and board came to nearly $1,000 a semester—a sum that did not include the many extra charges that the school levied. For my mother a typical semester's costs included $75 for horseback riding, $100 for piano lessons, $50 for lectures and athletics, a $50 registration fee, $19.25 for weekly hot oil shampoos and manicures, $7 for excess laundry charges, $2.70 for ladies' maid service, and $2.50 for her (required) seat in the church. Students were charged for uniforms, note pads, textbooks, and even cocoa. All in all, Knox would have cost Walter about $2,700 a year, which, when converted to 2016 dollars, is roughly equivalent to what a tony private boarding school costs parents today.

64. "Noted Author Has Article on Cheyenne Mountain Country Club in Country Life," *CSG*, August 20, 1920, 6.

65. David Shumway, "Fetishizing Fetishism: Commodities, Goods, and the Meaning of Consumer Culture," *Rethinking Marxism* 12, no. 1 (Spring 2000): 11; Lewis, *Babbitt*, 62.

66. In fact, the very same month that Walter declared his readiness to "go through with it," a Denver oilman and millionaire had settled out of court with a showgirl whom he had promised to marry. She collected $45,000. Undated news clipping about Denver oilman Frank Kistler, May 1929, Davis Family Archive.

67. Much of Colorado had limped along in the aftermath of World War I. However, the state's fortunes began to revive by decade's end. Pueblo's Colorado Fuel and Iron Company, the biggest steel plant west of the Mississippi, enjoyed such a profitable year in 1929 that the firm budgeted for $1 million of additional coke ovens. This account of the frenzy in the Springs appeared in the *Rocky Mountain News* and is cited in Leonard, *Trials and Triumphs*, 13. For pre-crash conditions in Colorado, see Leonard as well.

68. Parts of southeastern Colorado were part of the Dust Bowl. For the slump preceding the Great Depression in the Dust Bowl states of North and South Dakota, see Catherine McNicol Stock, *Main Street in Crisis: The Great Depression and the Old Middle Class on the Northern Plains* (Chapel Hill: University of North Carolina Press, 1992), 18. On stock exchanges after the crash, see Roth, *The Great Depression*, 7. On conditions in the fall of 1929 in Colorado Springs, see "Stock Market Crash Now Latest Alibi of Debtors," *CSG*, November 3, 1929; "Will Transfer Movie Studio to Springs," *CSG*, November 10, 1929, 1.

69. The number of his depositors varied according to newspaper and publication date. I have chosen to go with the number of 3,609 that the receiver and his lawyer supplied to the press. "Second Dividend on City Savings," *CSG*, October 18, 1936, 1.

4: Slipping Through Your Fingers

1. Much of this account is drawn from William E. Leuchtenburg, *Herbert Hoover* (New York: Times Books, 2009), 129–34.

2. This happened in Youngstown, Ohio, in the spring of 1932. See Roth, *The Great Depression*, xiii, 54.

3. "Fewer Desirable Rentals than a Year Ago," April 26, 1932, *CSET*, 14.

4. "Unemployment is Growing In City, Says Secretary," *CSG*, January 18, 1931.

5. McNicol Stock, *Main Street in Crisis*, 18; Leonard, *Trials and Triumphs*, 25–26.

6. "A.E. Carlton Estate Value Is $991,069," *CSET*, December 25, 1931, 16.

7. "Heywood Broun Interviews Manufacturer Who Calls Himself a 'Golf Bag Socialist,'" *RMN*, 6.

8. John F. Kasson, *The Little Girl Who Fought the Great Depression: Shirley Temple and 1930s America* (New York: W.W. Norton, 2014), 19.

9. See Cohen, *Making a New Deal*, 267.

10. Roth, *The Great Depression*, 26; Galbraith, *The Great Crash*, 154; "A Bank Swindle Linked with the Market Break," *NYT*, February 2, 1930. Nearly a year after their sentencing, only nine of these men were still in prison. See "Acquits Flint Banker in $3,500,000 Shortage," *NYT*, December 21, 1930.

11. "Californian Admits Theft of $7,500,000," *NYT*, December 13, 1930; "$8,000,000 Embezzler Heavy Loser in Stocks," *NYT*, December 19, 1930. Beesemyer pleaded guilty and was sentenced to forty years in prison. He served nine years in San Quentin, from which he was released in January 1940. The *Los Angeles Times* was tight-lipped when it came to the area's B&L failures. The paper noted that two years after the state seized control of his B&L, it had assets (almost entirely in real estate) of over $5 million. However, it would take years before the depositors would see any money. See "Guaranty Loan Set-Up Shifted," *LAT*, October 5, 1932. In 1936, almost six years after its crash, the receiver paid out its first dividend—at 10 percent. See "Guaranty Dividends Expected," *LAT*, April 7, 1936. It took seven years from the time of its reorganization for the liquidating corporation to operate at a profit. "Guaranty Profits of $44,152 Announced," *LAT*, May 18, 1937.

12. "Whitmore in Danger," *LAT*, December 17, 1930.

13. "Building Loan Offices Moved," *LAT*, August 3, 1933.

14. "Loan Official Gets Long Prison Term," *Pittsburgh Press*, June 24, 1932; "Accuse 40 Philadelphians," *NYT*, July 28, 1932; "Escaping Gas Kills Editor," *NYT*, November 9, 1929. The Newark B&Ler was also an editor of a Hungarian newspaper, and his troubles were exacerbated by a libel suit brought against him by another newspaper editor.

15. See article on John F. Vivian on page one of the December 10, 1931 edition of the *Gazette*. His own political career was ruined, but his son was elected governor of Colorado thirteen years later, in 1944.

16. Galbraith, *The Great Crash*, 150–51.

17. In a speech given for the Colorado State League of Building and Loan Associations, probably in 1928, Sims declared that a properly run association could not fail because it was backed by the best possible security, first mortgages on real estate. "Willis Sims Says a B&L Properly Managed Cannot Fail," *CSG*, January 19, 1928.

18. "Home Paper Predicts Early Reorganization of Nevada B.&L. Assn.," *Sikeston Standard*, June 10, 1932, 1.

19. "Loan Association Inquiry Finished," *CSG*, January 5, 1932, 10.

20. "Extension Is Granted for Assurance," *CSG*, February 6, 1932, 1.

21. "Assets of Closed Loan Firms Gain," *CSG*, September 22, 1936, 1.

22. *Assurance Liquidation Corporation vs. Buffalo Lodge, Etc.*, case no. 19082; *Grant McFerson, as State Bank Commissioner vs. Fidelity and Deposit Company of Maryland, Etc.*, Statement of Claim, no. 18886; *Assurance Liquidation Corporation vs. Grant McFerson, Etc.*, case no. 18997; *Assurance Liquidation Corporation vs. Buffalo Lodge*, case no. 19082, Box 46075, CSA.

23. "Broadmoor Golfers," *CSG*, July 13, 1933.

24. "R.D. Sims Takes Own Life by Gun," *SGT*, February 8, 1942, 4.

25. "Buffalo Lodge Is Sold for $99,000," *CSG*, November 27, 1941, 1.

26. "City Sued for $1,314.80 by Mrs. Edith Foersteman," *CSG*, June 8, 1932, 1. See also *Esther Foersteman vs. The City Savings Building and Loan Association*, case no. 18875, Box 46075, CSA. Esther and Edith appear to be the same woman, a divorced bookkeeper.

27. It's worth noting here that the *Denver Post's* tell-all coverage of the B&L scandal was driven in large part by politics. The paper opposed Democratic governor Billy Adams and tried to pin it on him. For examples of these upbeat articles, often published as "specials to" the newspaper in question, see "Building and Loan Associations Gain in Assets and Memberships," *Christian Science Monitor*, January 2, 1930, 24; "Building and Loan Associations," *Wall Street Journal*, October 26, 1931, 6; "Building and Loans Concerns' Good Position," *Christian Science Monitor*, February 11, 1933, 10.

28. Pratt quoted in C.H. Packard, "Debate on Spiritualism," *CSI*, February 13, 1930, 2.

29. The Pratts were early adopters of the term "racketeer" to describe unionist officials. See, for example, "Rackets Under Guise of Unions Boycott Trade," *CSW*, August 12, 1932, 1, and "Labor Racketeers Coerce Candidates at Every Election," *CSW*, August 26, 1932, 1. It was right-wing newspaperman Westbrook Pegler, columnist for the conservative newspaper chain Scripps-Howard, who was most responsible for getting the term into circulation, but not until the early 1940s. Pegler and other conservatives framed as "racketeering" legitimate union activities (dues collection, union shop contracts, and secondary boycotts) and in so doing helped to lay the foundation for the Taft-Hartley Act of 1947, which so undermined the labor movement. The term also helped delegitimate the New Deal. For scholarly discussions of the role played by labor racketeering and the discourse around it, see David Witwer, "The Racketeer Menace and Anticommunism in the Mid-Twentieth Century US," in *International Labor and Working Class History* 74, no. 1 (Fall 2008); David Witwer, "Labor History Symposium: David Witwer, *Shadow of the Racketeer*," and responses by Kim Phillips-Fein, Robert Zieger, Gerald Friedman, and James Jacobs, *Labor History* 52, no. 2, May 2011.

30. It is impossible to know when the Pratts began to go after the building and loan industry because the only surviving issues of the newspaper cover nothing more than the period from May 1932 until November 1932. But

certainly by April, if not sooner, the renegade paper was publicizing the situation and driving the panic. The Pratts did break with some other tax-slashing activists by supporting old-age pensions, and very briefly even FDR. See "My Stand on Old Age Pension," *CSW*, September 13, 1932, 1. For its views of FDR, see "The Farmers Seize the Donkey," in the September 23, 1932, issue and "Roosevelt Says Nothing" in the September 30, 1932, issue.

31. The state attorney general later said that this was not actually a legally binding requirement.

32. I should say that Sharer was no stranger to lawsuits. For example, in 1927 a thirty-three-year-old man whom Sharer had hired to work for the association off-site sued the B&L head, claiming that he had reneged on his promise to pay him $104 a month, plus the cost of his gasoline. It's also worth noting that some of the suits that would come to trial in 1932 concerned transactions several years old, perhaps because those with grievances against him felt that their cases might be taken seriously with Sharer now seemingly on the ropes. *Sharer vs. Glenn O. Elliott*, November 15, 1927, El Paso County District Court, case no. 16486, Box 37618, CSA.

33. Here I am drawing upon articles in the press as well as *Supreme Court of Colorado v. Shields*, case no. 13280, October 9, 1933 (93 Colo. 480, 27 P.2d 485).

34. In 1924 Sharer sold Forbes a forty-acre tract of land in the Black Forest, just north of Colorado Springs. The region was attracting a number of investors because it had become locally known that a California company believed it might contain oil and gas reserves. Sharer had arranged for Forbes to buy the land through a loan from the Dollar. At some point later, after having paid about half of his debt to the Dollar, Forbes reportedly approached Sharer again about buying more of the quickly appreciating land. After purchasing another thirty acres, Forbes owed the association $1,800. Soon thereafter the oil company lost interest in the region and land values in the Black Forest dropped. According to Sharer, Forbes, who had not succeeded in selling his land, grew disgruntled. Sharer reportedly claimed that he told Forbes he would allow him to pull out of the second transaction entirely. Sharer said that he wrote the Dollar a check to cover the purchase price of that now-canceled second land deal. And Forbes paid off the balance of the loan for the first land parcel. That should have been the end of story, but in March 1927 Sharer directed a clerk at the association to issue two checks to Forbes—one for $300 and the other for $700. According to the district attorney Sharer then signed Forbes's name on the back of each check and claimed $1,000 from the Dollar company's funds, with the intention of keeping the money for himself. Dollar employees said that Sharer explained he was due the money because of a business transaction with Forbes's son-in-law. "Sharer to Face Forgery Charges," *CSG*, August 12, 1932, 1.

35. Many depositors believed Sharer's story that Walter Davis, not Sharer, controlled the Dollar. It is true that from 1927 onward, Davis seems to have tried to keep the Dollar from closing, doubtless for self-interested reasons. He wanted to prevent any domino-like collapse of the B&L business in the Springs. The authorities also believed that Davis controlled the Dollar, but the evidence here is mixed. An official of the Dollar, its secretary, testified in court that Davis did not control the association. On the other hand a former employee claimed in court that it had been Davis who hired him to work as a clerk at the Dollar. It does seem that the affairs of the two associations were entangled in some complicated ways. However, Sharer's dubiousness in business matters and his propensity to lie were established well before 1927, and they were confirmed by the whistleblowing employee and the auditor who investigated that 1927 shortfall. The speculation that Davis encouraged Sharer to leave town because he believed the industry's collapse in the Springs was imminent seems unlikely. More than six weeks passed between Sharer's escape from Colorado Springs and Davis's. See "Davis Controlled Dollar Loan Association—Sharer," *CSG*, June 26, 1932, 1; "Sheriff Departs to Return Sharer," *CSG*, June 27, 1932, 1; "Auditor, Former Employees Tell About E.C. Sharer's Acts," *CSG*, September 28, 1932, 2.

36. Leonard, *Trials and Triumphs*, 34; "Record Number of Homeless," *CSET*, May 4, 1932; "Salvation Army Served 2,780 Meals in Week," *CSG*, May 1, 1932.

37. W. E. Sparling, "City's 'Hotel' Guests, Here for Night Only, Constantly Kept on the Move," *CSG*, December 29, 1931, 7.

38. Ibid.; "Street Cars Are Replaced by Buses," *CSG*, May 1, 1932, 1; "Little Trolley Cars," *CSG*, April 30, 1932, 1; "A Roaring Tornado in the Shadow of Pikes Peak," *RMN*, June 11, 1932, 1.

39. *W.A. Paulsen vs. The Home Savings Building and Loan, H.L. Armentrout and Fred N. Bentall*, June 22, 1932, case no. 18906, Box 46073, CSA.

40. "Bentall Held in County Jail for Embezzlement," *CSG*, June 30, 1932, 1; "Bentall Charged with Theft," *CSG*, June 31, 1932, 1; "Bentall Confesses Juggling Funds," *CSG*, July 1, 1932, 1; "$100,000 Shortage Denied by Home's Bentall," *CSG*, July 8, 1932, 1.

41. "Authorities Differ on Fingerprinting & Photographing Bentall and Sharer," *CSG*, August 28, 1932, 4; "DA Meikle Prepares 8 Charges," *CSG*, August 17, 1932, 1.

42. "Bentall Tells Meikle He's Pleading Guilty," *CSG*, August 20, 1932; "51-Year-Old Bentall Gets 16–35 Years," *CSG*, August 26, 1932, 1; "Bentall Denies Hiding Funds of Home," *CSG*, August 23, 1932, 1; "Bentall Now in State Prison in Canon City," *CSG*, August 27, 1932, 1; "Bentall Is Now in State Reformatory," *CSG*, September 2, 1933, 1; "Home Savings Will Pay First Dividend," *CSG*, December 12, 1934, 1; "Liquidation Soon for Home

Savings," *CSG*, December 11, 1936, 1; "Final Payment of Homes Savings Out," *CSG*, February 2, 1937; "Fred N. Bentall Freed on Parole," *CSG*, May 18, 1938, 1.

43. The description here is drawn from "Top Hat and Limousine," *RMN*, December 13, 1932.

44. Amity Shlaes, *The Forgotten Man: A New History of the Great Depression* (New York: HarperCollins, 2007), 139.

5: Sowing Grief

1. "Million Shortage Found in Springs Loan Concern," *DP*, June 23, 1932, 1; "Davis Affairs in Bad Shape After January 1," *CSG*, June 28, 1932, 3.

2. "Davis Affairs in Bad Shape." The initial communication about the house on Millionaires' Row was made in a telegram while Walter was traveling.

3. Mention of the representative is mentioned in "Court to Protect Borrowers from B&Ls," *CSG*, September 8, 1932, 5.

4. "Upholds Cornforth in Woody Decision," *CSG*, October 24, 1934, 10.

5. "Can Walter Davis Avoid Extradition Like Insull Is Now Doing in Greece?" *SGT*, October 16, 1932.

6. "Taxes Mount Up on B&L Properties," *CSG*, November 24, 1932.

7. "City Sued for $1,314.80 by Mrs. Edith Foersteman," *CSG*, June 9, 1932, 1.

8. Lula's lawyer, Horace Hawkins, made this claim at the trial for the railway officials, whom he was defending. See "Railway Loan Firm Officers Kept Secret Bank Account," *CSG*, January 11, 1934.

9. "Davis Said Threats Caused Him to Leave," *CSG*, June 28, 1932, 3.

10. "Human Vultures Thrive in Colorado Springs," *CSW*, May 27, 1932, 1; "Citizens Left Destitute," *CSW*, June 3, 1932, 4.

11. "Revealed That Railway Association's Attorney, Bernard Seeman of Denver," *CSG*, July 15, 1932, 1.

12. Hoover created the RFC in January 1932 and among its intended beneficiaries, some believed, were building and loan societies. Kennedy, *Freedom from Fear: The American People in Depression and War, 1929–1945* (New York: Oxford University Press, 2001), 84. Opinion differed about whether B&Ls were eligible for RFC assistance. See the Hearings on Home Loan Bank Bill, 1932, in *Hearing Before Committee on Rules, House of Representatives, Seventy-First Congress*, Third Session, on H.J. Res. 292 (Washington, DC: Government Printing Office, 1931).

13. These details (and, indeed, many of the other details here) appear in Walter Davis's Bureau of Investigation file.

14. "City Savings Loan Assn. Placed in Receivership," *CSG*, June 21, 1932; "Open Davis's Savings Deposit Boxes in Morning," *CSG*, June 22, 1932, 1.

15. "Walter Davis and $1,000,000 Are Missing," *CSG*, June 23, 1932, 1; "Warrant Charging Davis with Filing False Claims Issued," *CSG*, June 24, 1932, 1.

16. "Inspector of Colorado Springs Detectives Asks NYC Police to Arrest Davis," *DP*, June 23, 1932.

17. In the months leading up to the collapse of the City, Colorado newspapers carried a number of stories about men who killed themselves so that their insurance money could aid their heirs or favorite charity or cause. One such story featured the suicide of a well-known Denver businessman (whose wife was a niece of abolitionist John Brown) who reportedly killed himself to aid Colorado Woman's College. "Braukman Ends Life to Aid Woman's College with Insurance," *DP*, June 1, 1932, 1.

18. "Walter Davis and $1,000,000 Are Missing."

19. This would be Richard Sobel, a lawyer in Ann Arbor, Michigan.

20. "Legal Action to Be Filed by Meikle," *CSG*, June 25, 1932, 1.

21. Ibid.

22. "Police Arrest Eva Terry," *CSG*, June 24, 1932, 1.

23. "Denver Girl Who Worked for Firm to Be Questioned," *DP*, June 23, 1932, 1; "Terry Woman Refuses to Betray Davis," *CSG*, June 24, 1932, 1.

24. According to the *Colorado Springs Evening Telegraph*, Eva had undergone surgery for adhesions resulting from a recent operation for appendicitis. According to medical historian Lynn Sacco, appendicitis surgery for women was often code for a hysterectomy. The reason a code was even necessary was that sometimes a hysterectomy was required to deal with untreated gonorrhea that had resulted in pelvic inflammatory disease. Both female and male doctors discussed this practice of misnaming, which was generally viewed as the ethical option of choice, because to tell the wife she had gonorrhea was tantamount to outing her husband as a philanderer, which doctors saw as a violation of ethics. Of course, Eva may have actually suffered appendicitis. Email correspondence, Lynn Sacco, January 11, 2011.

25. "Denver Girl, Ex-Secretary of Fugitive Banker Arrested," *DP*, June 24, 1932, 1.

26. "Release Eva Terry Today," *CSG*, June 25, 1932, 1.

27. "Woman Still Held Thru Agreement," *CSET*, June 25, 1932, 2; "Police Arrest Eva Terry in Denver for Quiz," *CSG*, June 24, 1932, 1.

28. "Springs Loan Firm's Bonds Hunted Here," *RMN*, June 25, 1932, 1; "File Charges on Eva Terry & W.C. Davis," *CSG*, July 1, 1932, 1.

29. News clipping from Olathe, Colorado, May 14, 1931: "While Dems Are Grooming Lt. Governor Johnson the Republicans Should 'Get Busy Slicking Up Roy Davis.'" Also, "Boosts Roy Davis for Governorship," *Alamosa Press*, December 3, 1926. Alamosa was the hometown of Governor Billy Adams, with whom Roy Davis worked closely, despite the party difference.

Roy A. Davis Collection, S2010.18, Folder 1, D, Pioneers Museum, Colorado Springs.

30. "Mrs. W.C. Davis Promises to Aid Authorities," *CSG*, June 27, 1932, 1; "Daughter Is with Mother at Home Here," *CSET*, June 27, 1932, 7; "Wife of Davis Is Hysterical in Police Quiz," *DP*, June 27, 1932, 1; "Davis in America, Harper Believes," *CSG*, June 28, 1932, 1.

31. "Plot to Seize Daughter of Davis Feared," *RMN*, June 30, 1932, 1; "Plot to Kidnap Verner Z. Reed and His Two Sons," *CSG*, June 4, 1932, 1. For a useful history, see Paula Fass, *Kidnapped: Child Abduction in America* (New York: Oxford University Press, 1997).

32. "Depositors Ask Court to Offer Reward for WC Davis," *CSG*, September 1, 1932, 1.

33. Doma's views appeared in the July 17, 1932, edition of the *Denver Post*. Those who knew Roy's signature, which was very similar to his brother's, must have chuckled over Doma's sinister interpretation.

34. "Did Davis Have the Million or Had He Spent It?" June 25, 1932, *CSET*, 2.

35. "Can Walter Davis Avoid Extradition."

36. "Depositors Demand Arrest of Gross," *DP*, July 2, 1932, 1.

37. I have pieced together Eli Gross's career from multiple sources, including Martelle, *Blood Passion*, census reports, newspaper articles, and mentions in the *Cigar Makers Official Journal* and *The Miners Magazine*. For the cigar maker charge, see "That's That," *DP*, July 15, 1932, 2.

38. "Revealed That Railway Association's Attorney Bernard Seeman," *DP*, July 15, 1932, 1; "Gross Failed Civil Service Exam," *DP*, August 7, 1932.

39. "Depositors Ask Court to Offer Reward for WC Davis," *CSG*, September 1, 1932, 1; "Court to Protect Borrowers from B&Ls," *CSG*, September 8, 1932, 5.

40. For one such typical attack, see "Newton to Draw $1,000 a Month Salary as Receiver of Pueblo B&L," *DP*, July 27, 1932, 1.

41. Home Loan Bank Bill, House of Representatives, Committee on Rules, May 26, 1932, and June 7, 1932, in *Hearing Before the Committee on Rules, House of Representatives, Seventy-Second Congress* (Washington, DC: Government Printing Office, 1932). Quotations cited can be found in this order: 22, 22, 35, 35, 40, 27.

There was a disagreement about whether, legally, building and loan associations could accept federal money. I have found one newspaper article that shows that the RFC did loan money to B&Ls in Dayton, Ohio. However, this was a deal in which the HOLC exchanged $12 million of its bonds for mortgages in the seven associations, which would then be reorganized as federal savings and loan associations. My understanding is that this was not typical: most failing and frozen B&Ls were not revived in this fashion. "RFC Makes

$20,574,832 Loans to Aid Seven Dayton Building and Loan Groups," *NYT*, December 9, 1934, N7.

42. "People's Vote Urged on Beesemyer Bill," *LAT*, May 5, 1937. The tabling of the bill in the Senate Judiciary Committee led its supporters to consider pushing for a constitutional amendment so that victims of the massive B&L meltdown in California could file claims against the state for compensation. The logic behind the bill was that state liability was reasonable given the failure of state examiners to detect shortages. The man behind it was a Democratic assemblyman from the San Fernando Valley, Elmer Lore Sr., who was supported by Democrats Culbert Olson and Ralph Swing as well as Bradford Crittenden, a Republican.

43. Cohen, *Making a New Deal*, 233, 230, 276–77.

44. Anne O'Hare McCormick quoted in Bieto, *Taxpayers in Revolt*, 8.

45. El Paso County residents formed the association in 1880, and revived it as a corporation in 1917. Officers were Richard T. Clough, president, Charles N. Wheeler, secretary and E.J. Eaton, treasurer. "To the Taxpayers of El Paso County," statement of purpose, January 5, 1917, Special Collections, Tutt Library, Colorado College.

46. "Demand Slash Expenditure Public Cash," *CSG*, January 27, 1933, 1; "Foresees Slashes in City Activities," *CSG*, September 3, 1936.

47. What I am describing here resembles in many respects what Becky M. Nicolaides uncovered in her book about the white working people of the Los Angeles suburb Southgate. See *My Blue Heaven*.

48. Merrill Shoup made many of these points at a meeting of Denver's Taxpayers' Protective Association. See "Citizens Demand End of Officials' Spending Spree," *DP*, January 9, 1932, 1. On the efforts of the El Paso County Taxpayers Association to block the city's plans to pave the streets with gold, see "'Taxpayers Launch Campaign on Paving," *CSG*, March 5, 1920, Sec. 2, 2.

49. The consciousness of these working-class antitax activists may prefigure the hostility of formerly unionized private-sector workers toward unionized public-sector workers whom they regard as the beneficiaries of "special treatment." See Noam Scheiber, "Labor's Might Seen in Failure of Trade Deal," *NYT*, June 14, 2015. This hostility has enabled anti-statist politicians such as Wisconsin governor Scott Walker to successfully go after public-sector workers. Another recent study that may be useful in understanding the consciousness of some members of the EPCTA shows that support for raising the minimum wage is popular except among those who "make just above the minimum wage" and who figure that the beneficiaries of a wage increase might "leapfrog me." See Noam Scheiber, "Give to the Bottom? Sure, as Long as They Stay There," *NYT*, June 10, 2015.

50. "Citizens Demand."

51. The EPCTA brought together Republicans and Democrats, which caused conflict. The group's positions, particularly when it came to public ownership of utilities or development, often put it at odds with many within the Republican establishment. Although Judge Little slammed the city's decision to build an airport, claiming that it was so unused "not even a buzzard" had flown over it in months, other Republicans were for it. The airport would become a piece of the Springs' successful courtship of the U.S. military less than ten years later. See "Avery Offers to Battle," *CSG*, March 1, 1933, 1.

52. Here Oliver Shoup is paraphrasing the late President Harding. See "Shoup Opposes Council Plan," *CSG*, March 16, 1924. Shoup's view was not unusual among power brokers in the Springs. P.B. Stewart, president of the Colorado Springs Electric Company and the (unsuccessful) Republican nominee for governor in 1906, argued a year later that municipal ownership of public utilities was inefficient, needlessly expensive, and "socialistic." "'Municipal Ownership,'" *CSG*, March 22, 1907, 1. For more on Stewart, see his obituary in the *CSG*, July 22, 1957. Shoup's characterization of city-owned utilities as "socialistic" was echoed years later by a "taxpayer" who in a letter to the editor claimed it was "Russian." See *CSG*, February 28, 1933, 5. Another Springs corporation that battled with the town's public utilities commission was the Golden Cycle, which requested a restoration of its former light and power rates. When its request was refused, the corporation announced it would build its own power plant. "Golden Cycle to Build $200,000 Power Plant," *CSG*, May 4, 1918, 3.

53. See Lewis, *Babbitt*, 150.

54. Richard S. McElvaine, *The Great Depression: America, 1929–41* (New York: Three Rivers Press, 1984), 254–56.

55. "Mayor Replies to Handbill" and "Nine Mill Levy Is Up for Vote Today," *CSG*, April 4, 1933.

56. A favorable article in the *Denver Post* described the groups as composed of both "small homeowners, who are facing the loss of their modest properties through tax sales as well as prominent professional men and large property owners"; see "Citizens Demand." My research into the twenty-five members whose names appeared in the press (and who appeared in the city directory or census) suggests that the newspaper was not exaggerating. Figuring out the most useful way to categorize these individuals is not easy especially because there is a good deal of variation in many of these categories. Take the category of lawyer, say. Some lawyers did quite well for themselves, judging by their addresses, but not all lawyers were prosperous North End lawyers. My breakdown of these twenty-five is as follows: three widows of prominent professionals or businessmen, one salesman/clerk, four lower-level service workers (porter at a pool hall to census clerk), two laborers, three lawyers,

four merchants, two real estate salesmen, three wealthy businessmen, and three contractors/builders of modest means.

57. Particularly in the West, hostility to government—or certain kinds of government authority—did not originate with these taxpayer associations, but rather has a long history. However, these taxpayer associations have not been studied nearly enough, even though one can draw a line from them through to antitax initiatives later in the twentieth century. Conservative activist Grover Norquist helped to popularize the phrase "starve the beast." Norquist, a libertarian, has been instrumental in orienting the Republican Party toward a position hostile to big government. He was the author of the Taxpayer Protection Pledge, which has enjoyed overwhelming support from Republicans. He has said, "I'm not in favor of abolishing the government. I simply want to reduce it to the size where I can drag it into the bathroom and drown it in the bathtub." Norquist quoted in Monika Bauerlein and Clara Jeffrey, "The Job Killer," *Mother Jones*, November/December 2011. This view was restated by Rand Paul, who in February 2015 said, "We need to shut the damn thing down." Paul quoted in Peter Wehner, "Government Is Not the Enemy," *NYT*, March 1, 2015.

58. "City Fights Budget Bill," *CSG*, February 21, 1933, 1.

59. "Officials Rotten," *CSG*, March 30, 1933, 3. For more on Little, see "Little to Go on Bench Tomorrow," *SGT*, December 18, 1938, 1.

60. Take the example of the Community Chest of Colorado Springs, which like municipalities elsewhere pushed a plan for repatriating Mexicans. The town's charitable organization identified seventy-five local Mexican families that it deemed lucky enough to be "qualified to return" to Mexico, no matter what the families in question wanted. "75 Mexican Families Here Qualified to Return to Mexico," *CSG*, May 27, 1932. And in 1936, Colorado governor Ed Johnson established a blockade to keep Mexicans out of the state.

61. Lorena Hickok, *One Third of a Nation: Lorena Hickok Reports on the Great Depression*, ed. Richard Lowitt and Maurine Beasley (Urbana: University of Illinois Press, 1981), 243.

62. These groups are thought to have faded by the mid-thirties, but see "New Yorkers Set for Tax Rebellion," *CSG*, January 24, 1940, 1.

63. Bieto, *Taxpayers in Revolt*, xii.

64. The press was filled with denunciations of the New Deal, such as "New Deal Soaking Poor, Says Knox," *CSG*, October 1, 1936, 1. Locally, Little also attacked taxes, but in 1933 he was on record praising FDR. See "Officials Rotten."

65. "Rift Not Healed in Taxpayers' Bodies," *CSG*, February 21, 1933, 1; "Seek Special City Election," *CSG*, April 1, 1934, 1.

66. Robert G. Athearn is referring specifically to the New Deal years, but this attitude predates the Depression years. See *Mythic West*, 103.

67. This paragraph draws upon Albert Hurtado's "Whose Misfortune? Richard White's Ambivalent Region," *Reviews in American History* 22 (June 1994): 286–91.

68. Phillips-Fein, *Invisible Hands*, 118–19.

69. "Merrill Shoup," *CSGT*, July 16, 1964, 1.

70. Lassiter, *The Silent Majority*, 198.

71. Kuttner, *Revolt of the Haves*.

72. "Required Reading; Government One," *NYT*, January 27, 1983. Today, Americans' hostility to government dwarfs what it was during the Depression. Some analysts point to race as the key reason for this shift. During the thirties New Deal reforms routinely excluded people of color and targeted whites as beneficiaries, thereby blunting the public's objections to big government. A case in point: the Federal Housing Administration (FHA) insured homeowners' loans, making this linchpin of the American dream widely available to white Americans. However, the FHA routinely rejected the applications of minority homeowners on the grounds that they lived in neighborhoods too risky to refinance or were poor credit risks. Simply put, white Americans were less likely to object to a welfare state when they (or those who resembled them) were its beneficiaries. On a related issue, many people argue that the HOLC discriminated against minorities, but Adam Gordon argues that although the HOLC maps created the template for redlining, its own lending was not racially discriminatory. It was, he argues, the FHA who took those maps and ran with them. See Gordon, "The Creation of Homeownership: How New Deal Changes in Banking Regulation Simultaneously Made Homeownership Accessible to Whites and Out of Reach for Blacks," *Yale Law Journal* 115, no. 1 (October 2005).

73. "Can Walter Davis Avoid Extradition," *CSG&T*, October 16, 1932, Sec 2, 1.

74. "Chief Harper Is the President of the International Association," *CSG*, June 16, 1932, 1.

6: The Port of Missing Men

1. Richard H. Pells, *Radical Visions and American Dreams: Culture and Social Thought in the Depression Years* (New York: Harper Collins, 1974), 78.

2. McElvaine, *The Great Depression*, 137; Alan Dawley, *Struggles for Justice: Social Responsibility and the Liberal State* (Cambridge, MA: Harvard University Press, 1991), 348. In his film *American Madness*, Frank Capra succeeded in capturing the terrifying panic of a bank run.

3. Kyvig, *Daily Life in the United States*, 224.

4. McElvaine, *The Great Depression*, 92.

5. Ibid., 90.

6. "The Editor Says," *Sikeston Standard*, June 10, 1932, 1.

7. Quoted in McElvaine, *The Great Depression*, 136.

8. "Seven New Mexico Bankers Go to Pen," *CSG*, October 8, 1932, 1. Otis Seligman's father, the governor, died shortly before the sentencing of his son.

9. "That's That," *DP*, July 15, 1932, 2. See Robert Lynn Fuller, *"Phantom of Fear": The Banking Panic of 1933* (Jefferson, NC: McFarland, 2012), 64.

10. "Illinois Banker Under Investigation for Irregularities Found Terribly Beaten," *DP*, August 8, 1932, 1.

11. Walter Clyde Davis, FBI File 62-27247.

12. It would become semi-legendary as the Parkside Evangeline Residence for Young Women. Steven Kurutz, "On Gramercy Park, an Old-Fashioned Girl," *NYT*, September 25, 2005.

13. See *New York Herald Tribune*, December 13, 1932.

14. "Attorney to File Petition Today for Reward Order," *CSG*, September 2, 1932, 1.

15. "Betrays Self," *New York Herald Tribune*, December 13, 1932, 3; "Banker," *NYT*, December 12, 1932, 32.

16. Walter's FBI file included a copy of the letter.

17. "Davis Affairs in Bad Shape," *CSG*, June 28, 1932, 3; Eva quoted in *CSET*, June 24, 1932, 1. The *Denver Post* later claimed that not long after he went on the lam he wrote a letter in which he said he might commit suicide. "Walter Davis Uses Necktie to End Wild Financial Career," *DP*, December 12, 1932.

18. "N.Y. Realty Man Commits Suicide," *CSG*, April 23, 1932; "Charles Maag Hangs Himself," *CSG*, April 19, 1932. Maag was a butcher who lived on the west side.

7: Orphans in the Storm

1. My account of my grandfather's arrest and suicide is drawn from multiple newspaper articles. His arrest and suicide were covered in many of the country's newspapers. For before-and-after photos, see "Price Marks of Crime," *DP*, December 14, 1932, 1.

2. By the authorities I mean the DA, the police, and the receiver. "Will Press Search for Davis's Hidden Fortune," *CSG*, December 13, 1932, 1. Harper told the press the fortune was larger. See "Find Davis's Safety Deposit Box," *CSG*, December 16, 1932, 1.

3. "Suicide-Puzzle Quest Pushed Police," *LAT*, July 1, 1932, 2; "Davis Attended Walker Hearings," *RMN*, December 15, 1932; "Receives Tips on Davis and Fleagle," *CSG*, July 19, 1933.

4. It was known as the Pecora Committee because of its unrelenting and savvy chief counsel, Ferdinand Pecora. It is worth noting that Congress had

already passed some reform measures, including the Glass-Steagall Act, before the committee issued its final report in June 1934.

5. Ron Chernow, "Where Is Our Ferdinand Pecora?" *NYT*, January 6, 2009.

6. "That's That," *DP*, June 29, 1933, 2.

7. Quoted in Larry Doyle, *In Bed with Wall Street: The Conspiracy Crippling Our Global Economy* (New York: Macmillan, 2014), 149.

8. McElvaine, *The Great Depression*, 139–40.

9. Chernow, "Where Is."

10. The police found in his apartment masses of papers strewn about, and they were filled with numbers that, to them, looked like nonsense. To the journalists covering the story in Colorado, the nonsensical figures demonstrated either that loneliness and worry had completely unhinged him or that he was trying to "plant" an insanity defense. And then there was the little-reported information that he seemed to have been in communication with a New York lawyer who was trying to help him sort out his business affairs. "Find Mass of Papers in Davis' Room but Figures Mean Nothing; Insanity Defense Was 'Planted,'" *CSET*, December 13, 1932, 1; "Davis Planned to Use Gun or Poison," *CSG*, January 10, 1933, 10.

11. One detail he never took care of was writing his will. Perhaps he intended to elude the authorities for such a long time that he would be declared legally dead, at which point the insurance companies would pay out to the depositors and to Lula. But such a plan would have to have been predicated upon having enough money to last him for nearly a decade. In the famous case of the "Missingest Man in New York," Judge Joseph Crater, who disappeared in 1930, nine years passed before he was presumed legally dead. See "Crater Will Case Up May 26," *NYT*, April 28, 1939, 27.

12. "Funeral on the 17th," *CSG*, December 18, 1932, 1; "Davis' Deposit Box Found Almost Empty," *DP*, December 18, 1932, 1.

13. Report, or Sale Bill, of Sale of Personal Property, State of Colorado, County of El Paso in re Estate of Walter Clyde Davis, Deceased, no. 372, Box 36804, CSA. A December 31, 1932, article in the *Gazette* claimed that his total estate was his Cadillac.

14. "Harper and Fertig Enlist Aid of U.S. Justice Department," *CSG*, January 4, 1933; "Pay $1,000 to New York Detective," *CSG*, January 5, 1933.

15. The papers did print articles about the so-called code letter. See "Code Letter to Wife Davis Case Clue," *CSG*, December 20, 1932; "Search for Davis's Box Nears Crisis," *CSG*, December 21, 1932, 1; "Know Nothing of Any Code Letter," *CSG*, December 22, 1932, 1; "$500 of Davis's Money in Box," *CSG*, December 25, 1932, 1.

16. "Eva Terry Willing to Aid Authorities in Solution," *CSG*, December 13, 1932, 1; "Eva Terry to Keep Ring and $3,000," *CSG*, October 23, 1936, 1; "Mrs. Davis Mute on Hubby's Arrest," *CSG*, December 12, 1932, 1.

17. "Banker's Suicide Will Aid Victims," *RMN*, December 13, 1932, 1.

18. "Mrs. Davis Mute."

19. "Extended Time to File Claims on City Savings," *CSG*, December 30, 1932, 1.

20. Obituary, Horace Hawkins, *RMN*, May 25, 1947, sec. 2, 1.

21. "Petition District Court to Call Grand Jury," *CSG*, January 27, 1933, 1; "Gross Admits He Failed to Make Examinations," April 26, 1933, 1; "Sensational Cases," *CSG*, May 9, 1933, 1; "Validity of Grand Jury Is Attacked," *CSG*, May 19, 1933, 1; "Indictments Quashed by Judge Young," *CSG*, May 30, 1933; letter in Davis family archive.

22. "Services Today for C.T. Fertig," *CSG*, April 16, 1933, 5; "TC Turner, Fertig's Lawyer, and FW Haskew Named Co-receivers for City," *CSG*, April 19, 1933, 12.

23. Undated letter from Dorothy Davis to Horace Hawkins, Davis family archive.

24. State of Colorado, County of El Paso in re Estate of Walter Clyde Davis, no. 372, Box 36804, CSA.

25. Another $30,000 withdrawal that day went to buy the stock of the El Paso Industrial Bank.

26. "Damnation of Mitchell," *Time*, March 6, 1933.

27. "Mitchell's Trial to Appease Mob," *CSG*, May 17, 1933.

28. In Chicago's Cook County, fifty-seven bankers were indicted, but most of these cases were reversed on appeal. See Fuller, *"Phantom of Fear"*, 63–67.

29. *RMN*, June 30, 1936; Pueblo scandal editorial, *RMN*, July 16, 1932. "If Law Invalid May Get Sentence Slashed," *CSG*, October 8, 1932, 1. The article said that either Bentall would be pardoned by the governor at the expiration of his thirteen-year minimum for embezzlement or he could petition the state supreme court for revocation of the part of the sentence involving falsification of reports. "Depositors Ask Court to Offer Reward for WC Davis," *CSG*, September 1, 1932, 1. Moreover, the legal establishment had assumed that it was illegal for a building and loan officer to file false reports, but that wasn't what the law actually said. Nor did the law require an association founder to have any of his or her own money invested in said concern.

30. See Mason, *From Buildings and Loans*, 126. Mason also attributes the success of the S&L industry to the positive relationships thrift managers forged with their customers.

31. Only those thrifts that were federally chartered were members of the Federal Savings and Loan Insurance Corporation (FSLIC), which, like its bank counterpart, FDIC, offered deposit insurance. Ibid., 94.

32. "Savings and loan" was a locution already in existence in New York and in parts of Ohio, Washington, and elsewhere. See Hedges Ewalt, *A Business Reborn*, 9.

33. "Case Outlined Against Savings-Loan Officials," *LAT*, May 3, 1940.

34. Office rent, office expenses, accounting fees, trustee and title expenses, and taxes came to over $25,000. However, many of those expenses, as I have indicated, would have to have been paid by a liquidating corporation. "Loan Company's Assets $899,428," *CSG*, July 8, 1936, 1.

35. "Mighty Sqawk [*sic*] Set Up by Receivership Racketeers," *Lodi Sentinel*, August 25, 1934, 1.

36. "Newton to Draw $1,000 a Month Salary as Receiver," *DP*, July 27, 1932.

37. "Seek Cancellation of B.&L. Claims," *CSG*, February 14, 1935, 1.

38. "City Savings Checks Ready Next Monday," *CSG*, July 12, 1935, 1.

39. Roth, *The Great Depression*, 36, 50. In California, salesmen sometimes offered depositors what they called a "more safe investment" for surrendering their passbooks.

40. Lawyers for and officials of the CSLC claimed that the corporation did not issue stock, but the courts disagreed. And the case turned definitively against it when the regional Securities and Exchange Commission said that the "CSLC was not complying with federal statutes as they affect stock exchange or sale." "Will Get $180,000 from City Savings," *CSG*, n.d. (probably March or April 1936).

41. "Issues Warning on Stock Offers to B.&L. Victims," *CSG*, August 20, 1932, 1.

42. "4 Testify at Loan Probe," *San Jose News*, January 23, 1935.

43. "Building-Loan Revision Bill Signed by Merriam," *LAT*, May 14, 1935. New Deal Democrats wanted to do more, and fought unsuccessfully for the "Beesemyer Bill," which would have allowed victims of the B&L collapse to file claims for compensation from the state of California. The state's liability was reasonable, supporters argued, because state examiners failed to detect shortages. When it failed to get out of committee in May 1937, its backers even contemplated putting it forward as an amendment to the state's constitution, but that failed as well. See "People's Vote Urged on Beesemyer Bill," *LAT*, May 5, 1937.

44. Roosevelt's advisor is usually credited with coining the term in 1932. See Ronald Sullivan, "Stuart Chase, 97; Coined Phrase 'A New Deal,'" *NYT*, November 17, 1985. For the claim that Costigan used it before Roosevelt, see Leonard, *Trials and Triumphs*, 20–21.

45. On Colorado politics, see Leonard, *Trials and Triumphs*, 20–21.

46. "New B&L Measures Planned," *CSG*, January 7, 1933, 1; "Bill Introduced in Senate," *CSG*, January 14, 1933, 1.

47. "Adams Hears Protest on Two Measures," *Greeley Daily Tribune*, May 23, 1931, 1.

48. "Dust Bowl County Rejects Soil Plan," *CSG*, January 5, 1938, 1.

49. For the ad language, see *CSW*, September 2, 1932. The contest was announced in the same issue that carried an article on Pratt's candidacy. As for shutting down the campaign, I'm not sure this man was ever charged for his theft, or if he even existed. Perhaps the campaign was faltering.

50. "Seek Special City Election Next Autumn," *CSG*, April 1, 1934, 1.

51. "Million Dollars Missing," *Daily Mail*, March 19, 1935, 1.

52. Another source, a businessman who claimed to know him well, said he had run into Walter in Denver before the banker headed east and that he had on him a "fat bundle of securities." "Davis Known to Have Big Bundle of Bonds When He Left Denver," *DP*, June 26, 1932, 12; "Funeral on the 17th," *CSG*, December 18, 1932, 1.

53. In Pueblo alone, 77 of the 133 home loans that the City had made there were in default. "Court to Protect Borrowers from B&L's," *CSG*, September 8, 1932, 5.

54. "Davis Affairs in Bad Shape After January 1," *CSG*, June 28, 1932.

55. "Seeks Dividends on B&L Claims," *CSG*, October 20, 1934, 1.

56. Receiver Turner apparently outmaneuvered the Davises' lawyer, Hawkins. Among the policies Turner had allowed Lula to retain were quite a few that he knew had lapsed. In the end, the correspondence suggests that an expensive arrangement was brokered whereby Lula paid three different insurance companies nearly $20,000 to cover the back premiums and have the policies reinstated. None of this made its way into the press.

57. Ed Sharer's wife wrote to Lula suggesting that she contribute $750 toward her husband's court appeal. This was the man who, in order to save his own skin, had described himself as Walter's "hired man," as though that absolved him of responsibility for the fraud and forgery that juries had convicted him of. Then there was the letter from "A Tax Payer," who wrote to say that in light of the insurance settlement, Lula should "reimburse" Jim Fleming and his wife, who had suffered a heavy financial loss. I doubt that it surprised Lula that one of the many people making claims against the estate was none other than Eva Terry. She claimed that she should not have to pay a fine on shares of State Savings Bank stock she owned because they had been a gift from Walter. As a stockholder in Sims's failed State Savings Bank to the tune of $500, she owed Colorado's banking commissioner double that amount. Davis family archive.

58. These are part of the oral history collection at the Pioneers Museum, Colorado Springs. "Citizens Left Destitute," *CSW*, June 3, 1932, 4; "Can Walter Davis Avoid Extradition Like Insull is Now Doing in Greece?" *SGT*, October 16, 1932, sec. 2, 1.

59. See "State Senator Roy Davis Speaks to Manitou Kiwanis Club," *CSG*, November 24, 1931, 2; J. Herbert Pratt, "My Stand on the Old-Age Pension," *CSW*, September 13, 1932, 1.

60. Editorial, *CSG*, February 19, 1934, 4. For articles on the Taxpayers' Association's legal challenge, see "Age Pension Said Invalid by Taxpayers," January 21, 1937, 1, and "Payment Sped as Pension Is Decided Valid," *CSG*, January 27, 1937, 1.

61. "Push Investigations of Age Pensioners," *CSG*, June 11, 1936, 5.

62. "Vets Who Receive Bonus Off Relief," *CSG*, June 15, 1936, 1.

63. "Relief Snowball Here," *CSG*, January 24, 1937, 1.

64. For attitudes toward relief, see journalist Lorena Hickok's fascinating reporting collected in Hickok, *One Third of a Nation*. Hickok traveled across the country in her capacity as an internal reviewer of the government's relief efforts. She reported back to Harry Hopkins, who ran the federal government's Works Progress Administration.

65. White, *It's Your Misfortune*, 474; "Democratic Solon Assails Spending," *CSG*, October 1, 1936, 1.

66. Even during the first year of the New Deal, Colorado resisted some of its programs. For example, the state legislature released money to help fund relief efforts under the Federal Emergency Relief Administration (FERA), a New Deal agency, only after Denver nearly exploded as poor people rioted and armed mobs gathered to pillage grocery stores. According to FERA guidelines, the federal government would provide $1 for every $3 provided by states for relief. However, the Colorado state legislature decided against providing the required matching funds. FERA's first administrator, Harry Hopkins, advanced the state half a million dollars a month until the end of 1933 when, fed up, he cut off the funds. After the rioting in Denver the legislature finally increased the state's gas tax in order to provide matching funds. White, *It's Your Misfortune*, 473–74.

67. Also, in California's 1934 gubernatorial race one sees the Republican Party successfully uniting voters across class lines to defeat the left-leaning Upton Sinclair. Olmsted, *Right Out of California*, 171–91.

68. Johnson quoted in Leonard, *Trials and Triumphs*, 239.

69. Athearn, *Mythic West*, 99. Much of the state's press treated the poor, the beneficiaries of that aid, as an inherently suspect category. And yet the press gave a pass to those large corporations that manipulated relief for their own benefit. Two of the worst offenders were the Great Western Sugar Company and Rockefeller's Colorado Fuel & Iron Company (CF&I). To even get on relief, beet workers for GWS had to be approved by a company man. They needed supplementary relief because the company paid so little. In Pueblo, officials of the CF&I dominated the committee coordinating federal relief. Relief administrators there mandated that full-time male employees who

were in debt receive supplementary relief—on average $10 to $20 a month—but in the form of dispersing orders for food and clothing to be cashed at CF&I's company store. New Dealer Lorena Hickok, who traveled across the country investigating the government's relief efforts, wrote that what she found in Colorado was "complete domination by industry using us to subsidize itself." See Hickok, *One Third*, xii.

70. "'Taxpayers' Evade Issue; Says Unemployed Committee," *CSG*, January 30, 1931. The criticism that those on relief rejected paid work was a common complaint. Yet it really made no sense for an unemployed person to get off relief for what might be just a few weeks of paid work when getting approved for relief was so very difficult.

71. "Unemployed Council Presents Demands to City Council," *CSG*, March 5, 1933, 2.

72. "Agitator Arrested for Disturbance," *CSG*, April 26, 1933, 3.

73. The editor in question was John C. McCreary. F.B. Morris, "The Politics in the Women's WPA," *CSI*, September 24, 1936, 3. It's true that relief administrators everywhere, concerned to limit the number of cases, aimed to make the experience uncomfortable. But, according to the *Independent*, conditions for relief workers in the Springs were much worse than in neighboring cities. In Pueblo and Denver the WPA filled workers' orders for shoes, clothing, milk, and fruit, and without any reduction in what was allowed them for food, rent, and fuel. By comparison, the Springs provided a bare-bones program of relief. The paper said it wasn't as much the New Deal as the "Raw Deal." The term "Raw Deal" was usually deployed not by the left but by the right. William Randolph Hearst, who opposed Roosevelt and the New Deal, wanted all Hearst wire service chiefs and editors to use the term in all editorials and news stories about the New Deal. See David Nasaw, *The Chief: The Life of William Randolph Hearst* (New York: Mariner Books, 2001), 515. The *Colorado Springs Independent*'s coverage of the WPA is fascinating.

74. I have searched the local Colorado Springs papers through 1941 for any mention of that final dividend payment. However, after the December 7, 1941, bombing of Pearl Harbor the dailies were filled with war news, and finding such a notice became very much a needle-in-the-haystack proposition. However, a Google search indicated that the International Typographical Union's journal might reveal when that final check was mailed out and what the percentage of payout was. In a small notice about a deceased member who had willed his tiny estate to the union's retirement home, located in Colorado Springs, I learned that as late as November 1942 the union was still waiting on the final dividend check, projected to be 10 percent. If this information is accurate, it means that depositors were reimbursed at 41 percent. See *Typographical Journal* (Milwaukee, Wisconsin), November 1942, 903.

75. Some have argued that the HOLC discriminated in favor of the middle classes—an assumption that Cohen challenges in *Making a New Deal*, 274. My sense from the figures in the local Springs press is that the HOLC was helpful to a broad range of homeowners, not just to the middle class. Of course, the HOLC maps did establish the template for the insidious practice of "redlining," which ensured the decline of neighborhoods consisting primarily of racial and ethnic minorities.

76. Calder, *Financing*, 281; Cohen, *Making a New Deal*, 273.

77. Cohen, *Making a New Deal*, 233; "Grand Jury Action into Building, Loan Charges Demanded," *CSG*, May 6, 1937; "Convictions upon Embezzling Upheld," *CSG*, February 3, 1942.

78. Either Sharer was very lucky or his political connections saved him from serving a long sentence. In October 1932 he had been sentenced to between eleven and fourteen years for a single forgery charge. He had been allowed to stay at the county jail—certainly more agreeable than the state penitentiary—pending his appeal of that conviction. The Colorado Supreme Court reversed his forgery convictions twice on the grounds that the district attorney's office had sent the wrong canceled checks on to the Court. One thing is for sure: the one judge on the state Supreme Court who always ruled in Sharer's favor always included as part of his judgment his view that Sharer was just acting on orders from Walter Davis. For the final court action, see "Charges Against Sharer Dismissed," *CSG*, April 16, 1935, 1; see also "E.C. Sharer, Former Springs Resident, Dies in Los Angeles," *CSG*, August 16, 1947.

79. "Fred N. Bentall Freed on Parole," *CSG*, May 18, 1938.

80. "Organize Federal Savings and Loan Association Here," *CSG*, September 18, 1933, 1.

81. The reason that HOLC records provide such a useful gauge of public attitudes toward B&Ls is that many of those facing foreclosure had obtained their mortgage through a B&L. To keep those folks in their homes the HOLC needed to work with B&Ls, including those in receivership.

82. HOLC memo, R.L. Olson to Corwin A. Fergus, August 19, 1938. A full 20 percent of those surveyed reported that the question was moot because they had no savings. A mere 12 percent reckoned that a building and loan association might be "okay." Records of the Federal Home Loan Bank Board, 195.3, Records of the Home Owners' Loan Corporation (HOLC), 1933–51, Textual Records, National Archives.

83. "Summary: Survey of Pueblo, Colorado," by the Mortgage Rehabilitation Division, Field Report, dated April 10, 1936. This same report indicted the Railway Savings B&L, noting that it charged exorbitant interest on its mortgage loans—between 7 and 10 percent. It also noted that in 1929 Pueblo banks had paid 4 percent on savings, a figure that subsequently dropped to

3 percent on the first $5,000 and 2 percent over $5,000. Records of the Federal Home Loan Bank Board, 195.3, Records of the Home Owners' Loan Corporation (HOLC), 1933–51, Textual Records, National Archives.

84. John A. Noakes, "Bankers and Common Men in Bedford Falls," *Film History* 10, no. 3 (January 1998).

85. Bosley Crowther, "The Spirits Move," *NYT*, January 12, 1947.

86. My discussion of the movie has been influenced by Jonathan Munby, "A Hollywood Carol's Wonderful Life," in *Christmas at the Movies: Images of Christmas in American, British and European Cinema*, ed. Mark Connelly (New York: I.B. Tauris, 2000), 39–57. Mark Harris described Capra as having "scattershot politics." See Harris, *Five Came Back: A Story of Hollywood and the Second World War* (New York: Penguin Books, 2014), 422; James Chandler, *An Archeology of Sympathy: The Sentimental Mode in Literature and Cinema* (Chicago: University of Chicago Press, 2013), particularly ch. 2; John Bodnar, *Blue-Collar Hollywood: Liberalism, Democracy, and Working People in American Film* (Baltimore: Johns Hopkins University Press, 2003). *It's a Wonderful Life* came to be compulsory TV watching every holiday season because in 1974 the studio holding its copyright failed to renew it and the film became public domain.

87. For more about race and real estate finance, see Beryl Satter's illuminating *Family Properties*, 41.

88. Snowden, "Transition," 158.

89. Dick Netzer, "Savings and Loans Were Always a Scandal," letter to the editor, *NYT*, April 24, 1990.

90. Taper was one of the developers of Lakewood, California, a white working-class south Los Angeles neighborhood. See D.J. Waldie, *Holy Land: A Suburban Memoir* (New York: W.W. Norton, 2005).

91. "Cripple Creek Mines Pour out $5,083,000 in Gold," *CSG*, December 26, 1937, 1; "State's Mines Add Millions in New Wealth," *CSG*, January 10, 1938, 1. By the early fifties, Cripple Creek was a largely abandoned mining town that from the road looked like a "tiny disorder." This is how a character in Patricia Highsmith's 1952 novel *The Price of Salt* (New York: W.W. Norton, 2004) describes it (214–15).

92. Ann Markusen, Peter Hall, Scott Campbell, and Sabrina Deitrich, *The Rise of the Gunbelt: The Military Remapping of Industrial America* (New York: Oxford University Press, 1991), 176. My account of the transformation of the Springs draws heavily from this book.

93. Ibid., 178; Charles Banks oral history, interview by Brenda Hawley and Norman Sams, May 18, 1973, Pikes Peak Library District Oral History Project, OH IV, Pikes Peak Library District, Special Collections, 7. "Springs Named Big Army Camp" and "Defense School Is Allotted $58,518," *CSG*, July 17, 1941, 1. Actually, the efforts at a partnership between the town's

leading businessmen and the military began at least as far back as 1922 when the city tried to pursue the building of a military aviation field in the springs. "City After Flying Field Again: Denver Not to Get It," *CSG*, July 2, 1922; Mia Gray and Ann R. Markusen, "Colorado Springs: A Military-Anchored City in Transition," in *Second Tier Cities: Rapid Growth Beyond the Metropolis*, ed. Ann R. Markusen, Yong-Sook Lee, and Sean DiGiovanna (Minneapolis: University of Minnesota Press, 1999), 313.

94. Markusen et al., *Rise of the Gunbelt*.

95. Philip Deloria, "Polarized Tribes: Colorado, Wyoming, and Montana," in *Religion and Public Life in the Mountain West: Sacred Landscapes in Transition*, ed. Jan Shipps and Mark Silk (Walnut Creek, CA: AltaMira Press, 2004), 121.

96. Markusen et al., *Rise of the Gunbelt*, 192.

97. "City Charter Bars Unions," *CSGT*, February 7, 1949, 1.

98. Markusen et al., *Rise of the Gunbelt*, 175.

99. A year after Hoiles acquired the *Gazette*, the paper's printers, among the very few unionized workers in town, went on strike. Mary Ann Milbourn, "Hoiles: Dynasty to Bankruptcy," *Orange County Register*, May 3, 2010; Carl Watner, "The Uncompromising R.C. Hoiles," *Orange County Register*, November 27, 2007; "Gazette-Telegraph Is Placed in Hands of New Publishers," *CSG*, January 11, 1946, 1; Aldo Svaldi, "Freedom Communications Sells *Gazette* in Colorado Springs, Six Others," *DP*, June 11, 2012. In the end, the striking workers formed an alternative paper, the *Colorado Springs Sun*, which was also eventually bought by Hoiles's newspaper empire for a reported $30 million. "Two Colorado Springs Papers Will Merge into One," *LAT*, January 27, 1986.

100. "Taxpayers Assn. Protests Proposed Tax on Cigarets," *CSGT*, September 26, 1955, 8; "Taxpayers Assn. to Probe Schools' Reckless Spending," *CSGT*, May 20, 1955; "Opposes Proposed Bond Issue for New Police Station," *CSGT*, February 26, 1955.

101. "The Every Day Diary," November 20, 1934, Roy Davis Collection, Folder 1, S2010.18, Pioneers Museum, Colorado Springs. According to Roy's diary, he was among the first people Ed Sharer visited upon his release from the county jail. Ed Sharer and Roy Davis had been next-door neighbors. Still, it says a lot about Roy's feelings toward his older brother that he met with Sharer, a man who consistently blamed Walter. Roy did note that he slept poorly after the visit. His "Year Book, 1942," includes a June entry where he mentions that he sold seventy typewriters and rented out another forty to the army.

102. Lawrence J. White, "The Savings and Loan Debacle: A Perspective from the Early Twenty-First Century," in *The Savings and Loan Crisis: Lessons from a Regulatory Failure*, ed. James R. Barth, Susanne Trimbath, and Glenn Yago (Boston: Milken Institute, 2004), 18.

103. My account is largely drawn from Kitty Calavita, Henry N. Pontell, and Robert H. Tillman, *Big Money Crime: Fraud and Politics in the Savings and Loan Crisis* (Berkeley: University of California Press, 1997). If one were to add interest over the next thirty years, the authors argue, the cost to taxpayers is closer to $500 billion. See also Snowden, "Transition," 158.

104. Eric Weiner, "Subprime Bailout: Good Idea or 'Moral Hazard'?" NPR, November 29, 2007.

105. Deloria, "Polarized Tribes," 133.

106. Bruce also became notorious for being convicted of tax evasion in 2011. See "TABOR to Be Bruce's lasting legacy," *CSG*, April 6, 2009.

107. "TABOR Has Decimated Education, Critics Say," *CSG*, October 29, 2012. The most recent debate about TABOR concerns the state's marijuana law. Because of TABOR, Colorado, the first state to allow recreational marijuana sales, was threatened with having to return over $60 million in marijuana taxes to taxpayers. The legalization of pot was meant to raise revenue for the state and its schools, but TABOR limits how much money the state can take in before it has to return some of it to taxpayers. In the end, voters did pass a ballot initiative enabling lawmakers to spend the money on school construction and substance abuse programs. See Jack Healy, "In Colorado, Marijuana Taxes May Have to Be Passed Back," *NYT*, April 2, 2015; Kristen Wyatt, "Colorado May Have to Refund as Much as $30 Million in Pot Taxes," *Huffington Post*, February 4, 2015; John Frank, "Colorado Allowed to Spend Marijuana Tax," *DP*, November 3, 2015.

108. This question is posed by Garrett Epps in his article "Does a State Have the Right to Self-Destruct?," *Atlantic Monthly*, August 8, 2012.

Epilogue

1. During the twelve-year period between the insurance settlement and Lula's death, Lula appears to have withdrawn only $8,000 of the $65,000 worth of insurance from one of the companies.

2. Email exchange with Karen Halttunen, February 21, 2016.

Index

Page numbers in italics refer to images, photographs, and captions.

About the Author

Alice Echols is a professor of history and the Barbra Streisand Chair of Contemporary Gender Studies at the University of Southern California. She is author of several books including *Scars of Sweet Paradise: The Life and Times of Janis Joplin*, and *Hot Stuff: Disco and the Remaking of American Culture*. She lives in Los Angeles.

Celebrating 25 Years of Independent Publishing